ARTIFICIAL INTELLIGENCE, EXPERT SYSTEMS, COMPUTER VISION, AND NATURAL LANGUAGE PROCESSING

Artificial Intelligence Expert Systems Computer Vision and Natural Language Processing

by

William B. Gevarter
Office of Aeronautics and Space Technology
National Aeronautics and Space Administration
Washington, DC

np NOYES PUBLICATIONS
Park Ridge, New Jersey, USA

Copyright © 1984 to Noyes Publications
Library of Congress Catalog Card Number: 84-6014
ISBN 0-8155-0994-4
Printed in the United States

Published in the United States of America by
Noyes Publications
Mill Road, Park Ridge, New Jersey 07656

10 9 8 7 6 5 4 3 2

Library of Congress Cataloging in Publication Data

Gevarter, William B.
    Artificial intelligence, expert systems, computer vision, and natural language processing.

    Includes bibliographies and index.
    1. Artificial intelligence. I. Title.
Q335.G48 1984 001.53'5 84-6014
ISBN 0-8155-0994-4

Foreword

An overview of artificial intelligence (AI), its core ingredients, and its applications is presented in this volume. AI is a field with over a quarter century of history; however, it wasn't until the 1980s that AI received economic and popular acclaim and went through the transition from a primary research area to potential commercial applications. The full impact of AI's transition has yet to be felt. Recently, AI was made the basic thrust of Japan's Fifth Generation computer research effort. Success in this venture could project the Japanese into a dominant position in information sciences in the 1990s. Similar importance has been placed on AI by the U.S., Great Britain, and France.

The real payoff for AI will be in applications. Intelligent computer programs are now emerging from the laboratory into practical applications. This book presents overviews of key application areas—expert systems, computer vision, natural language processing, speech interfaces, and problem solving and planning. Basic approaches to these systems, the state of the art, existing systems, participants, and future trends are detailed. The book should be useful to engineering and research managers, potential users and others seeking a basic understanding of the rapidly evolving area of artificial intelligence and its applications.

The information in the book is from:

> *An Overview of Artificial Intelligence and Robotics. Volume I—Artificial Intelligence, Part A—The Core Ingredients,* by William B. Gevarter, Office of Aeronautics and Space Technology, National Aeronautics and Space Administration, June 1983.
>
> *An Overview of Artificial Intelligence and Robotics. Volume I—Artificial Intelligence, Part B—Applications,* by William B. Gevarter, Office of Aeronautics and Space Technology, National Aeronautics and Space Administration, October 1983.

v

An Overview of Artificial Intelligence and Robotics. Volume I—Artificial Intelligence, Part C—Basic AI Topics, by William B. Gevarter, Office of Aeronautics and Space Technology, National Aeronautics and Space Administration, October 1983.

The table of contents is organized in such a way as to serve as a subject index and provides easy access to the information contained in the book.

Advanced composition and production methods developed by Noyes Publications are employed to bring this durably bound book to you in a minimum of time. Special techniques are used to close the gap between "manuscript" and "completed book." In order to keep the price of the book to a reasonable level, it has been partially reproduced by photo-offset directly from the original reports and the cost saving passed on to the reader. Due to this method of publishing, certain portions of the book may be less legible than desired.

NOTICE

The materials in this book were prepared as accounts of work sponsored by the National Aeronautics and Space Administration and the National Bureau of Standards. Publication does not signify that the contents necessarily reflect the views and policies of the contracting agency or the publisher.

It is not the intent of NASA or the National Bureau of Standards or the publisher to recommend or endorse any of the manufacturers or organizations named in this report, but simply to attempt to provide an overview of the AI field. However, in a diverse and rapidly changing field such as AI, important activities, organizations and products may not have been mentioned. Lack of such mention does not in any way imply that they are not also worthwhile. The author would appreciate having any such omissions or oversights called to his attention so that they can be considered for future reports.

Contents and Subject Index

PART A
ARTIFICIAL INTELLIGENCE—
THE CORE INGREDIENTS

I. ARTIFICIAL INTELLIGENCE—WHAT IT IS 3
   Definition 3
   The Basic Elements of AI 4
      Heuristic Search 4
      Knowledge Representation 4
      Common Sense Reasoning and Logic. 5
      AI Languages and Tools 5
   Principal AI Application Areas 5
      Natural Language Processing (NLP). 5
      Computer Vision. 5
      Expert Systems. 5
      Problem Solving and Planning 5
   Is AI Difficult? 6
   References 7

II. THE RISE, FALL AND REBIRTH OF AI 8
   The First 15 Years 8
   The Decade of the 70's 11
   1980 to the Present 12
   References 14

III. BASIC ELEMENTS OF AI 15
   Heuristic Search 15
   Knowledge Representation 17
      Logical Representation Schemes. 17

viii   Contents and Subject Index

    Semantic Networks 17
    Procedural Representations and Production Systems 17
    Analogical or Direct Representations. 18
    Property Lists. 19
    Frames and Scripts 19
    Semantic Primitives 20
Computational Logic 21
    Propositional Logic 21
    Predicate Logic. 22
Logical Inference. 23
    Resolution Method 23
    Factors Which Affect the Efficiency of Deductive Reasoning. 23
    Non-Resolution Theorem Proving. .23
Common Sense Reasoning. 24
Non-Deductive Problem Solving Approaches. 25
    Elements of a Problem Solver 25
    Problem Reduction 25
    Difference Reduction ("Means-Ends" Analysis). 26
    More Efficient Tactics for Problem Solving. 27
        Hierarchical Planning and Repair 27
        Problem Solving by Creating and Then Debugging Almost-
          Right Plans. 27
        Special Purpose Subplanners 27
        Constraint Satisfaction. 28
        Relevant Backtracking (Dependency-Directed or Non-
          Chronological Backtracking) 28
        Disproving. 28
        Pseudo-Reduction 28
        Goal-Regression 28
    Production Systems. 28
AI Languages, Tools and Computers 32
    Programming Needs of AI. 32
    List Representations 32
    LISP. 35
        Background 35
        Basic Elements of LISP. 35
        Variables 35
        Defining New Functions. 36
        Predicates 36
        Conditional Branching 36
        Recursive Functions. 36
        Review of Program Features of LISP. 37
        LISP Today 37
    PROLOG. 38
        History 38
        Nature of PROLOG. 38
        PROLOG Today 40
    Other AI Languages 40
    AI Computational Facilities. 41

Contents and Subject Index ix

```
          Requirements..................................41
          AI Machines...................................41
          Future........................................43
       Summary and Forecast............................43
     References........................................44

IV.  APPLICATIONS.......................................45

V.   THE PRINCIPAL PARTICIPANTS.........................49

VI.  STATE-OF-THE-ART...................................52
     General...........................................52
     Basic Core Topics.................................52
     Expert Systems....................................52
     Natural Language..................................53
     Computer Vision...................................53
     Conclusions.......................................53
     References........................................54

VII. TOWARDS THE FUTURE.................................55
     General...........................................55
     Expert Systems....................................55
     Natural Language..................................55
     Computer Vision...................................55
     Intelligent Robots................................56
     Industrial Applications...........................56
     Computers for Future Automation...................56
     Computer Aided Instruction (CAI)..................56
     Learning by Computers.............................57
     The Social Impacts................................57

SOURCES FOR FURTHER INFORMATION........................58
     Journals..........................................58
     Conferences.......................................58
     Recent Books......................................58

GLOSSARY...............................................59
```

PART B
APPLICATIONS—EXPERT SYSTEMS, COMPUTER VISION, NATURAL LANGUAGE PROCESSING, ETC.

```
I.   EXPERT SYSTEMS.....................................71
     Introduction......................................71
     What Is an Expert System?.........................71
     The Basic Structure of an Expert System...........71
     The Knowledge Base................................73
     The Control Structure.............................73
     Uses of Expert Systems............................73
```

Architecture of Expert Systems 73
  Existing Expert Systems. 78
  Constructing an Expert System 78
  Summary of the State-of-the-Art 83
  Future Trends. 84
  References. 86

II. COMPUTER VISION. 87
  Introduction. 87
  Definition 87
  Relation to Human Vision. 87
  Basis for a General Purpose Image Understanding System 89
  Basic Paradigms for Computer Vision 91
    Hierarchical Bottom-Up Approach 91
    Hierarchical Top-Down Approach. 91
    Heterarchical Approach 91
    Blackboard Approach. 93
  Levels of Representation. 93
  Research in Model-Based Vision Systems 94
  Industrial Vision Systems 98
    General Characteristics. 98
    Examples of Efforts in Industrial Visual Inspection Systems 98
    Examples of Efforts in Industrial Visual Recognition and
      Location Systems 99
    Commercially Available Industrial Vision Systems 99
  Who Is Doing It. 99
    Research Oriented 99
      Universities Funded Under DARPA IU Program 99
      Other Active Universities 99
      Non-Profits 104
      U.S. Government. 104
    Commercial Vision Systems Developers 104
  Summary of the State-of-the-Art 104
    Human Vision. 104
    Low and Intermediate Levels of Processing. 104
    Industrial Vision Systems 105
    General Purpose Vision Systems. 105
  Applications and Future Trends. 106
    Techniques. 106
    Hardware and Architecture 106
    AI and General Vision Systems 106
    Modeling and Programming. 108
    Knowledge Acquisition. 108
    Sensing 108
    Industrial Vision Systems 108
    Future Applications. 109
  Conclusion. 109
  References. 109

III. NATURAL LANGUAGE PROCESSING (NLP) 111
Introduction. 111
Applications. 111
Approach. 112
Type A: No World Models 112
Key Words or Patterns 112
Limited Logic Systems 112
Type B: Systems That Use Explicit World Models. 113
Type C: Systems That Include Information About the Goals and Beliefs of Intelligent Entities 113
The Parsing Problem 113
Grammars 113
Phrase Structure Grammar—Context Free Grammar 113
Transformational Grammar. 114
Case Grammar 114
Semantic Grammars. 114
Other Grammars. 114
Semantics and the Cantankerous Aspects of Language 115
Multiple Word Senses. 115
Pronouns. 115
Ellipsis and Substitution. 115
Knowledge Representation 115
Procedural Representations. 115
Declarative Representations. 116
Case Frames. 116
Conceptual Dependency. 116
Frame. 116
Scripts. 116
Syntactic Parsing. 116
Template Matching 116
Transition Nets. 116
Other Parsers 119
Semantics, Parsing and Understanding. 119
Natural Language Processing (NLP) Systems. 119
Kinds 119
Question Answering Systems. 119
Natural Language Interfaces (NLI's) 119
Computer-Aided Instruction (CAI). 120
Discourse. 120
Text Understanding. 120
Text Generation 120
Research NLP Systems. 120
Commercial Systems 120
State of the Art. 122
Principal U.S. Participants in NLP. 122
Research and Development 122
Non-Profit. 122
Universities 123
Industrial. 123

xii Contents and Subject Index

        Principal U.S. Government Agencies Funding NLP Research 124
        Commercial NLP Systems 124
        Non-U.S. 124
    Forecast 124
    References 125

IV. **SPEECH RECOGNITION AND SPEECH UNDERSTANDING** 127
    Introduction 127
    Applications 127
    The Nature of Speech Sounds 127
    Isolated Word Recognition 129
    Recognizing Continuous Speech 131
    Speech Understanding 131
    The ARPA Speech Understanding Research (SUR) Project 133
        Introduction 133
        HEARSAY II 133
        HARPY 135
        HWIM 135
        Summary of the ARPA SUR Program 135
    State of the Art 139
        Speech Recognition 139
        Speech Understanding 139
    Who Is Doing Speech Recognition Related Work 139
        Commercial Organizations 139
        Universities 141
    Problems and Issues 141
    Future Trends 142
    References 142

V. **SPEECH SYNTHESIS** 144
    Introduction 144
    Why Synthesis 144
    Human Speech 144
    Electronic Simulation of the Speech Mechanism 146
    Synthesis in Speech Compression and Regeneration 146
    Parametric Coding Schemes 148
        Introduction 148
        Format Coding 148
        Linear Predictive Coding (LPC) 148
        PARCOR 148
        Line Spectrum Pair (LSP) 148
        Parametric Waveform Coding (PWC) 149
    Waveform Coding Schemes 149
        ADPCM 149
        Mozer's Waveform Coding 149
    Coding the Words to Be Stored 149
    Generating Speech from Text 150
    State of the Art 151

Some Available Commercial Systems. 153
Problems and Issues. 153
Forecast 153
References. 156

VI. PROBLEM SOLVING AND PLANNING. 157
    Introduction. 157
    Planning Defined. 157
    Basic Planning Paradigm 157
    Paradigms for Generating Plans 160
        Nonhierarchical Planning 160
        Hierarchical Planning. 160
        Utilization of Skeleton Plans 162
        Opportunistic Planning. 162
    Planners. 162
    Trends. 162
    References. 178

PART C
BASIC AI TOPICS—AUTOMATION, SEARCH-ORIENTED PROBLEM SOLVING, KNOWLEDGE REPRESENTATION, COMPUTATIONAL LOGIC

I. ARTIFICIAL INTELLIGENCE AND AUTOMATION 181
    Mechanization and Automation 181
    Tools, Machines, Teleoperators, Robots. 181
    Computation and Artificial Intelligence. 182
    Relationship of AI to Automation 183
    AI and Other Fields. 183
    References. 187

II. SEARCH-ORIENTED AUTOMATED PROBLEM SOLVING AND
    PLANNING TECHNIQUES. 188
    AI as Problem Solving. 188
    Elements of a Problem Solver 188
    State Graphs as an Aid to Problem Representation. 188
    Reasoning Forward and Backward 191
    Problem Solving Using Blind Search 192
        Breadth-First Search 192
        Depth-First Search. 192
        Backward Chaining 192
        Problem Reduction 192
    Heuristic State-Space Search 194
    Game Tree Search 194
        Representation 194
        The Minimax Search Procedure 195
        Searching a Partial Game Tree 195
        Heuristics in Game Tree Search 196

Other Considerations 196
Difference Reduction ("Means-Ends" Analysis)—Another Basic
Approach. 196
More Efficient Tactics for Problem Solving. 196
Future Directions for Research 196
    Integrating a Significant Number of Tactics 198
    Flexible Control Structure 198
    Planning for Parallel Execution 198
    Partial Goal Fulfillment 198
    Feedback of Lessons Learned from Plan Execution to Plan
    Generation. 198
Current Research. 198
Current State of the Art 198
Forecast 199
References. 200

III. KNOWLEDGE REPRESENTATION. 201
Introduction. 201
Purpose. 201
Techniques. 201
    Logical Representation Schemes. 202
    Semantic Networks 202
    Procedural Representations and Production Systems 202
    Analogical or Direct Representations. 206
    Property Lists. 206
    Frames and Scripts 206
    Semantic Primitives 209
Representation Languages. 211
State of the Art. 212
Issues 212
Some Research Needs. 213
Who Is Doing It. 214
    Universities 214
    Other 214
Future Directions 214
References. 215

IV. COMPUTATIONAL LOGIC 216
Introduction. 216
Propositional Logic 216
Predicate Logic. 218
Resolution. 219
Computational Logic Today 221
    Theorem Proving. 221
    Logic Programming 221
    Non-Monotonic Logic 221
    Multi-Valued and Fuzzy Logics 222
Future Directions 222
References. 225

PART A

ARTIFICIAL INTELLIGENCE— THE CORE INGREDIENTS

The information in Part A is from *An Overview of Artificial Intelligence and Robotics. Volume I— Artificial Intelligence, Part A—The Core Ingredients,* by William B. Gevarter, Office of Aeronautics and Space Technology, National Aeronautics and Space Administration, June 1983.

ACKNOWLEDGMENTS

I wish to thank the many people and organizations who have contributed to this report, both in providing information, and in reviewing the report and suggesting corrections, modifications and additions. I particularly would like to thank Jerry Cronin of U.S. Army Signal Warfare Lab., Ted Hopp and Len Haynes of NBS, Bob Hong and his associates at Grumman Aerospace Corp., Karen Hagedorn of Symbolics, Mache Creeger of LISP Machine, Inc., Fred Blair of IBM T.J. Watson Research Center, Jude Franklin of the U.S. Navy Center for Applied Research in AI, and David H. Brown of SRI International for their review of this report and their many helpful suggestions. However, the responsibility of any remaining errors or inaccuracies must remain with the author.

I. ARTIFICIAL INTELLIGENCE—WHAT IT IS

Definition

Artificial Intelligence* (AI) is an emerging technology that has recently attracted considerable publicity. Many applications are now under development. One simple view of AI is that it is concerned with devising computer programs to make computers smarter. Thus, research in AI is focused on developing computational approaches to intelligent behavior. This research has two goals: 1) making machines more useful and 2) understanding intelligence. This report is primarily concerned with the first goal.

The computer programs with which AI is concerned are primarily symbolic processes involving complexity, uncertainty, and ambiguity. These processes are usually those for which algorithmic solutions do not exist and search is required. Thus, AI deals with the types of problem solving and decision making that humans continually face in dealing with the world.

This form of problem solving differs markedly from scientific and engineering calculations that are primarily numeric in nature and for which solutions are known that produce satisfactory answers. In contrast, AI programs deal with words and concepts and often do not guarantee a correct solution—some wrong answers being tolerable as in human problem solving.

Table I-1 provides a comparison between AI and conventional computer programs. A key characteristic of AI programs is "heuristic search." Baraiko (1982, p. 448) quotes Minsky as saying "If you can't tell a computer how best to do something, program it to try many approaches." However, in complex problems the number of possible solution paths can be enormous. Thus, AI problem solving is usually guided by empirical rules—rules of thumb—referred to as "heuristics"—which help constrain the search.

TABLE I-1. Comparison of AI with Conventional Programming.

Artificial Intelligence	Conventional Computer Programming
• Primarily symbolic processes	• Often primarily numeric
• Heuristic search (solution steps implicit)	• Algorithmic (solution steps explicit)
• Control structure usually separate from domain knowledge	• Information and control integrated together
• Usually easy to modify, update and enlarge	• Difficult to modify
• Some incorrect answers often tolerable	• Correct answers required
• Satisfactory answers usually acceptable	• Best possible solution usually sought

---

*Also sometimes referred to as machine intelligence or heuristic programming. The relationship of AI to automation is discussed in Chapter I of Part C of this report.

Another aspect of AI programs is the extensive use of "domain knowledge." Intelligence is heavily dependent on knowledge. This knowledge must be available for use when needed during the search. It is common in AI programs to separate this knowledge from the mechanism that controls the search. In this way, changes in knowledge only require changes in the knowledge base. In contrast, domain knowledge and control in conventional computer programs are integrated together. As a result, conventional computer programs are difficult to modify, as the implications of the changes made in one part of the program must be carefully examined for the impacts and the changes required in other parts of the program.

The Basic Elements of AI

Nilsson (1982, see also Brown, 1981), a pioneer in AI and currently head of the SRI AI Center, likes to characterize the components of AI in terms of what he calls the onion model (see Figure 1). The inner ring depicts the basic elements from which the applications shown in the next ring are composed. We will first consider the quadrant designated as heuristic search.

Heuristic Search

Much of the early work in AI was focused on deriving programs that would search for solutions to problems. Note that every time one makes a decision, the situation is changed opening up new opportunities for further decisions. Therefore there are always branch points. Thus, one of the usual ways of representing problem solving in AI is in terms of a tree (see, e.g., Figure 1, Chapter III), starting at the top with an initial condition and branching every time a decision is made. As one continues down the tree many different decision possibilities open up, so that the number of branches at the bottom can get to be enormous for problems requiring many solution steps. Therefore, some way is needed to efficiently search the trees.

Initially, there were "blind" methods for searching trees. These were orderly search approaches that assured that the same solution path would not be tried more than once. However for problems more complex than games and puzzles, these approaches were inadequate. Therefore, rules of thumb (empirical rules), referred to as "heuristics," were needed to aid in choosing the most likely branches, so as to narrow the search. As an example, a simple heuristic to help choose which roads to follow when driving in the evening on back roads from Washington, DC to San Francisco is: "head for the setting sun." This may not produce the most optimum path, but can serve to help advance one toward one's goal. Heuristic rules like this can help guide search—reducing search enormously.

Knowledge Representation

Early on, AI researchers discovered that intelligent behavior is not so much due to the methods of reasoning, as it is dependent on the knowledge one has to reason with. (As humans go through life they build up tremendous reservoirs of knowledge.) Thus, when substantial knowledge has to be brought to bear on a problem, methods are needed to efficiently model this knowledge so that it is readily accessible. The result of this emphasis on knowledge is that knowledge representation is one of the most active areas of research in AI today. The needed knowledge is not easy to represent, nor is the best representation obvious for a given task.

Common Sense Reasoning and Logic

AI researchers found that common sense (virtually taken for granted in humans) is the most difficult thing to model in a computer. It was finally concluded that common sense is low level reasoning, based on a wealth of experience. In acquiring common sense we learn to expect that when we drop something it falls, and in general what things to anticipate in everyday events. How to represent common sense in a computer is a key AI issue that is unlikely to be soon solved.

Another area that is very important in AI is logic. How do we deduce something from a set of facts? How can we prove that a conclusion follows from a given set of premises? Computational logic was one of the early golden hopes in AI to provide a universal problem solving method. However, solution convergence proved to be difficult with complex problems, resulting in a diminishing of interest in logic. Logic is now enjoying a revival based on new formulations and the use of heuristics to guide solutions.

AI Languages and Tools

In computer science, specific high level languages have been developed for different application domains. This has also been true for AI. Currently, LISP and PROLOG are the principal AI programming languages. To date, LISP (List Processing Language, developed in the late 50's by John McCarthy then at M.I.T.) has been the prime language in the U.S. for AI. Utilizing LISP, software tools have been devised for expressing knowledge, formulating expert systems, and basic programming aids.

Principal AI Application Areas

Based on these basic elements, Nilsson identified four principal AI application areas (shown in the outer ring of Figure I-1.)

Natural Language Processing (NLP)

NLP is concerned with natural language front ends to computer programs, computer-based speech understanding, text understanding and generation, and related applications. A detailed overview of NLP is given in Gevarter (1983).

Computer Vision

Computer Vision is concerned with enabling a computer to see—to identify or understand what it sees, to locate what it is looking for, etc. A detailed overview of Computer Vision is given in Gevarter (1982B).

Expert Systems

Expert Systems is perhaps the "hottest" topic in AI today. How do we make a computer act as if it was an expert in some domain? For example, how do we get a computer to perform medical diagnosis or VLSI design? A detailed overview of Expert Systems is given in Gevarter (1982A).

Problem Solving and Planning

There are many problems for which there are no experts, but nevertheless computer programs for their solutions are needed. In addition there are some basic planning systems that are more concerned with solution techniques than with knowledge. A comprehensive overview of problem solving and planning is given in Chapter VI of Part B and Chapter II of Part C of this report.

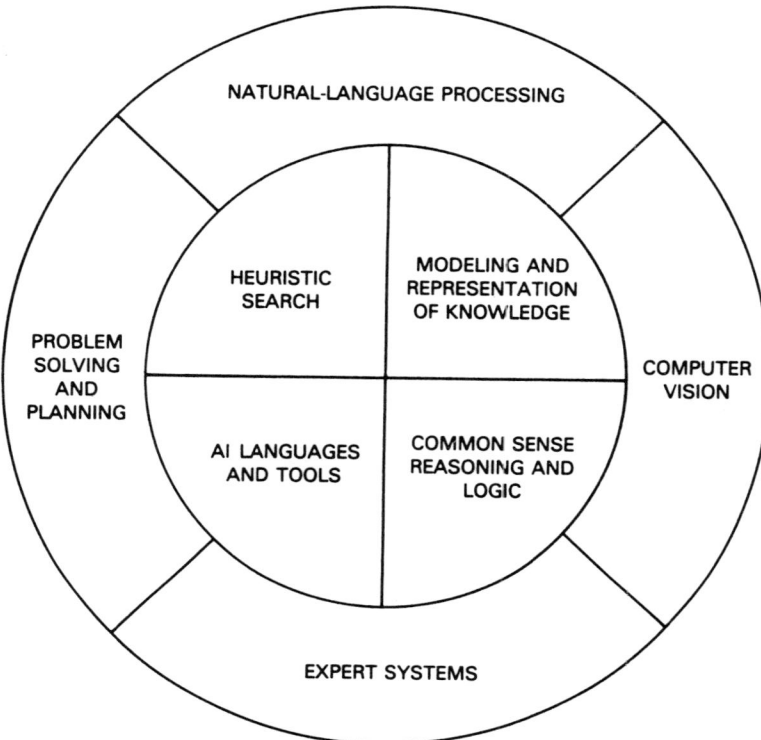

Figure I-1. Elements of AI.

Is AI Difficult?

The popular view that the study of AI is difficult has been partly due to the awe associated with the notion of intelligence*. It has also been due to the nomenclature used in AI and to the large size of some of the AI computer programs. However, the basic ideas of AI are readily understandable, even though in complex applications, the "bookkeeping" associated with such programs can be arduous.

Before we go into details on these basic ideas, it is illuminating to review the history of AI, which we will do in Chapter II. Then in Chapter III, the basic elements of AI will be discussed in some

---

*Indeed researchers can not even agree on a definition of intelligence itself. One paradoxical definition is "Intelligence is what an intelligence test measures."

detail (and elaborated upon further in Part C of this report). Chapters IV and V present the principle players in the AI drama and an indication of the unfolding applications area. (A more complete overview of AI applications is given in Part B of this report.) The current state of the art in AI and its future directions will be covered in Chapters VI and VII.

A list of sources for further information and a glossary of AI terms are provided at the end of this report.

CHAPTER I REFERENCES

- Boraiko, A.A., "The Chip," *National Geographic,* Oct. 1982, pp. 421-456.
- Brown, D.R., "Applications of Artificial Intelligence in Space Tracking and Data Systems," SRI Project 2203, SRI International, Menlo Park, CA, April 1981.
- Gevarter, W.B., *An Overview of Computer-Based Natural Language Processing*, NASA TM 85635 (also NBS 83-2687), NASA, Wash., D.C., April 1983.
- Gevarter, W.B., *An Overview of Computer Vision*, NBSIR-2582, National Bureau of Standards, Wash., D.C., September 1982.
- Gevarter, W.B., *An Overview of Expert Systems*, NBSIR-2505, National Bureau of Standards, Wash., D.C., May 1982 (Revised October 1982).
- Nilsson, N.J., "Artificial Intelligence: Engineering, Science or Slogan," *AI Magazine,* Vol. 3, No. 1, Winter 1981/1982, pp. 2-9.

II. THE RISE, FALL AND REBIRTH OF AI*

The First 15 Years

In 1956, ten scientists convened a conference at Dartmouth College from which emerged the present field of AI. The predictions made by those scientists were that in 25 years, we would all be involved in recreational activities, while computers would be doing all the work. In 1981, at the International Joint Conference on AI in Vancouver, Canada, a panel of five of these same scientists recalled that conference and their over-optimistic forecasts.

In 1956, it was assumed that intelligent behavior was primarily based on smart reasoning techniques and that bright people could readily devise ad hoc techniques to produce intelligent computer programs.

Figure II-1 lists some of the key AI activities during the first 15 years. The major initial activity involved attempts at machine translation. It was thought that natural language translation could be readily accomplished using a bilingual dictionary and some knowledge of grammar. However, this approach failed miserably because of factors such as multiple word senses, idioms and syntactic ambiguities. A popular story is that the saying "The spirit is willing but the flesh is weak," when translated into Russian and back again into English, came out "The wine is good but the meat is spoiled." Schwartz (1980, p. 27) reports that "Twenty million dollars of mechanical translation brought results so disappointing, that . . . by 1967 opinion had soured so dramatically that the National Academy of Sciences all but created a tombstone over the research." In fact it has only been recently that substantial work in mechanical language translation has reappeared.

Weizenbaum (1966) at MIT designed a natural language understanding program that simulated a non-directive psychotherapist. The program (ELIZA) bluffed its way through the interaction by picking up on key words and providing stock answers. When it did not find a recognizable key word, it would select a reply such as "Please continue." Though Weizenbaum wrote the program in part to show how ridiculous it was to expect true natural language understanding by a machine, the program nevertheless became popular and some of its basic techniques are used in commercial Natural Language Interfaces today.

In 1961, Slagle at M.I.T. devised a heuristic computer program to do symbolic integration. This proved to be the forerunner of a successful series of symbolic mathematical programs culminating

---

*An interesting history of the early years of AI is given by McCorduck (1979).

in MACSYMA, in use at M.I.T. today and available over the "ARPA Net" to other AI researchers.

Game playing was also one of the early areas of AI research, with Samuel's (1963) work at IBM on machine learning in checkers proving to be one of the early successes.

Solving puzzles was another area of early success in AI, leading to the development of problem solving techniques based on 1) search and 2) reducing difficult problems into easier subproblems.

Early work in vision involved image processing and pattern recognition (which was concerned with classifying two-dimensional patterns). Pattern recognition split off from AI and became a field in itself, but now the two disciplines have become much more unified.

Activities

- Attempts at Machine Translation
- ELIZA—Key Word and Template Matching
- Symbolic Integration
- Game Playing—Checkers, Chess
- Pattern Recognition
- Computational Logic
- General Problem Solver

Lessons Learned

- AI Much More Difficult Than Expected
- Heuristic Search Required To Limit Combinatorial Explosion
- Lack of Contextual Knowledge Severely Limits Capability
- Expectation Is a Human Characteristic of Intelligence
- Difficult To Handle a Broad Domain (e.g., Common Sense)

Figure II-1. A Condensed History of AI—1956-1970.

The pioneering work in computer vision was Robert's (1965) program designed to understand polyhedral block scenes. This program found the edges of the blocks using the spatial derivatives of image intensity, and from the resulting edge elements produced a line drawing. It then utilized simple features, such as the numbers of vertices, to relate the objects in the line drawing to stored 3D models of blocks. The resulting candidate model was then scaled, rotated, and projected onto the line drawing to see if the resultant match was adequate for recognition.

Another important area was computational logic. Resolution, an automatic method for determining if the hypothesized conclusion indeed followed from a given set of premises, was one of the early golden hopes of AI for universal problem solving by computer. Using resolution, Green (1969) devised a general-purpose, question-answering system, QA3, that solved simple problems in a number of domains such as robot movements, puzzles, and chemistry. Unfortunately, resolution, though it guarantees a solution, devises so many intermediate steps that turn out not to be needed for the final solution, that for large problems its use results in a combinatorial explosion of search possibilities.

Another approach, originally thought to have broad applicability, was the General Problem Solver (GPS) devised by Newell et al. (1960). The generality resulted from GPS being the first problem solver to separate its problem-solving methods from knowledge of the specific task currently being considered. The GPS approach was referred to as "means-ends analysis." The idea was that the differences between the current problem state and the goal state could be measured and classified into types. Then, appropriate operators could be chosen to reduce these differences, resulting in new problem states closer to the goal states. This procedure would then be iteratively repeated until the goal was reached. The series of operators used would then form the solution plan. Unfortunately, classifying differences and finding appropriate operators turned out to be more difficult than expected for non-trivial problems. In addition, computer running times and memory requirements rapidly become excessive for the more difficult problems.

AI proved much more difficult than originally expected. By 1970, AI had had only limited success. Natural Language Translation had already collapsed. "Toy" problems or well constructed problems such as games proved tractable, but real complex problems proved to be beyond the techniques thus far devised, or resulted in combinatorially explosive search that exceeded the then current computer capabilities. Similarly, real world computer vision efforts tended to be overwhelmed by the noise and complexities in real scenes.

In 1971, Sir Lighthill of Cambridge University was called upon by the British Government to review the AI field. The Lighthill Report (1972) found that "In no part of the field have the discoveries made so far produced the major impact that was promised." Further, he found that respected AI scientists were then predicting that ". . . possibilities in the 1980's include an all-purpose intelligence on a human-scale knowledge base; that awe-inspiring possibilities suggest themselves based on machine intelligence exceeding human intelligence by the year 2000"—the same sort of forecasts as were made 15 years earlier. Lighthill saw no need for a separate AI field and found no organized body of techniques that represented such a field. He felt that the work in automation and computer science would naturally come together to bridge whatever gap existed. The Lighthill report eventually brought work in AI in England to a virtual halt and cast a pall over AI work in the U.S.

However, the AI efforts of the 1950's and 1960's were not without merit. A great deal was learned about what really had to be done to make AI successful.

It was found that expectation is a human characteristic of intelligence. That perception, both visual and in language, is based upon knowledge, models and expectations of the perceiver. Thus communication via language was found to be based upon shared knowledge between the participants and that only cues are needed to actualize the models (in the receiver's head) from which to construct the complete message.

Thus in attempting communication or problem solving, lack of contextual knowledge was found to severely limit capability. Reasoning techniques alone proved inadequate. Knowledge is central to intelligence. Lacking this knowledge, it is difficult to handle a broad domain. An example is "common sense," found to be elementary reasoning based upon massive amounts of experiential knowledge.

It was also found that heuristics are necessary to guide search to overcome the combinatorial explosion of possible solutions that pervade complex problems—for each time one makes a decision, one opens up new possibilities.

The Decade of the 70's

As indicated in Figure II-2, in the 1970's AI researchers began to capitalize on the lessons learned. New knowledge representation techniques appeared. Search techniques began to mature. Interactions with other fields such as medicine, electronics and chemistry took place. Feasible approaches were demonstrated for language processing, speech understanding, computer vision, and computer programs that could perform like experts.

Activities

- Feasible Approaches Demo'd for:
    Language Processing
    Computer Vision
    Expert Systems
    Speech Understanding

- New Knowledge Representation Techniques Appear

- Search Techniques Begin To Mature

- Interaction with Other Fields Takes Place

Lessons Learned

- Knowledge Central to Intelligence

- Future Complex Systems Proved Feasible

Figure II-2. The Decade of the 70's.

SHRDLU was a natural language program at M.I.T. devised by Terry Winograd (1972) to interface with an artificial "blocks world." It was the first program to successfully deal in an integrated way with natural language by combining syntactic and semantic analysis with a body of world knowledge.

From 1971-1976, ARPA sponsored a five-year speech understanding program. HEARSAY II at Carnegie Mellon University was a winner, being able to understand sentences, with 90% accuracy, from continuous speech based on a 1000-word vocabulary. (The "blackboard" system architecture, devised for HEARSAY II to deal with multiple knowledge sources, has since found use in other AI applications.) A compiled network architecture system called HARPY, which handled the same vocabulary as HEARSAY II, was able to achieve a 95% accuracy. (A more detailed review is given in Part B of this report.)

At SRI, Gleason and Agin (1979) developed the SRI Vision Module as a prototype system for use in industrial vision systems. This system, which used special lighting to produce a binary image (silhouette) of an industrial workpiece, was able to extract edges by a simple continuous scan process, and was to prove the basis for several sophisticated commercial vision systems.

In the 70's, following an earlier successful effort called DENDRAL, a variety of prototype computer programs—called Expert Systems—designed to capture and utilize the expertise of a human expert in a narrow domain (such as medical diagnosis, crystallography, electrical circuitry, prospecting, etc.) made their appearance. MYCIN, a medical diagnosis and treatment consultant, devised by Shortliffe (1976) at Stanford University has been one of the most publicized.

Thus, the 70's found the AI research community developing the basic tools and techniques needed, and demonstrating their applicability in prototype systems. Future complex systems were proved feasible. The emphasis on knowledge, as essential to intelligence, led to the subfield of "Knowledge Engineering" associated with the building of expert systems.

1980 to the Present

The decade of the 70's set the framework from which the successes of the 80's emerged. In the 80's, expert systems proliferated. Dozens of prototype expert systems were devised in such areas as medical diagnosis, chemical and biological synthesis, mineral and oil exploration, circuit analysis, tactical targeting, and equipment fault diagnosis.

But the big news of the 80's (see Figure II-3) is that AI has gone commercial. AI companies (founded mostly by AI researchers) have formed to exploit applications. Computer, electronic, oil, and large diversified companies have set up AI groups. The military has also joined the fray, setting up their own AI groups and seeking early applications. The U.S. Defense Science Board views AI as one of the technologies that has the potential for an order of magnitude improvement in mission effectiveness.

In the expert systems area, DEC reports that R1—a system designed to configure VAX computer systems—is already saving them some 20 million dollars a year. MOLGEN—a system for planning molecular genetic experiments—is in regular commercial use. Shlumberger—a multi-billion dollar oil industry advisory company—seeing AI as a key to the company's growth in the 80's, has established four separate AI groups. The Palo Alto group has already created the expert system DIPMETER ADVISOR, to evaluate oil-drilling core samples.

In natural language front ends, some half dozen systems are now commercially available, with INTELLECT from Artificial Intelligence Corporation already boasting well over a hundred installations.

Highlighted by Texas Instruments' Speak and Spell, many commercial speech output systems have appeared. Limited speech recognition systems are also on the market, some using signal processing rather than AI techniques.

Hundreds of companies are now involved in computer vision systems, with dozens of commercial products already on the market for simplified vision applications.

Personal computers that are specially designed to run LISP—the List Processing Language favored by the U.S. AI community—are now commercially available from several companies.

The other indication that AI has now emerged as a viable discipline is that the existing AI technology is now becoming codified and therefore made broadly available to everyone, not just the core group of several hundred researchers of the 70's.

ARPA sponsored a three volume *AI Handbook* which was published in 1981 and 1982. Individual technology texts—in Vision, Natural Language, Expert Systems and LISP—are beginning to appear in numbers. NASA has sponsored this NBS set of overviews in Artificial Intelligence and Robotics.

Computer software tools for structuring knowledge and constructing expert systems are also becoming available.

In 1982, the Japanese officially began a 10 year, one-half billion dollar, research project to create a *Fifth Generation Computer*. The main features of this computer are that it is to have 1) intelligent interfaces (speech, text, graphics, etc.) 2) knowledge base management and 3) automatic problem solving and inference capabilities. All these capabilities are predicated on the use of AI techniques. The machine itself is visualized as a non-Von Neumann computer featuring parallel processing and having the capability of one billion logical inferences per second.

The Japanese are now considering the European AI language—PROLOG (Programming in Logic)—as the basis for their machine. Using PROLOG, logic problem-solving systems (heuristically guided) are reemerging (from the earlier failure of pure resolution) to handle complex problems.

With the advent of the Japanese Fifth Generation Computer Project, European nations, such as France and Britain, as well as the U.S., are putting renewed effort into their AI activities (Warren, 1982).

Activities

- Expert Systems Proliferate
- AI Goes Commercial
    - Expert Systems: RI, DIP-METER ADVISOR, MOLGEN
    - Natural Language Front Ends—INTELLECT
    - Speech Output—Speak and Spell
    - Vision Systems
    - AI Groups and Companies Form To Exploit Applications
    - LISP Machines Become Available
- AI Technology Becoming Codified
    - AI Handbook
    - Individual Technology Texts: Natural Language, Vision, etc.
    - NBS/NASA Overviews

Conclusions

- AI Tools and Systems Become Available
- Logic Systems (Heuristically Guided) Reemerge—PROLOG
- AI Techniques Sufficiently Perfected for Early Applications

Figure II-3. 1980-Present.

In summary then, we can conclude that AI tools and systems are now becoming available, and AI techniques are now sufficiently perfected for early applications. Further, the importance of AI is being recognized internationally and substantial sums of money in the U.S. and abroad are now beginning to be committed to developing AI applications.

CHAPTER II REFERENCES

- Gleason, G.J. and Agin, G.J., "A Modular System for Sensor-Controlled Manipulation and Inspection," *Proc. of the Ninth Inter. Symp. of Ind. Robots,* SME and RIA, Wash., DC, 1979, pp. 57-70.
- Green, C.C., "The Application of Theorem-Proving to Question Answering Systems," *IJCAI-1,* 1969, pp. 219-237.
- Lighthill, J., "Artificial Intelligence: A General Survey," Scientific Research Council of Britain, SRC 72-72, March 1972.
- McCorduck, P., *Machines Who Think,* San Francisco, W.H. Freeman, 1979.
- Newell, A., Shaw, J.C. and Simon, H.A., "A Variety of Intelligent Learning in a General Problem Solver," In M.C. Yovits and S. Cameron (Eds.), *Self Organizing Systems,* New York, Pergamon Press, 1960, pp. 153-189.
- Roberts, L., "Machine Perception of Three-Dimensional Solids," In J. Tippitt (Ed.), *Optical and Electro-Optical Information Processing,* Cambridge, Mass, MIT Press, 1965, pp. 159-197.
- Samuel, A.L., "Some Studies in Machine Learning Using the Game of Checkers," In E.A. Feigenbaum and J. Feldman (Eds.), *Computers and Thought,* New York, McGraw Hill, 1963.
- Schwartz, R.D., "Refocus and Resurgence in Artificial Intelligence," *IEEE Proc. of the Nat. Aerospace and Electronic Conference: NACON-1980,* Dayton, Ohio, May 20-22.
- Shortliffe, E.H., *Computer-Based Medical Consultations,* MYCIN, New York: American Elsevier, 1976.
- Slagle, J.R., "A Heuristic Program that Solves Symbolic Integration in Freshman Calculus: Symbolic Automatic Integrator (SAINT)," Rep. No. 5G-001, Lincoln Lab., M.I.T., Cambridge, Mass., 1961.
- Weizenbaum, J., "Eliza—A Computer Program for the Study of Natural Language Communication Between Man and Machine," *CACM* 9, 1966, pp. 36-45.
- Winograd, T., *Understanding Natural Language,* New York, Academic Press, 1972.
- Warren, D.H.D., "A View of the Fifth Generation and Its Impact," *The AI Magazine,* Vol. III, No. 4, Fall 1982, pp. 34-39.

III. BASIC ELEMENTS OF AI

Heuristic Search

AI problem solving can often be viewed as a search among alternative choices. It is thus possible to represent the resulting search space as a hierarchical structure called a tree, an example of which is shown in Figure III-1. (Figure III-1 is a search tree for the elementary problem of finding the simplest route, from city A to the destination city D, from among the network of roads illustrated by the state graph of Figure III-2.) The solution paths run from the initial state (root node) along the branches of the tree and terminate on the leaves (terminal nodes) labeled "goal state."

For a large complex problem, it is obviously too cumbersome to explicitly draw such trees of all the possibilities and directly examine them for the best solution. Thus, the tree is usually implicit; the computer generating branches and nodes as it searches for a solution.

In searching for a solution we may reason forward as in Figure III-1, or backward from the goal (searching an equivalent tree where the root node is the goal).

For fairly simple problems, a straightforward, but time-consuming, approach is blind search, where we select some ordering scheme for the search and apply it until the answer is found. There

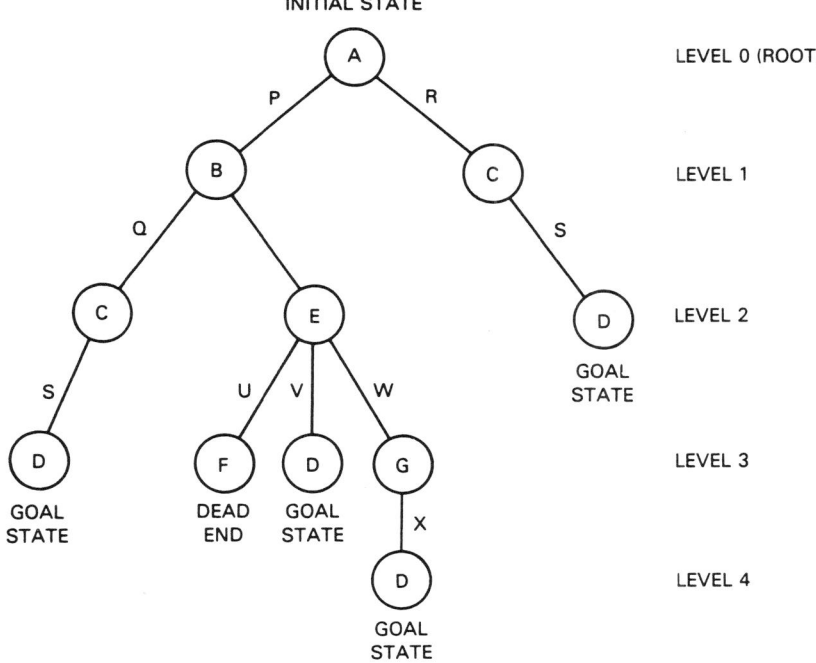

Figure III-1. Tree Representation of Paths Through the State Graph of Figure III-2.

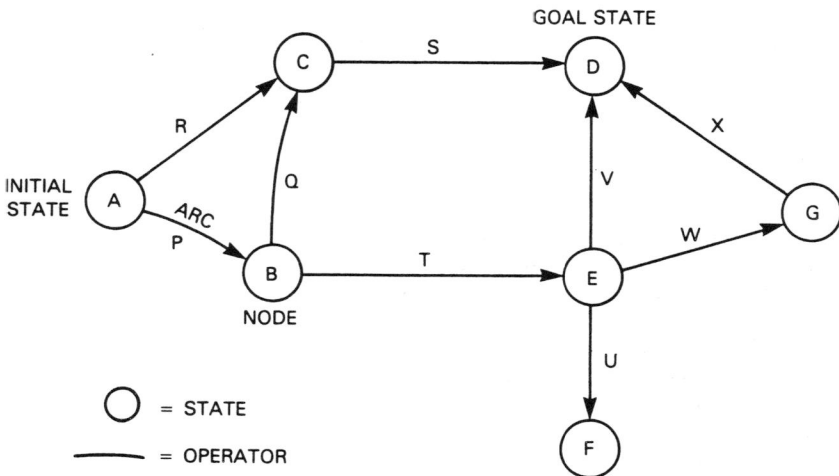

Figure III-2. State Graph for a Simple Problem.

are two common blind search procedures, breadth-first search and depth-first search. In breadth-first search, the nodes of the search tree are generated and examined level by level starting with the root node. In a depth-first search, a new node (at the next level) is generated from the one currently being examined, the search continuing in this way deeper and deeper until forced to backtrack.

Blind search does not make any use of knowledge about the problem to guide the search. In complex problems, such searches often fail, being overwhelmed by the combinatorial explosion of possible paths. If on the average there are n possible operators that can be applied to a node, and the search space is searched to a depth of d, then the size of the search space tends to grow in relation to n^d. Heuristic methods have been designed to limit the search space by using information about the nature and structure of the problem domain. Heuristics are rules of thumb, techniques or knowledge that can be used to help guide search. Heuristic search is one of the key contributions of AI to efficient problem solving. It often operates by generating and testing intermediate states along a potential solution path.

One straightforward method for choosing paths by this approach is to apply an evaluation function to each node generated and then pursue those paths that have the least total expected cost. Typically, the evaluation function calculates the cost from the root to the particular node that we are examining and, using heuristics, estimates the cost from that node to the goal. Adding the two produces the total estimated cost along the path, and therefore serves as a guide as to whether to proceed along that path or to continue along another, more promising, path among those thus far examined. However, this may not be an efficient approach to minimize the search effort in complex problems.

Search techniques are now relatively mature and are codified in the *AI Handbook* (Barr and Feigenbaum, 1981) and various AI texts. More detailed information on search techniques are given in Chapter II of Part C of this report.

Knowledge Representation*

The purpose of knowledge representation (KR) is to organize required information into a form such that the AI program can readily access it for making decisions, planning, recognizing objects and situations, analyzing scenes, drawing conclusions, and other cognitive functions. Thus knowledge representation is especially central to expert systems, computational vision, and natural language understanding.

Representation schemes are classically classified into declarative and procedural ones. Declarative refers to representation of facts and assertions, while procedural refers to actions, or what to do. A further subdivision for declarative ("object oriented") schemes includes relational (semantic network) schemes and logical schemes.

The principal KR schemes are briefly discussed in the following paragraphs.

Logical Representation Schemes

The principal method for representing a knowledge base logically is to employ First Order Predicate Logic. In this approach, a knowledge base (KB) can be viewed as a collection of logical formulas which provide a partial description of the world. Modifications to the KB result from additions or deletions of logical formulas.

An example of a logical representation is:

$$\text{IN (SHUTTLE ORBIT)} = \text{The shuttle is in orbit}$$

Logical representations are easy to understand and have available sets of inference rules needed to operate upon them. A drawback of logical representation is its tendency to consume large amounts of memory.

Semantic Networks

A semantic network is an approach to describing the properties and relations of objects, events, concepts, situations or actions by a directed graph consisting of nodes and labelled edges (arcs connecting nodes). A simple example is given in Figure III-3. Because of their naturalness, semantic networks are very popular in AI.

Procedural Representations and Production Systems

In procedural representations, knowledge about the world is contained in procedures—small programs that know how to do specific things (how to proceed in well specified situations). Classification of procedural representation approaches are based on the choice of activation mechanisms for the procedures, and the forms used for the control structures.

The two common approaches consist of procedures representing major chunks of knowledge — subroutines—and more modular procedures, such as the currently popular "production rules." The common activation mechanism for procedures is matching the system state to the preconditions needed for the procedure to be invoked.

---

*A more detailed presentation of knowledge representation is given in Chapter III of Part C.

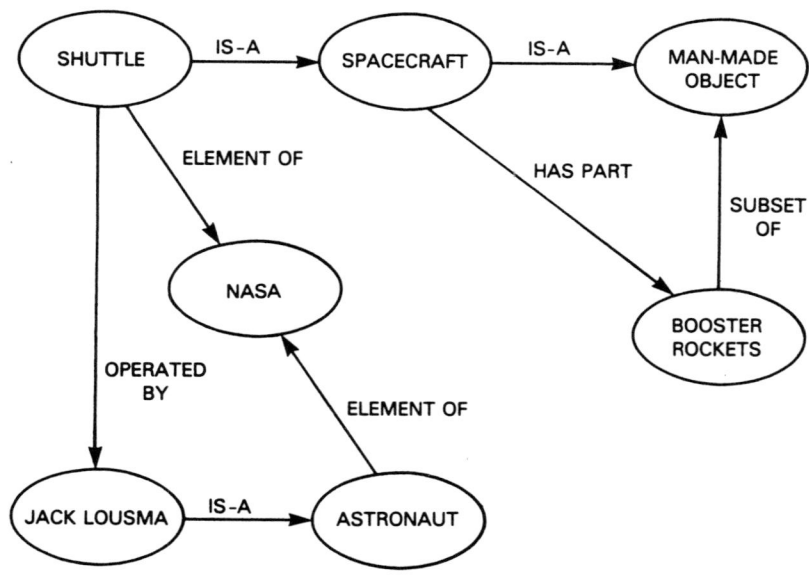

Figure III-3. Simple Example of a Semantic Network.

Production rules (PR) are characterized by a format of the type:
>Pattern, Action
>If, Then
>Antecedent, Consequent
>Situation, Procedure

e.g., If the shuttle power supply fails,
>and a working power supply is available,
>and the situation causing the problem no longer exists,

>Then switch to the backup.

Because of their modular representation of knowledge and their easy expansion and modifiability, PR's are now probably the most popular AI knowledge representation, being chosen for most expert systems.

Analogical or Direct Representations

In many instances it is appropriate to use natural representations such as an array of brightness values for an image, or a further reduced "sketch map" of the scene delineations in a computer vision system. These natural representations are useful in computational vision, spatial planning, geometric reasoning and navigation.

This form of representation has the advantages of being easy to understand, simple to update, and often allows important properties to be directly observed, so that they don't have to be inferred.

Property Lists

One approach to describe the state of the world is to associate with each object a property list, that is a list of all those properties of the object pertinent to the state description. The state, and therefore the object properties, can be updated when a situation is changed.

Frames and Scripts

A large proportion of our day-to-day activities are concerned with stereotyped situations such as going to work, eating, shopping, etc. Minsky (1975) conceived of "frames," which are complex data structures for representing stereotyped objects, events or situations. A frame has slots for objects and relations that would be appropriate to the situation. Attached to each frame is information such as:
—how to use the frame
—what to do if something unexpected happens
—default values for slots.

Frames can also include procedural as well as declarative information. Frames facilitate expectation-driven processing—reasoning based on seeking confirmation of expectations by filling in the slots. Frames organize knowledge in a way that directs attention and facilitates recall and inference.

An example of a frame is:
   Airplane Frame:
   Type:
     range: (fighter, transport, trainer, bomber, light plane, observation)
   Manufacturer:
     range: (McDonnell-Douglas, Boeing . . .)
   Empty Weight:
     range: (500 lbs to 250,000 lbs)
   Gross Weight:
     range: (500 lbs to 500,000 lbs)
     if needed: (1.6 × empty weight)
   Max Cruising Range:
     if needed: (look up in table cruising range appropriate to type and gross weight)
   Number of Cockpit Crew:
     range: (1 to 3)
     default: 2

Scripts are frame-like structures designed for representing stereotyped sequences of events such as eating at a restaurant or a newspaper report of an apartment fire.

Semantic Primitives:

For any knowledge representation scheme, it is necessary to define an associated vocabulary. For semantic nets, there has been a real attempt to reduce the relations to a minimum number of terms (semantic primitives) that are non-overlapping. A similar effort has emerged for natural language understanding, for which several attempts have been made to describe all of the world's aspects in terms of primitives that are unique, unambiguous representations into which natural language statements can be converted for later translation into another language or for other cognitive actions.

Schank (see, e.g., Schank and Riesbeck, 1981) has developed a "conceptual dependency" theory for natural language, in an attempt to provide a representation of all actions in terms of a small number of primitives. The system relies on 11 primitive physical, instrumental and mental ACT's (propel, grasp, speak, attend, etc.), plus several other categories, or concept types. There are two basic kinds of combinations or conceptualizations. One involves an actor doing a primitive ACT; the other involves an object and a description of its state. Attached to each primitive act is a set of inferences that could be associated with it.

An example of a representation in conceptual dependency is:

"Armstrong flew to the moon."

Actor:	Armstrong
Action:	flew
Direction to:	the moon
From:	unknown

Computational Logic*

Logic is a formal method of reasoning. Graham (1979, p. 163) observes that:

> Computational logic—doing logical reasoning with a computer—is based on what is traditionally known as symbolic logic, or mathematical logic. This, in turn, is divided into two (principal) parts, the simpler *"propositional logic"* and the more complex *"predicate logic"*.

Propositional Logic

In logic, a "proposition" is simply a statement that can be true or false. Rules used to deduce the truth (T) or falsehood (F) of new propositions from known propositions are referred to as "argument forms."

To make more interesting statements we can join propositions together with the following connectives:

Connective	Symbol	Meaning
And	$\wedge$ or $\cap$	both
Or	$\vee$ or $\cup$	either or both
Not	$\neg$ or $\sim$	the opposite
Implies	$\supset$ or $\rightarrow$	If the preceding term is true, then the term following will also be true
Equivalent	$\equiv$	has the same truth value

The simplest argument form is the "conjunction," which utilizes the connective AND. It states that if proposition p is true and proposition q is true, then the conjunction "p AND q" are true. In symbolic form we have

$$
\begin{array}{ll}
p & \text{(premise)} \\
\underline{q} & \text{(premise)} \\
p \wedge q & \text{(conclusion)}.
\end{array}
$$

That is, the conclusion is true if the premises are true.

Deduction involves deriving answers to problems based on a given set of premises. In mathematical logic, deductive procedures are sometimes referred to as "formal inference."

---

*A more complete discussion of computational logic is presented in Chapter IV of Part C.

A simple form of deduction is the "syllogism." For example:

> All Greeks are mortal.
> Socrates is a Greek.
> Therefore, Socrates is mortal.

This type of reasoning can be represented as a mathematical form of argument called "Modus Ponens" (MP):

> p   (premise)
> p implies q (premise)
> q   (conclusion)

or in logical notation as:

$$(p \land (p \rightarrow q)) \rightarrow q$$

Predicate Logic:

Propositional logic is limited in that it deals only with the T or F of complete statements. Predicate logic remedies this situation by allowing you to deal with assertions about items in statements, and allows the use of variables and functions of variables.

Propositions make assertions about items (individuals). A "Predicate" is the part of the proposition that makes an assertion about the individuals, and is written as:

$$\text{Predicate (individual, individual, ...)}$$

with "individual, individual, ..." being the arguments of the predicate.

For example,

> "The box is on the table," (proposition) is denoted as:
> ON (BOX, TABLE)

The predicate, together with its arguments, is a proposition. Any of the operations of propositional logic may be applied to it.

By including variables for individuals, Predicate Logic enables us to make statements that would be impossible in Propositional Logic. This can be further extended by the use of functions of variables. Finally, by use of the universal and existential quantifiers $\forall$ (for all) and $\exists$ (there exists), we arrive at First Order Predicate Logic (FOPL). FOPL permits rather general statements to be made, e.g.

For all Earth satellites, there exists a point y on the satellite that is closest to Earth:

$$\forall(x) \; \text{SATELLITE}(x) \rightarrow \exists(y) \; (\text{CLOSEST}(y, \text{Earth}) \land \text{ON}(y, x))$$

Various inference rules exist for the manipulation of quantifiers, the substitution of connectives, and other syntactic operations that assist in performing logical reasoning.

Logical Inference*

Resolution Method

Logical inference—reaching conclusions using logic—is normally done by "theorem proving." The most popular method for automatic theorem proving is the resolution procedure developed by Robinson (1965). This procedure is a general automatic method for determining if a hypothesized-conclusion (theorem) follows from a given a set of premises (axioms). First, using standard identities, the original premises and the conclusion to be proved are put into clause form. The conclusion to be proved is then negated. New clauses are then automatically derived using resolution and other procedures. If a contradiction is reached, then the theorem is proved.

Basically, resolution is the cancellation between clauses of a proposition in one clause with the negation of the same proposition in another clause.

Unfortunately, resolution has been unable to handle complex problems, as the search space generated by the resolution method grows exponentially with the number of formulas used to describe a problem. Thus for complex problems, resolution derives so many clauses not relevant to reaching the final contradiction, that it tends to use up the available time or memory before reaching a conclusion. Several domain-independent heuristics have been tried to constrain the search, but have proved to be too weak.

Factors Which Affect the Efficiency of Deductive Reasoning

Cohen and Feigenbaum (1982, pp. 80-81) state that "One kind of guidance that is often critical to efficient system performance is information about whether to use facts in a *forward-chaining* or *backward-chaining* manner . . . Early theorem-proving systems used every fact both ways leading to highly redundant searches . . ."

Another factor that can greatly affect the efficiency of the deductive reasoning is the way in which a body of knowledge is formalized. "That is, logically equivalent formalizations can have radically different behavior when used with standard deduction techniques."

Non-Resolution Theorem Proving

Cohen and Feigenbaum (1982, p. 94) observe that "In *non-resolution* or *natural deduction* theorem-proving systems, a proof is derived in a goal-directed manner that is natural for humans using the theorem prover. Natural-deduction systems represent proofs in a way that maintains a distinction between goals and antecedents, and they use inference rules that mimic the reasoning of human theorem-proving." They also tend to use domain-specific heuristics that help guide the search, and many proof rules to reduce goals to subgoals. The result is much more complex than the simpler, but less effective, resolution procedure.

Though requiring help from the programmer, the non-resolution Boyer and Moore (1979) Theorem Prover is one of the most powerful theorem provers available.

Special higher order languages (such as PROLOG, that helps structure the deduction problem and provides various built-in aids), coupled with domain-specific formulation and heuristic guidance rules, appears to be the direction that computational logic is proceeding in an attempt to handle complex real world problems.

---

*A more detailed discussion is given in Chapter IV of Part C.

Common Sense Reasoning

Common sense reasoning is low level reasoning based on a vast amount of experiential knowledge. An example is reasoning about falling objects, based upon experience rather than upon Newton's Laws. The same sort of reasoning tells us what is the appropriate thing to do in everyday social situations. While it is a simple matter for humans, it is very difficult to achieve in present AI systems with current techniques.

Nilsson (1980, p. 154) states:

> ... many common sense reasoning tasks that one would not ordinarily formalize can, in fact, be handled by predicate calculus theorem-proving systems. The general strategy is to represent specialized knowledge about the domain as predicate calculus expressions and to represent the problem or query as a theorem to be proved.

Nilsson (1980, p. 423) also observes that, "Much common sense reasoning (and even technical reasoning) is inexact in the sense that the conclusions and the facts and rules on which it is based are only approximately true. Yet people are able to use uncertain facts and rules to arrive at useful conclusions about everyday subjects such as medicine. A basic characteristic of such approximate reasoning seems to be that a conclusion carries more conviction if it is independently supported by two or more separate arguments." Several of the AI expert systems, such as Mycin and Prospector, make use of this approach.

AI approaches to approximate and plausible reasoning such as fuzzy set theory and default reasoning, and non-monotonic logic are given in Nilsson (1980) and Cohen and Feigenbaum (1982).

Non-Deductive Problem Solving Approaches*

Elements of a Problem Solver

All problems have certain common aspects: an initial situation, a goal (desired situation) and certain operators (procedures or generalized actions) that can be used for changing situations. In solving the problem, a control strategy is used to apply the operators to the situations to try to achieve the goal. This is illustrated in Figure III-4 where we observe a control strategy operating on the procedures to generate a sequence of actions (called a plan) to transform the initial conditions in the situation into the goal conditions. Normally, there are also constraints (specifying the conditions necessary for a specific procedure to be applied) which must be satisfied in generating a solution. In the process of trying to generate a plan, it is necessary for the problem solver to keep track of the actions tried and the effects of these actions on the system state. Figure III-5 is a restatement of Figure III-4 in which we can view the operators as impacting the data base to change the current situation (system state).

Problem Reduction

One simple form of problem solving is "divide and conquer," usually referred to as "problem reduction". Very often several subproblems (conjuncts) must be satisfied simultaneously in order to achieve a goal.

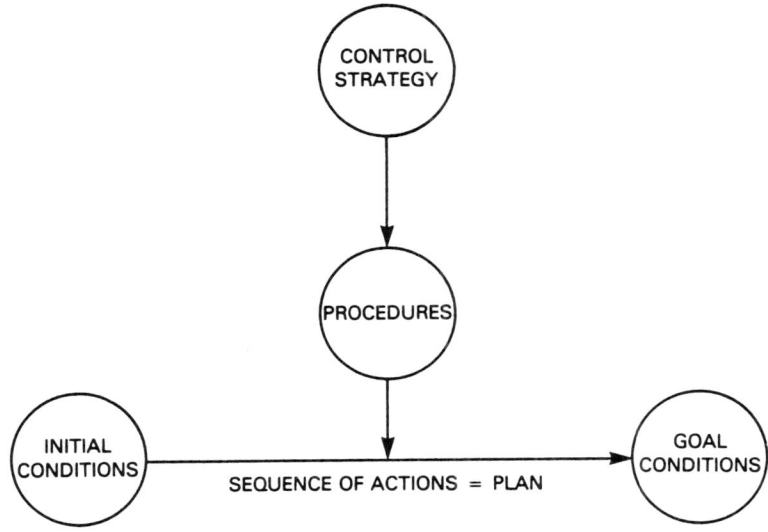

Figure III-4. Problem Solving.

---

*A more complete presentation is given in Chapter II of Part C.

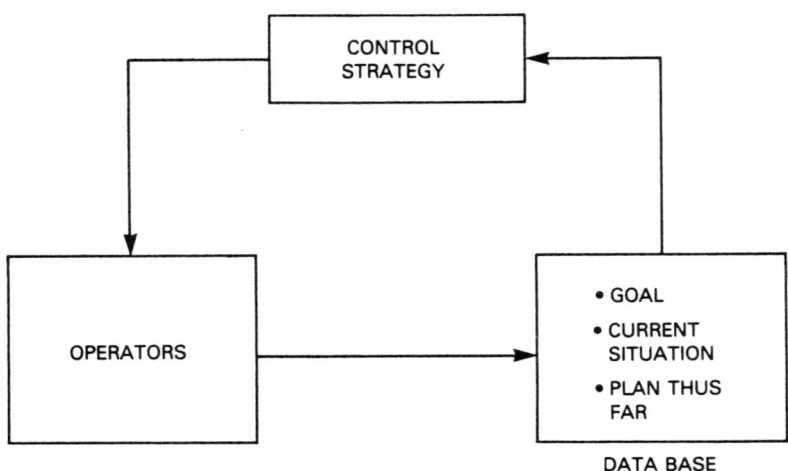

Figure III-5. Automatic Problem Solving Relationships

Problem reduction often fails without specific problem knowledge, as there is otherwise no good reason to attack one interacting conjunct before another. Lack of such knowledge may lead to an extensive search for a sequence of actions that tries to achieve subgoals in an unachievable order.

Difference Reduction ("Means-Ends" Analysis)

Difference reduction was introduced by the General Problem Solver (GPS) Program developed by Newell, Shaw and Simon, beginning in 1957. This was the first program to separate its general problem-solving method from knowledge specific to the current problem.

The means-ends analysis first determines the difference between the initial and goal states and selects the particular operator that would most reduce the difference. If this operator is applicable in the initial state, it is applied and a new intermediate state is created. The difference between this new intermediate state and the goal state is then calculated and the best operator to reduce this difference is selected. The process proceeds until a sequence of operators is determined that transforms the initial state into the goal state.

The difference reduction approach assumes that the differences between a current state and a desired state can be defined and the operators can be classified according to the kinds of differences they can reduce. If the initial and goal states differ by a small number of features, and operators are available for individually manipulating each feature, then difference reduction works. However, there is no inherent way in this approach to generate the ideas necessary to plan complex solutions to difficult problems.

More Efficient Tactics for Problem Solving

For more efficient problem solving it is necessary to devise techniques to guide the search by making better use of initial knowledge about the problem or of the information that can be discovered or learned about the problem as the problem solver proceeds through the search.

Sacerdoti (1979) indicates that information relevant to planning that can be learned during the exploration process includes:
- order relationships among actions
- hierarchical links between actions at various levels of abstraction
- the purpose of the actions in the plan
- the dependence among objects (or states) being manipulated

There are two opposing ways to improve the efficiency (solution time) of a problem solver:
- use a cheap evaluation function and explore lots of paths that might not work out, but in the process acquire information about the interrelationships of the actions and the states as an aid in efficiently guiding a subsequent search.
- use a relatively expensive evaluation function and try hard to avoid generating states not on the eventual solution path.

The following methods are attempts to achieve more efficient problem solving through employing various ratios of exploration and evaluation.

a. Hierarchical Planning and Repair

As in planning by humans, one can start by devising a general plan and refine it several times into a detailed plan. The general plan can be used as a skeleton for the more detailed plan. Using this approach, generating rather complex plans can be reduced to a hierarchy of much shorter, simpler subproblems. As the detailed plans are generated, the results should be checked to see that the intended general plan is being realized. If not, various methods for patching up the failed plan can be applied.

Another approach is to observe that some aspects of a problem are significantly more important than others. By utilizing this hierarchical ranking, a problem solver can concentrate most of its efforts on the critical decisions or more important subgoals first.

b. Problem Solving by Creating and then Debugging Almost-Right Plans

This approach deliberately oversimplifies the problem so it can be more readily solved and then corrects the solution using special debugging techniques (associated with errors due to the simplification). An everyday example is the general tactic by which people use road maps: find a simple way to get to the vicinity of your destination and then refine the plan from there.

c. Special Purpose Subplanners

This approach uses built-in subroutines to plan frequently occurring portions of a problem, such as certain moves or subgoals in robotics.

d. Constraint Satisfaction

This technique provides special purpose subplanners to help insure that the action sequences that are generated will satisfy constraints.

e. Relevant Backtracking (Dependency-Directed or Non-Chronological Backtracking)

The focus here is on sophisticated post-mortem analysis gained from several attempts that failed. The problem solver then uses this information to backtrack, not to the most recent choice point, but to the most relevant choice point.

f. Disproving

In this approach, attempts are made to prove the impossibility of the goal, both to avoid further pursuing an intractable problem, and to employ the resultant information generated to help suggest an action sequence to achieve the goal for a feasible problem.

g. Pseudo-Reduction

For the difficult case where multiple goals (conjuncts) must be satisfied simultaneously, one approach is to find a plan to achieve each conjunct independently. The resultant solutions to these simpler problems are then integrated using knowledge of how plan segments can be intertwined without destroying their important effects. By avoiding premature commitments to particular orderings of subgoals, this tactic eliminates much of the backtracking typical of problem solving systems.

h. Goal-Regression

This tactic regresses the current goal to an earlier position in the list of goals to be satisfied. This approach can be useful in cases where conjunctive subgoals must be satisfied, but where the action that satisfies one goal tends to interfere with the satisfaction of the others.

Table III-1 (derived from Sacerdoti, 1979, p. 15) indicates where the emphasis lies in the various problem-solving techniques discussed—either in the computational effort employed in evaluating the information gained thus far from the searched region, or in the effort expended in choosing the next move based only on local information.

Production Systems

Production rules (PR's), such as:

>If the Shuttle Power Supply fails
>and a backup is available,
>and the cause of failure no longer exists,
>Then switch to the backup.

have proved such a convenient modular way to represent knowledge, that they now form the basis of most Expert Systems.

The basic automatic problem solving relationships of Figure III-5 can be recast as a production system as shown in Figure III-6. A production system consists of a knowledge base of production rules (consisting of domain facts and heuristics), a global data base (GDB) which represents the

TABLE III-1. Primary Emphasis of Problem Solving Tactics.

Relationship	Learn and Evaluate	Choose New Move Based on Local Information
Sequencing Order	• Pseudo Reduction (Plan Generation Portion)	
	• Relevant Backtracking	
	• Disproving	
Hierarchy	• Plan and Repair	• Special Purpose Subplanner
Purpose of Actions	• Creating Almost-Right Plans	• Goal Regression
	• Pseudo Reduction (Plan Repair Portion)	
Dependency Among Objects	• Relevant Backtracking	• Constraint Satisfaction

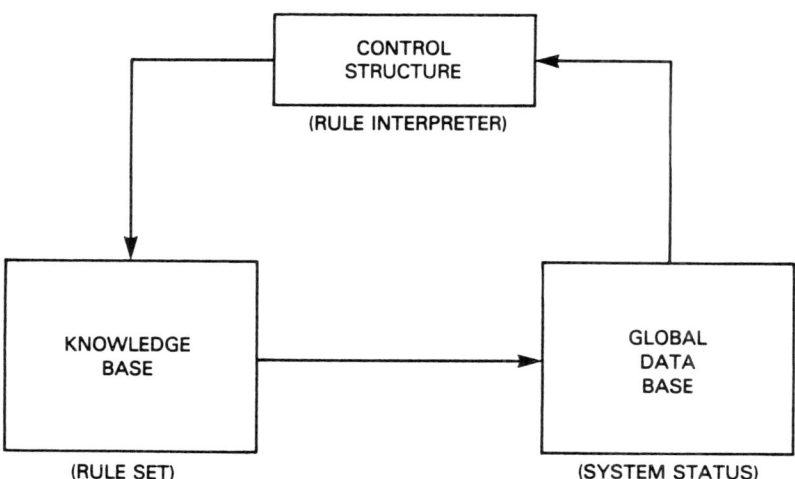

Figure III-6. A Production System.

system status, and a rule interpreter (control structure) for choosing the rules to execute. In a simple production rule system, the rules are tried in order and executed if they match a pattern in the GDB.

However, in more complex systems, such as used in Expert Systems, a very complex control structure may be used to decide which group of PR's to examine, and which to execute from the PR's in the group that match patterns in the GDB. In general, these control structures work in a repetitive cycle of the form:
1. Find the "conflict set" (the set of competing rules which match some data in the GDB).
2. Choose a rule from among the conflict set.
3. Execute the rule, modifying the GDB.

Production rule systems can be implemented for any of the problem-solving approaches discussed earlier. Thus, we may use a "top-down" approach, employing the rules to chain backwards from the goal to search for a complete supportive or causal set of rules and data ("goal-driven," or "model-driven" control structure). Or, we can use a "bottom-up" approach employing forwarding-chaining of rules to search for the goal ("event-driven" or "data-driven" control structure).

In complex systems (employing many rules) the control structure may contain meta-rules which select the relevant rules from the entire set of rules, and also focuses attention on the relevant part of the data base. This reduces the search space to be considered. The control structure then employs further heuristics to select the most appropriate rule from the conflicting rules which match the preconditions in the global data base. Johnson (1980, p. 7) describes this approach as follows:

> ... event-driven logic operates in the forward direction, comparing the left-hand sides of the rules in the rule-set with the data in the data base. The "best" of the matching rules found is selected and fired, causing the righthand side of that rule to make some modification in the global data base. This process is repeated until a goal rule matches the data and terminates the process ... a goal rule is one which tests whether the problem is done.
>
> In a "pure" production rule interpreter, the generalized repeating process takes the form shown in Figure III-7. That idealization may be considered as a four-cycle logical process with activation, matching, conflict-resolution, and execution subcycles. For generality, the subcycle machinery in Figure III-7 is shown to be controlled by additional sets of higher-order rules about rules, which are called meta-rules. In practice, one often finds part or all of the meta-rule machinery of Figure III-7 replaced by simpler mechanisms. In practical programs many variations of this basic scheme exist because of efficiency considerations, the characteristics of the particular applications, and programmer preferences.

A simple example of an event-driven production system can be visualized for a Shuttle Flight in which the power supply status is observed to be out of limits in the Global Data Base. The strategy meta-rules indicated in Figure III-7 then select, from the tens of thousands of rules in the Knowledge Base having to do with Shuttle Flight Operations, those rules having to do with power and the use of power. Similarly, the focusing meta-rules select from the GDB the relevant part having to do with the status of the power supply, and the Shuttle's and the experiments' use of power. The relevant rules are then compared with the relevant part of the GDB to determine which rules are appropriate for the current system status. The scheduling metarules (using priorities) then select the most appropriate rule (such as switching in the backup, or turning off the less important experiments). Executing the selected rule changes the system status, and the cycle repeats.

Basic Elements of AI   31

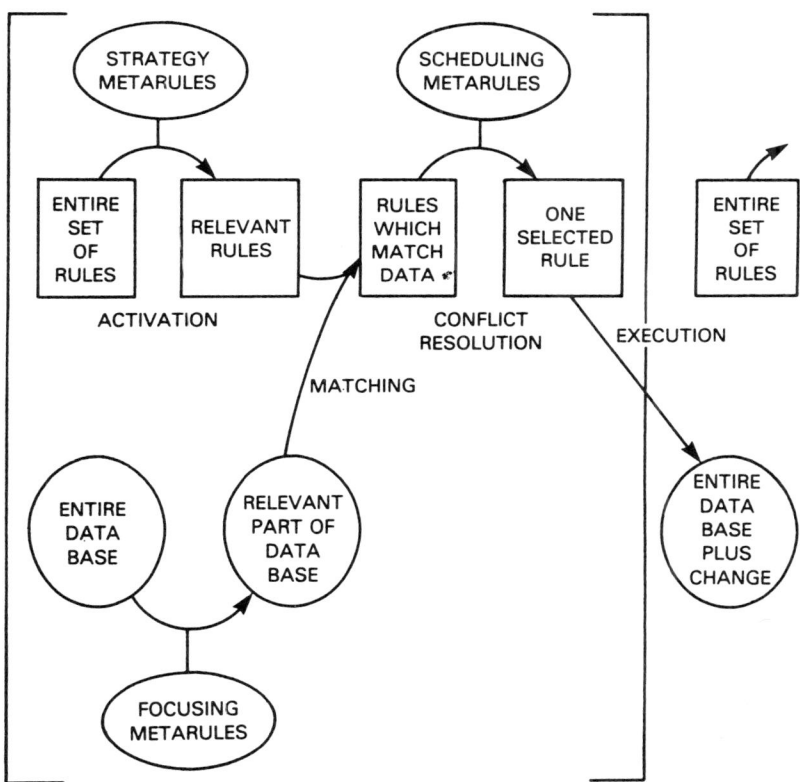

SOURCE: JOHNSON, 1980.

Figure III-7. Idealized Event-Driven Control Scheme.

AI Languages, Tools and Computers

Programming Needs of AI

AI research has been an experimental science trying to develop computer programs that exhibit intelligent behavior. This has proved to be a difficult endeavor requiring the best programming tools. AI programs tend to develop iteratively and incrementally. As the programs are thus evolutionary, creating AI programs requires an interactive environment with built-in aids such as dynamic allocation of computer memory as the program evolves, rather than advance memory allocation as in most other programming domains. More importantly, the unpredictable intermediate forms of the data (as the program evolves) also influence the form of the programming languages and the management of memory.

Another unusual aspect of AI programming is that AI researchers found that expressing functions recursively (defined in terms of themselves) was a great simplification in writing programs. Thus, AI programming languages tend to support recursive processing. Finally, AI programs are primarily concerned with symbol manipulation, rather than numeric computation. All AI languages thus support this feature.

Barr and Feigenbaum (1982, p. 32) observe that, "AI programs are among the largest and most complex computer programs ever developed and present formidable design and implementation problems . . . AI researchers in their capacity as language designers and programmers have pioneered an interactive mode of programming in environments with extensive support: editors, trace and debugging packages, and other aids for the construction of large complex systems.

Two basic general AI languages—LISP and PROLOG—have evolved in answer to these programming requirements. LISP has been the primary AI programming language. PROLOG, a logic-based language, has appeared more recently and has gained favor in Europe and Japan.

Various derivatives and dialects of LISP exist. Special high level programming languages, for such purposes as assisting in knowledge representation and constructing expert systems, have been built on top of LISP.

In recent years, nearly all AI programs were developed on the DEC PDP-10 and PDP-11 computers. AI programming is now transitioning to the DEC VAX computers and the new personal AI machines.

List Representations

List processing was originally introduced in their IPL programming language by Newell, Shaw and Simon (1957) to deal with symbol manipulation. Lists form associations of symbols which allow computer programs to build data structures of unpredictable shape and size. To handle such unpredictably shaped data structures IPL used primitive data elements (called cells).

The same idea is used in LISP in the form of CONS cells. Each CONS cell is an address (a computer word) that contains a pair of pointers to other locations in computer memory.* The left portion of the cell points to the first element (the "CAR") of the list. The right portion points to

---

*One can thus view the basic data object in LISP to be pointers, with lists as one interpretation placed upon the resultant pair structure.

another CONS cell representing the remainder (the "CDR") of the list. Thus, as indicated in Figure III-8, representing a sequence of words or symbols in memory can be visualized as a binary tree structure using these memory cells.

The problem of unpredictable size of data structures was solved by having a free list of memory cells that could be dynamically allocated as required.

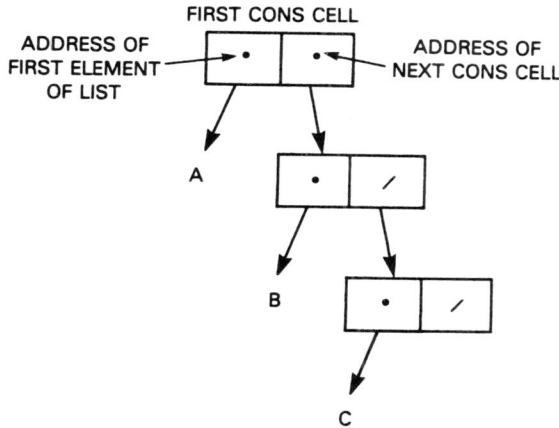

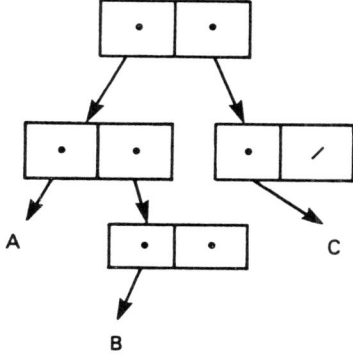

Figure III-8. Representation of List Structures in Memory.

A list is a sequence of zero or more elements enclosed in parentheses, where each element is either an atom (an indivisible element) or a list. Lists can be used to represent virtually any type of data. Lists are therefore useful for representations in such AI areas as language understanding, computer vision, and problem solving and planning.

Tree structures (used to represent search spaces) are ubiquitous in AI. A list representation for a tree structure is shown in Figure III-9. It will be observed that the resultant representation is a list (as indicated by parentheses) consisting of elements, some of which are also lists. These nested structures are common in list representations.

Predicate logic expressions such as
  IN(x,A) OR IN(x,B)
  meaning x is in A or in B
can be conveniently expressed, using prefix notation, in list form as
  (OR (IN x A) (IN x B))

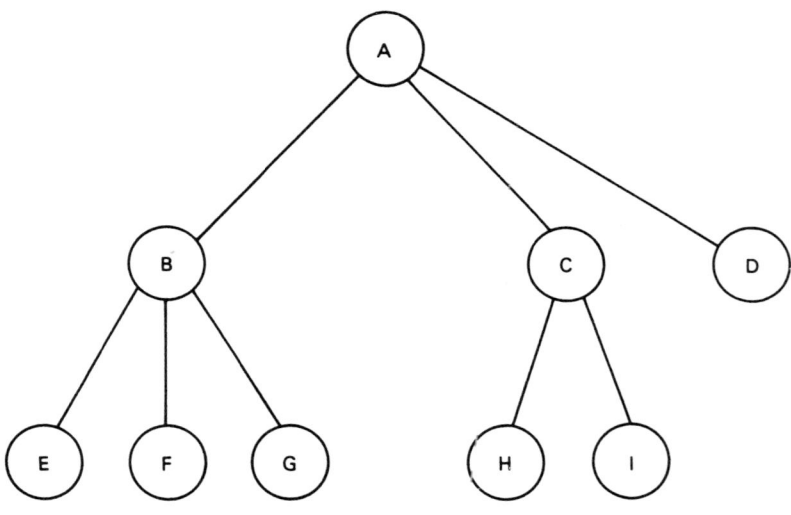

(A (B E F G) (C H I) D)

WHERE (B E F G), (C H I) AND D ARE THE SUBTREES
OF THE ROOT NODE A.

Figure III-9. List Representation of a Search Tree.

LISP

a. Background

Around 1960, John McCarthy at M.I.T. developed LISP as a practical list processing language with recursive-function capability for describing processes and problems. Since then, LISP has been the primary AI programming language—the one most used in AI research.

b. Basic Elements of LISP

All LISP programs and data are in the form of symbolic expressions (S-expressions) which are stored as list structures. LISP deals with two kinds of objects: atoms and lists. Atoms are symbols (constants or variables) used as identifiers to name objects which may be numeric (numbers) or non-numeric (people, things, robots, ideas, etc.). A list is a sequence of zero or more elements enclosed in parentheses, where each element is either an atom or a list.

Graham (1979, p. 226) observes, "A LISP system is a function-evaluating machine. The user types in a function and its arguments. LISP types back the result of applying the function and its arguments." For example for addition:

    User input: (PLUS 6 2)

    LISP response: 8

To manipulate lists, LISP has three basic functions (related to the memory cell structure storage for lists):

    CONS, to join a new first member to a list.

    CAR, to retrieve the first member of a list.

    CDR, (pronounced coud-er) to retrieve the list consisting of all but the first member of a list.

Thus:

    User: (CONS 'Z '(C D E))

    LISP (Z C D E)

where the quote symbol, ', is used to indicate that the expression following is not to be evaluated. Normally, LISP evaluates all expressions (starting with the innermost parentheses) before carrying out other operations.

    User: (CAR '(John Mary X Y))

    LISP: John

    User: (CDR '(John Mary X Y))

    LISP: (Mary X Y)

c. Variables

In LISP, the SET function assigns a value to a variable. Thus:

    User: (SET 'Z George)

    LISP: George

    User: Z

    LISP: George

Atoms are used for variables in LISP. When quoted, an atom stands for itself, otherwise LISP automatically substitutes its value during processing.

d. Defining New Functions

Programming in LISP involves defining new functions. Thus, we could define SECOND (the second atom of a list) by:

    User: (DEFUN SECOND (Y) (CAR(CDR Y)))
        where Y is a dummy variable.
    LISP: SECOND
    User: (SECOND '(JOHN FRANK MARY JANE))
    LISP: FRANK

e. Predicates

A predicate is a function which returns either NIL (false) or T (true). As a programming convenience, any none-NIL value is also considered to be true. (NIL is actually the name of the empty list.)

Thus, the predicate GREATERP returns T if the items in the series are in descending order.

    User: (GREATERP 6 5 2)
    LISP: T

f. Conditional Branching

It is often necessary in AI to use conditional branching. For example, if so and so is true, then do X, if not, if thus and so is true, then do Y, if not do Z.

The COND function in LISP has this role. Its form is:

    (COND (condition 1 expression 1)
           (condition 2 expression 2)
                •
                •
                •
           (condition m expression m))

where each condition is an expression that will evaluate to NIL or something else. The COND function evaluates the conditions in order until one of them evaluates to other than NIL. It then returns the value of the corresponding expression.

g. Recursive Functions

It is often much easier to define a function recursively—in terms of itself—than to define it as an explicit series of steps. This recursive feature is an important characteristic of LISP. A simple illustration is the factorial example (Barr and Feigenbaum, 1982, P. 6):

$$N! = \begin{cases} 1 & \text{if } N=1 \\ N \times (N-1)! & \text{if } N > 1 \end{cases}$$

This factorical function (FACTORIAL) can be written as:
(DEFUN FACTORIAL (N)
  (COND (EQUAL N 1) 1)
    (T (TIMES N (FACTORIAL (DIFFERENCE N 1)))))

h. Review of Program Features of LISP

It should be noted that LISP programs and data are both in the same form - lists. Thus, AI programs can manipulate other AI programs. This allows programs to create or modify other programs, an important feature in intelligent applications. It also allows programming aids for debugging and editing to be written in LISP, providing great interactive flexibility for the LISP programmer, who can thus tailor things to suit his needs.

Other notable aspects of LISP are (Barr and Feigenbaum, 1982, p. 17)

—LISP is an interactive interpreted language and therefore relatively slow. (However, it can be compiled, often resulting in an order of magnitude improvement.)
—Memory allocation is automatic.
—LISP expressions are very simple and regular. All expressions are made up of atoms and compositions of atoms.
—Control is normally applicative—the flow of control being guided by the application of functions to arguments, in contrast to the sequential control structure of most programming languages.
—Dynamic Scoping of Variables—usually a non-local variable will have its value locally assigned by the function evaluating it, unless it was assigned a value by the function calling the evaluating function.
—For real-time operation, LISP requires a sophisticated garbage collection system to recycle memory cells no longer being used.
—LISP is a huge package and until the advent of the special personal LISP machines, the full capabilities of LISP could only be implemented on large computers.
—The use of nested parentheses in LISP can be confusing, but the confusion can be reduced somewhat by indenting expressions according to their level of nesting.

i. LISP Today

There are two major LISP dialects today:
  MACLISP developed at M.I.T.
  INTERLISP developed at BBN and XEROX-PARC.

Both offer very similar programming environments with editing and debugging facilities. Both offer many LISP functions and optional features. The emphasis in INTERLISP has been to provide the best possible programming environments, even at the expense of speed and memory space. MACLISP has had more emphasis on efficiency, conservation of address space and flexibility for building tools and embedding languages.

INTERLISP has been the much better-supported version, with complete documentation and many users. It runs on DEC and XEROX operating systems.

Out of the need to standardize the various MACLISP dialects has evolved "Common LISP" and "LISP Machine LISP" for personal AI computers. This new dialect—Common LISP—appears destined to be used on most of the new personal AI machines and operating systems. Common LISP is intended to be efficient and portable, with stability a major goal.

Because of the rapid development of LISP features by the user community, other more local LISP versions (such as FRANZLISP at U. of CA, Berkeley) exist at several university AI labs.

A good text on LISP programming is *LISP* by Winston and Horn (1981).

PROLOG (PROgramming in LOGic)

a. History

PROLOG is a logic-oriented language developed in 1973 at the University of Marseille AI Laboratory by A. Colmerauer and P. Roussel. Additional work on PROLOG has been done at the University of Edinburgh in Great Britain. Development of PROLOG in France has continued to the present, achieving a documented system that can be run on nearly all computers (Colmerauer et al., 1981).

b. Nature of PROLOG

PROLOG is a theorem-proving system. Thus, programs in PROLOG consist of "axioms" in First-Order Predicate Logic together with a goal (a theorem to be proved). The axioms are restricted to implications, the left- and right-hand sides of which are written in "Horn-clause" form.

A Horn clause consists of a set of statements joined by logical AND's. Thus, the form of a typical PROLOG axiom is:

$$A \cap B \cap C \cap X \longrightarrow Y \cap Z$$

That is, A AND B AND C AND X together IMPLY Y AND Z.

when read declaratively. It can also be read procedurally as:

To prove Y AND Z, try to prove A AND B AND C AND X.

Looked at this way, a PROLOG program consists of a group of procedures, where the left side of a procedure is a pattern to be instantiated* to achieve the goals on the right side of the procedure.

$$\text{PROCEDURE:} \quad \text{PATTERN} \longrightarrow \text{GOALS}$$

(Note the similarities of these modular rules to the IF, THEN production rules used in constructing Expert Systems. It is this modularity which promotes clear, accurate, rapid programming—that is one of the reasons for PROLOG's popularity.)

---

*An instance is found that satisfies it.

EXAMPLE: Find the geopolitical entities in Europe:
DATA: written as a relational data base in Horn clause form:
$$\text{PARTOF (London, England)}$$
$$\cap \text{ PARTOF (England, Europe)}$$
$$\cap \text{ PARTOF (Boston, U.S.)}$$
$$\cap \text{ PARTOF (Tokyo, Japan)}$$

PROCEDURES:
   (1)   PARTOF(X,Y) ⟶ IN(X,Y)
That is, to prove X is in Y, try to prove X is part of Y.
   (2)   PARTOF(X,Y) $\cap$ IN(Y,Z) ⟶ IN(X,Z)
That is, to prove X is in Z, try to prove X is part of Y and Y is in Z.

GOAL (Theorem to be Proved):
$$\text{IN(X, Europe)}$$
That is, What X's are in Europe?

By matching the goal to the right-hand side of the first procedure we instantiate the procedure by letting
$$\text{Europe} = Y$$
Then matching the data to this procedure we find
$$X = \text{England}$$
Matching the goal to the right-hand side of the second procedure, we instantiate it by letting
$$\text{Europe} = Z$$
Now, matching the data to the two procedures, we instantiate them by letting
$$Y = \text{England}$$
$$X = \text{London}$$
Thus we have two instances:
$$X = \text{England}$$
$$X = \text{London}$$
that satisfy the goal.

As indicated by the example, PROLOG solves a problem by pattern-matching, which can be viewed as unification (the carrying out of instantiations) in the sense of First Order Predicate Logic. (PROLOG incorporates a very powerful pattern-matching mechanism.) If the pattern-matching fails as PROLOG searches through its procedures, then it automatically backtracks to its previous choice point, resulting in a depth-first type of search.

The solution process starts with the system searching for the first clause whose right side matches (unifies with) the goal. Thus, the search process can be guided by the programmer by choosing the order for the procedures, the data, and the goals in the clauses.

PROLOG can be considered as an extension of pure LISP coupled with a relational data base query language (as exemplified by the Horn clause form for expressing the basic data) which utilizes virtual relations (implicit relations defined by rules). Like LISP, PROLOG is interactive and uses dynamic allocation of memory.

c. PROLOG Today

PROLOG is a much smaller program than LISP and has now been implemented on a variety of computers (including microcomputers). A documented highly portable version of PROLOG has been written in France (Colmerauer, et al, 1981.) The execution of PROLOG is surprisingly efficient and in its compiled version it is claimed to be faster than compiled LISP. PROLOG has proved very popular in Europe and is now targeted as the language for Japan's Fifth Generation Computer project. PROLOG's design (and its powerful pattern matcher) is well suited to parallel search and therefore an excellent candidate for such powerful future computers incorporating parallel processing. Substantial interest in PROLOG is now arising in the U.S., with some of PROLOG's features being implemented in LISP.

PROLOG's principal drawback appears to be its depth-first search approach which could be a concern in certain complex problems that tend toward combinatorial explosions in the size of the search space.

PROLOG was originally developed for natural language understanding applications, but has since found use in virtually all AI application areas.

Other AI Languages

A number of AI languages have been developed as extensions of, improvements upon (e.g., special features for knowledge organization and search), or alternatives to, LISP. These include (see Barr and Feigenbaum, 1982):

- *System Programming Languages* (LISP-level)
    - —SAIL (Stanford AI Language) (1969)
    - —QA4 and QLISP (at SRI 1968, 1972)
    - —POP-2 (at U. of Edinburgh 1967)
- *Deduction/Theorem-Proving Languages*
    - —PLANNER and MICROPLANNER (M.I.T., 1971)
    - —CONNIVER (M.I.T., 1972)
    - —POPLER (U. of Edinburgh, 1972)
    - —PROLOG (U. of Marseille, 1973)
    - —AMORD (M.I.T., 1977)

LISP and POP-2 are designed to simplify the building of new languages within or on top of them—QLISP being embedded in INTERLISP, POPLER embedded in POP-2. POP-2 remains popular in England, but has not caught on elsewhere.

Most of the above AI languages are no longer supported and have fallen into disuse. However, they were experiments that helped pave the way for the modern AI languages now in use, such as the LISP dialects, PROLOG, and POP-2. For instance, PROLOG's style of programming is similar to that demonstrated in QA3 and PLANNER.

Other special languages have been built for Knowledge Representation, Knowledge Base Management, writing rule-based systems (such as Expert Systems), and for special application areas. These languages are treated in the appropriate sections of this report.

AI Computational Facilities

a. Requirements

Good AI people are still scarce, expensive and dedicated. It therefore behooves an organization supporting an AI group to provide the best facilities available (commensurate with cost) so as to maximize the productivity of their AI people.

Fahlman and Steele (1982) state that desirable features of an AI Programming Environment are:
- Powerful, well-maintained, standardized AI languages.
- Extensive libraries of code and domain knowledge (A facility should support the exchange of code with other AI research facilities).
- Excellent graphic displays: high resolution, color, multiple windows, quick update, and software to use all of these easily.
- Good input devices.
- Flexible, standardized inter-process communication.
- Graceful, uniform user-interface software.
- A good editor that can deal with a program based on the individual program structure.

They suggest that:
- Sticking with the hardware and systems that major AI centers are using is important, so that the time can be spent getting work accomplished, not reinventing the wheel.
- $50K-$100K per researcher for computing facilities is appropriate.
- Your AI product can be developed in the best available environment. Once developed, it can be ported to other languages and machines, as appropriate.
- Isolated machines are nearly useless. Good network interfaces, internal and external are critical.*
- AI people spend roughly 80% of their time editing, reading and communicating. Thus, facilities for this must be excellent.

b. AI Machines

The computers used for AI research for the past several years have been primarily the DEC system-10 and DEC system-20 family of time-shared machines. These are now being superseded by the more economical DEC VAX time-shared computers and the newer personal AI machines. However, Brown (1981) sees this as a mixed blessing, as the newer machines are still deficient in software, as compared to the older DEC 10's and 20's with their rich software libraries.

The newer machines tend to have 32-bit words, sorely needed for address space, as most AI programs are huge.

Fahlman and Steele (1982) see the DEC VAX, with a UNIX operating system, as the best time-sharing machine today for AI purposes. Several LISP dialects are available. The VAX is the current choice of many universities.

M.I.T. designed a personal machine specially microcoded for LISP. This M.I.T. LISP Machine has been licensed to LMI and Symbolics. Table III-2 lists some of the current Personal AI

---

*Brown (1981) sees an ARPANET link as essential for a NASA AI lab. "The ARPANET links most U.S. AI research centers and provides an electronic bulletin board, electronic mail, file transfer, and access to remote data bases, software tools and computing power."

TABLE III-2. Some Personal AI Computers Now Available.

Machine/Company	Approx. Price	Characteristics
3600 Symbolics, Inc. Cambridge, MA	$75K	A new complete redesign of MIT LISP Machine. Very fast and flexible. Extensive software.
Lambda LISP Machines, Inc. Los Angeles, CA	$73K	A recent redesign of MIT LISP Machine. Software from MIT.
PERQ1a 3 Rivers Computer Corp. Pittsburgh, PA	$30K	SPICE Software from CMU, including Common LISP. Much less powerful than LISP machines.
XEROX 1100 Series XEROX Electro-Optical Systems Pasadena, CA	$25K*/up	A mature INTERLISP system available in several versions having different memory capacities.

*Mainframe computer support desirable.

Machines. Several other personal machines of lesser capacity are also being offered for AI applications.

These new AI personal machines represent unusually powerful interactive exploratory programming environments in which system design and program develop together (Sheil, 1983). This is in sharp contrast to the more traditional structured programming approach in which software program specifications are first written, with the software development following in rigid adherence to the specifications.

To further enhance the exploratory programming approach, the user-friendly object-oriented programming languages have been devised. An object (such as an airplane, or a window on a computer screen) can be encoded as a package of information with attached descriptions of procedures for manipulation of that information. Objects communicate by sending and receiving messages that activate their procedures. A class is a description of one or more similar objects. An object is an instance of a class and inherits the characteristics of its class. The programmer developing a new system creates the classes that describe the objects that make up the system and implements the system by describing messages to be sent. Use of object-oriented programming reduces the complexity of large systems. The notion of class provides a uniform framework for defining system objects and encourages a modular, hierarchical (top-down) program structure (Robinson, 1981). "Smalltalk" is an object-oriented language available on the Xerox machines. "Flavors" is available on the M.I.T.-based LISP machines. LOOPS being developed at Xerox PARC is a further extension of the Smalltalk system. ROSS at RAND Corp. is an object-oriented programming language for use in symbolic simulation of activities such as air combat.

The new AI personal machines tend to come with interactive facilities for program development, editing, debugging, etc. For key portions of AI programs, microcode allows key inner loops to be run very fast. This is especially important in graphics and vision programs. The efficiency of computers microcoded for AI applications and suppporting large memories make these personal computers especially attractive.

ZETALISP derived from MACLISP is an integrated software environment for program development and program execution as the Symbolics 3600. ZETALISP has available nearly 10,000 compiled functions making it an exceptionally powerful and functional form of the LISP programming language. Similar capabilities are available on the LMI Lambda machines.

Interlisp-D, used on the Xerox 1100 machines, provides a comprehensive programming environment particularly suited for the development and delivery of expert and other knowledge-based systems.

c. Future

It is expected that the price of good AI personal computers that run LISP will rapidly drop below $50K as competition heats up and demand escalates. It is thus anticipated that one personal AI machine per AI person will be the standard of the future.

Parallel architectures are now being considered for future AI machines. This is especially attractive for PROLOG because its structure facilitates parallel search. Japan intends to build sequential PROLOG personal computers by 1985, featuring 10K logical inferences per second. In the 1990 time frame, Japan's Fifth Generation Computer project is projected to yield an enormously powerful AI parallel processing machine running PROLOG at one billion logical inferences per second (about 10,000 times more powerful than the DEC-KL-10 on which the AI community grew up).

Summary and Forecast

It now appears that LISP dialects designed specifically for personal computers will become commonplace. It is also expected that software portability will improve substantially. PROLOG and its derivatives, now prevalent throughout Europe, will become incorporated with LISP in the U.S.

Powerful Personal AI Computers under $50K will rapidly appear and become the AI standard for the next several years. In the longer term, powerful parallel computers, such as the Japanese Fifth Generation Computers, will probably become the standard as the number of AI practitioners expands and more difficult problems are addressed.

The rapidly increasing capability and ease of development of VLSI chips, promises to move AI computing power for developed applications out of the laboratory and into the field and products as needed.

An emerging trend is the increased use of object-oriented programming to ease the creation of large exploratory programs. The use of objects is also a good way to program dynamic symbolic simulations, which will become more important as the quest for utilizing deeper knowledge accelerates and the demand for increased reliability of knowledged-based systems is pursued. Object-oriented programming also holds promise for distributed processing, as each object could be implemented on a separate processor in a linked network of processors.

Finally, it is anticipated that the AI exploratory software development approach will slowly infuse conventional software practices.

CHAPTER III REFERENCES

- Barr, A. and Feigenbaum, E.A. (Eds.), *The Handbook of Artificial Intelligence,* Vol. I, Los Altos, CA, W. Kaufmann, 1981.
- Barr, A., and Feigenbaum, E.A. (Eds.), *The Handbook of Artificial Intelligence,* Vol. II, Los Altos, CA, W. Kaufmann, 1982.
- Boyer, R.S., and Moore, J.S., *A Computational Logic,* New York, Academic Press, 1979.
- Brown, D.R., "Recommendations for an AI Research Facility at NASA/GSFC," SRI Project 2203, SRI Inter., Menlo Park, CA, October 1981.
- Cohen, P.R. and Feigenbaum, E.A. (Eds.), *The Handbook of Artificial Intelligence,* Vol. III, Los Altos, CA, W. Kaufmann, 1982.
- Colmerauer, A., Kanoui, H., Van Canegham, M., "Last Steps Toward an Ultimate PROLOG," *IJCAI-81,* Vancouver, Canada, Aug. 1981, pp. 947-948.
- Fahlman, S.E., and Steele, G.L., "Tutorial on AI Programming Technology: Language and Machines," AAAI-82, Pittsburgh, PA, August 16, 1982.
- Graham, N., *Artificial Intelligence,* Blue Ridge Summit, PA, Tab Books, 1979.
- Johnson, C.K., "Programming Methodology of Artificial Intelligence," *Computing in Crystallography,* Diamond, R., and Kenkatsan, S.R. (Eds.), Bangladore, India, Indian Academy of Sciences, 1980, pp. 28.01-28.16.
- Minsky, M., "A Framework for the Representing Knowledge," In P. Winston (Ed.), *The Psychology of Computer Vision.* New York, New York, McGraw-Hill, 1975, pp. 211-277.
- Newell, A., Shaw, J.C. and Simon, H.A., "Programming the Logic Theory Machine," *Proc of the Western Joint Computer Conf.,* 1957, pp. 230-240.
- Newell, A., Shaw, J.C. and Simon, H.A., "A Variety of Intelligent Learning in a General Problem Solver," In M.C. Yovits and S. Cameron (Eds.), *Self Organizing Systems,* New York, Pergamon Press, 1960, pp. 153-189.
- Nilsson, N.J. *Principles of Artificial Intelligence,* Palo Alto, CA, Tioga Pr., 1980.
- Robinson, D., "Object-Oriented Software Systems," *BYTE,* Aug. 1981, pp. 74-86.
- Robinson, J.A., "A Machine-Oriented Logic Based on the Resolution Principle," *J. ACM,* Vol. 12, 1965, pp. 33-41.
- Sacerdoti, E.D., "Problem Solving Tactics," TN189, SRI Inter., Menlo Park, CA, July 1979.
- Schank, R.C. and Riesbeck, *Inside Computer Understanding,* Hillsdale, N.J.: Lawrence Erlbaum, 1981.
- Sheil, B., "Power Tools for Programmers," *Datamation,* Feb. 1983, pp. 131-144.
- Winston, P.H. and Horn, B.K.P., *LISP,* Reading, Mass., Addison-Wesley, 1981.

IV. APPLICATIONS

The potential range of AI applications is so vast that it covers virtually the entire breadth of human intelligent activity. Detailed listings of focused applications are given in Part B of this volume, in each of the sections on applications: expert systems, computer vision, natural language processing, and problem solving and planning. This section just summarizes some of the key applications. Generic applications are listed in Table IV-1. Examples of specific applications of AI are listed in Table IV-2. Potential functional applications for NASA are indicated in Table IV-3. The opportunities this opens up for NASA are listed in Table IV-4. Similar opportunities are available in many other public and private domains.

TABLE IV-1. Generic Applications of AI.

Knowledge Management
- Intelligent data base access
- Knowledge acquisition
- Text understanding
- Text generation
- Machine translation
- Explanation
- Logical operations on data bases

Human Interaction
- Speech understanding
- Speech generation

Learning and Teaching
- Intelligent computer-aided instruction
- Learning from experience
- Concept generation

Fault Diagnosis and Repair
- Humans
- Machines
- Systems

Computation
- Symbolic mathematics
- "Fuzzy" operations
- Automatic programming

Communication
- Public access to large data bases via telephone and speech understanding
- Natural language interfaces to computer programs

Operation of Machines and Complex Systems

Autonomous Intelligent Systems

Management
- Planning
- Scheduling
- Monitoring

TABLE IV-1. (cont'd)

Sensor Interpretation and Integration
- Developing meaning from sensor data
- Sensor fusion (integrating multiple sensor inputs to develop high level interpretations)

Design
- Systems
- Equipment
- Intelligent Design Aids
- Inventing

Visual Perception and Guidance
- Inspection
- Identification
- Verification
- Guidance
- Screening
- Monitoring

Intelligent Assistants
- Medical Diagnosis, Maintenance Aids and Other Interactive Expert Systems
- Expert System Building Tools

TABLE IV-2. Examples of Domain-Specific Applications of AI.

Medical
- Diagnosis and Treatment
- Patient Monitoring
- Prosthetics
  —Artificial Sight and Hearing
  —Reading Machines for the Blind
- Medical Knowledge Automation

Science and Engineering
- Discovering
  —physical and mathematical laws
  —determination of regularities and aspects of interest
- Chemical and Biological Synthesis Planning
- Test Management
- Data Interpretation
- Intelligent Design Aids

Industrial
- Factory Management
- Production Planning and Scheduling
- Intelligent Robots
- Process Planning
- Intelligent Machines
- Computer-Aided Inspection

TABLE IV-2. (cont'd)

Military
- Expert Advisors
- Sensor Synthesis and Interpretation
- Battle and Threat Assessment
- Automatic Photo Interpretation
- Tactical Planning
- Military Surveillance
- Weapon-Target Assignment
- Autonomous Vehicles
- Intelligent Robots
- Diagnosis and Maintenance Aids
- Target Location and Tracking
- Map Development Aids
- Intelligent Interactions with Knowledge Bases

International
- Aids to Understanding and Interpretation
  —goals, aspirations and motives of different countries and cultures
  —cultural models for interpreting how others perceive
- Natural Language Translation

Services
- Intelligent Knowledge Base Access
  —airline reservations
- Air Traffic Control
- Ground Traffic Control

Financial
- Tax Preparation
- Financial Expert Systems
- Intelligent Consultants

Executive Assistance
- Read Mail and Spot Items of Importance
- Planning Aids

Natural Resources
- Prospecting Aids
- Resource Operations
  —Drilling Procedures
  —Resource Recovery Guidance
- Resource Management Using Remote Sensing Data

Space
- Ground Operations Aids
- Planning and Scheduling Aids
- Diagnostic and Reconfiguration Aids
- Remote Operations of Spacecraft and Space Vehicles
- Test Monitors
- Real-time Replanning as Required by Failures, Changed Conditions or New Opportunities
- Automatic Subsystem Operations

TABLE IV-3. Potential Functional Applications of AI in NASA.

- Planning and Scheduling

- Test and Checkout

- Symbolic Computation

- Information Extraction

- Operations Management
  —Monitoring
  —Control
  —Sequencing

- System Autonomy
  —Subsystem Management
  —Fault Diagnosis

- Intelligent Assistants

TABLE IV-4. AI and NASA.

AI Opens up an Opportunity for NASA to

- Dramatically
  —Reduce Costs
  —Increase Productivity
  —Improve Quality
  —Raise Reliability
  —Utilize Facilities and People More Effectively

- Provide New Mission Capabilities

- Enable New Missions

- Improve Aerospace Science and Technology

By using AI techniques to increase human productivity and to help automate many activities previously requiring human intelligence.

V. THE PRINCIPAL PARTICIPANTS

Originally, AI was principally a research activity—the principal centers being Stanford U., M.I.T., Carnegie Mellon U. (CMU), SRI, and the U. of Edinburgh in Scotland. Research successes during the 1970's encouraged other universities to also become involved.

In the 1980's, it became apparent that AI had a large commercial and military potential. Thus, existing large computer, electronic, and multinational corporations, as well as some aerospace firms, started forming AI groups. Schlumberger, a multi-billion dollar oil exploration advisory firm, was the first to pursue AI in a big way. They now have AI groups in France, Connecticut, Texas and California.

In 1980, the Navy committed itself to building an AI Laboratory at Bolling AFB, Washington, DC to help transfer AI to Navy Applications from research at the universities. The lab now has some 20 people including Navy personnel and visiting scientists. By 1982, the Army and the Air Force also decided to form AI organizations and are now in the process of doing so.

In response to a perceived market in natural language processing, computer vision and expert systems, new small AI companies began to form, headed by former (and present) university researchers. Several dozen such companies now exist.

The computer science departments at major universities have also recently become involved, so that AI courses and beginning AI research now is evident at many universities.

Abroad, France and Great Britain have now joined Japan in evidencing major concern. The largest major commitment to AI has been by Japan, which has initiated a 10 year, one half billion dollar program to develop a "Fifth Generation Computer." This computer is to incorporate a parallel processing architecture, natural language interfacing, knowledge base management, automatic problem solving, and image understanding as the basis for a truly fast, intelligent computer. In the U.S., a new cooperative organization—Microelectronics Computer Technology Corporation (MCC)—made up of U.S. computer and electronics manufacturers, has recently been formed to be a sort of American version of the Japanese Fifth Generation Computer research project.

Thus, the AI research sponsored by DARPA, NIH, NSF, ONR and AFOSR for the past two decades has now spawned such a burgeoning AI community that it is no longer an easy task to list all those involved. (A list of participants in each of the application areas is given in the associated volumes in this series). However, Table V-1 provides an indication of the current principal players. These are given by application area, as even most research efforts initially have a specific application domain as a focus, with the results of the research usually being later generalized to cover a broader area.

TABLE V-1. The Principal Participants in AI.

1. Universities

Expert Systems	Computer Vision	Natural Language Processing
Stanford	CMU	Yale
MIT	U. of MD	U. of CA (Berkeley)
CMU	MIT	U. of IL
Rutgers	Stanford U.	Brown
	U. of Rochester	Stanford
	U. of MA	Rochester

2. Non-Profit

Expert Systems	Computer Vision	Natural Language Processing
SRI	JPL	SRI
RAND	SRI	
JPL	ERIM	
MITRE		

3. U.S. Government

Expert Systems	Computer Vision	Natural Language Processing
NRL AI Lab, Washington, DC	NBS, Wash., D.C.	NRL AI Lab
NOSC, San Diego		

4. Diversified Industrial Corporations

Expert Systems	Computer Vision	Natural Language Processing
Schlumberger	G.E.	BBN
Hewlett Packard	Hughes	IBM
Bell Labs	GM	TRW
Hughes	Westinghouse	Burroughs
IBM		SDC
DEC		Hewlett Packard
GM		Martin Marietta
Martin Marietta		Texas Instruments
Texas Instruments		Bell Labs
TRW		Sperry Univac
Xerox PARC		Lockheed Electronics Corp.
AMOCO		
United Technologies Corp.		
ATARI		
Grumman Aerospace Corp.		
Lockheed Palo Alto		
Westinghouse Electric Corp.		

TABLE V-1. (cont'd)

5. New AI Companies

Expert Systems	Computer Vision	Natural Language Processing
AIDS, Mt. View, CA	Automatix, Inc., Burlington, MA	AIC, Waltham, MA
Applied Expert Systems, Cambridge, MA	Machine Intelligence Corp., Sunnyvale, CA	Cognitive Systems Inc., New Haven, CT
Brattel Research Corp., Boston, MA	Octek, Burlington, MA	Symantec, Sunnyvale, CA
Daisy, Sunnyvale, CA		Computer Thought, Richardson, TX
Intelligent Software, Van Nuys, CA		Machine Intelligence Corp., Sunnyvale, CA
Jacor, Alexandria, VA		Weidner Communications Corp., Provo, UT
Kestrel Institute, Palo Alto, CA		
Smart Systems Technology, Alexandria, VA		
Systems Control, Inc., Palo Alto, CA		
Teknowledge, Inc., Palo Alto, CA		
IntelliGenetics, Inc., Palo Alto, CA		

6. AI Computer Manufacturers

LISP Machines, Inc., Cambridge, MA, Culver City, CA
Symbolics, Cambridge, MA
Three Rivers Corp., Pittsburgh, PA
DEC, Hudson, MA
Xerox PARC, Palo Alto, CA
Daisy, Sunnyvale, CA
BBN, Cambridge, MA
MMC, Austin, TX (U.S. Fifth Generation Computer Research Consortium)

7. Major Foreign Participants

Japan

Electromechanical-Technology Lab, Tsukiba	Fifth Gen. Computer
Fujitsu-Fanuc, Ltd., Kawasaki	Fifth Gen. Computer
Hitachi, Ltd., Tokyo	Fifth Gen. Computer
Mitsubishi Elec. Corp., Tokyo	Fifth Gen. Computer
Nippon Electric Co., Ltd., Tokyo	Fifth Gen. Computer
Nippon Tele and Tele Corp., Tokyo	Fifth Gen. Computer

Great Britain
Imperial College, London
University of Edinburg, Scotland
University of Sussex, Sussex
Intelligent Terminals, Ltd.

France
University of Marseilles, Marseilles

Italy
University of Milan

VI. STATE-OF-THE-ART

General

The state-of-the-art of AI is moving rapidly as new companies enter the field, new applications are devised and existing techniques are formalized. The cutting edge of AI today is Expert Systems, with some one hundred demonstration systems having been built. With the advent of personal LISP machines and the general reduction in computing costs, development of commercial AI systems are now underway. A number of Natural Language Interfaces and Computer Vision Systems are already on the market.

Japan has focused on AI capabilities as the basis for its "Fifth Generation Computer" (Warren, 1982), and has already initiated research toward this one-half billion dollar, ten-year goal.

Britain's Industry Department has formed a study group to coordinate British AI efforts. The European Space Agency (ESA) has published a substantial survey of AI (Berger et al., 1981) from a point of view of space applications. In the U.S., DARPA has been spending in the order of $20 million annually on AI research and appears to be expanding its efforts. The U.S. Navy, Army and Air Force are all initiating substantial AI efforts. The Navy has established a major NRL AI applied research center at Bolling AFB. The Air Force is focusing their inhouse AI research efforts at Rome Air Development Center and Wright Patterson AFB.

Basic Core Topics

AI basic theory and techniques are now being codified. *The AI Handbook* (1981, 1982) (funded by DARPA) has been a major contribution in pulling together the basic theory and making it available at the graduate level for students and practitioners of AI.

Search theory is now relatively mature and well documented. A number of knowledge representation techniques have been devised and are now supported by representation languages. Basic programming languages have continued to evolve, with INTERLISP being the best supported, but Common LISP is beginning to emerge from MIT's MACLISP as the language of AI personal computers. PROLOG, a logic-based programming language, popular in Europe, appears to be the language of choice for Japan's Fifth Generation Computer, and is beginning to awaken interest in the U.S. PROLOG holds promise of reinvigorating First Order Predicate Logic as a major factor in AI for knowledge representation and problem-solving.

A large number of problem solving techniques developed during the last two decades are now forming the basis for the inference engines in Expert Systems.

Though much work remains to be done, the core topics of AI are now in a sufficient state of readiness for use in initial AI applications.

Expert Systems

Many prototype expert systems (ES) have now been built, so that ES's are no longer a rarity. However, only a few, such as MOLGEN, R1, ONCOCIN, DENDRAL, DIP-METER ADVISOR, and PUFF, are in actual commercial use on a regular basis. Expert systems are still restricted to a narrow domain of expertise and require laborious construction via interaction with human experts.

Further, these systems tend to have the characteristics of:
—Providing satisfactory, rather than optimum solutions
—Providing satisfactory answers only a percentage of the time
—Some of the time being unable to provide an answer

This is in contrast to normal engineering solutions that are algorithmic in nature and virtually always provide a satisfactory answer when supplied with appropriate inputs. This "sometimes the answer is wrong" characteristic of ES is also characteristic of human decision-making. Thus, at the moment, expert systems tend to be used as human assistants (with humans making the final decisions) rather than as "stand-alone" autonomous systems.

Natural Language

Natural language interfaces (NLI's) were the first commercial AI product. ROBOT, (now INTELLECT, by the Artificial Intelligence Corp., Waltham, MA), in 1980 was the first in the market and now exists in over 200 installations. Some half dozen other commercial NLI systems are now available. All these systems are restricted to limited sets of natural language and exhibit occasional failures in understanding or processing a user's input. However, with a little training of the users, NLI's have proved very useful.

Several commercial Machine Translation Systems are also now available. These are not used as completely automatic systems, as in many cases their translation is very rough or even incorrect. However, as an aid to a human translator, they can improve productivity by a factor of 2 to 10, depending on the system and the material being translated.

Text Understanding and Text Generation are still in the research stage.

Computer Vision

Computer Vision has entered the commercial market, with some dozen companies offering sophisticated commercial vision systems. These systems are operating successfully in specialized environments on low level problems of verification, inspection, recognition, and determination of object location and/or orientation. Current commercial vision systems deal primarily with two dimensional images—they can't handle three-dimensional analysis needed to recognize objects from arbitrary viewpoints.

Though quite a number of high level research vision systems have been explored, no general vision system is available today or is imminent. Major current efforts in this area are ACRONYM at Stanford U., VISIONS at the U. of Mass, and the robotic vision effort at NBS.

Conclusions

Figure VI-1 is a list of overall conclusions on the current state of AI. Summarizing, it appears that technology is now ready for early applications. However, the fact that current AI systems are prone to error, suggests that current AI applications should be focused on intelligent aids for humans, rather than on truly autonomous systems.

- Basic principles and techniques devised and demonstrated
- Initial languages, programs and tools developed
- Software portability a problem
- A few initial applications already in use
- Technology is now ready for early applications
- Current technology more appropriate for intelligent assistants than for autonomous systems
- Customizing, adapting and usually writing own programs necessary
- Because of huge potential benefits, utilization will be explosive as technology is further rationalized

Figure VI-1. Conclusions on the Current State-of-the-Art in AI.

CHAPTER VI REFERENCES

- Berger, G., Havas, R. and Prajoux, R., "Survey of the State-of-the-Art in Robotics and Artificial Intelligence," MATRA Report 0361/DX60, European Space Agency, August 1981.
- Warren, D.H.D., "A View of the Fifth Generation Computer and its Impact," *AI Magazine,* Vol. 3, No. 4, Fall 1982, pp. 34-39.
- Barr, A. and Feigenbaum, E.A. (Eds.), *The Handbook of Artificial Intelligence,* Vols. I and II, Los Altos, CA, W. Kaufmann, 1981, 1982.
- Cohen, P.R. and Feigenbaum, E.A. (Eds.), *The Handbook of Artificial Intelligence,* Vol. III, Los Altos, CA, W. Kaufmann, 1982.

VII. TOWARDS THE FUTURE

General

Today's initial AI systems can primarily be regarded as intelligent assistants. These are taking the form of expert systems, natural language interfaces, computer vision systems and intelligent computer-aided instruction systems. They—like humans—are all prone to failures, but unlike humans, they are not capable of drawing on deep knowledge when needed to achieve graceful degradation, so that their failures are more abrupt. Thus, researchers are currently engaged in developing a new set of advanced systems, based on deep knowledge—which includes such aspects as causal models and scientific knowledge.

Expert Systems

Utilizing emerging expert-system building tools, AI developers are expected to eventually put expert medical, financial and legal advice at the fingertips of anyone with access to a personal computer (though this will probably have to await the arrival of a new generation using 32 bit microprocessors). Expert systems will also put expertise in the hands of less-trained, lower-salaried workers.

Natural Language

Speech recognition appears to be emerging as a key man-machine interface. Researchers have found that the psychological problems inherent in talking to a machine are a barrier to the acceptance of speech interfaces. Overcoming the psychological problems may be even more important than reducing cost. To achieve practical continuous speech recognition, systems will have to expand today's vocabularies by an order of magnitude, increase speed by two orders of magnitude, and get costs below $1,000. Such systems are estimated to still be five years away.

Natural language interfaces appear to be the way to vastly increase the number of people who can interact with computers. Systems with near natural-language capabilities are available now, though it will be years before the systems can handle truly unrestricted dialogue. It is estimated that public access to large data bases via computer using restricted speech understanding may begin to appear within three years. This can be expected to open up a whole new industry of automated reservation, shopping and information services accessed by telephone.

Another emerging aspect of natural language processing are systems that understand text by utilizing world knowledge. Such systems could read and summarize news stories (as is now being done in research) but more likely would be applied to such tasks as reading mail and informing the recipient of important items, or in general, processing large amounts of information for humans trying to escape from overload.

Computer Vision

Computer vision will increasingly be used in industry for inspection, identification, verification, part location, and other purposes. Vision provides the most general purpose sensory input for intelligent robots. It is likely that roughly 25% of all robots will utilize vision by the end of the decade. Vision is also expected to play a large part in military automation, remote sensing, and as aids to the handicapped.

Intelligent Robots

The development of AI is making intelligent robots feasible. As intelligence is added to robots, they will not only be able to perform more flexibly in manufacturing, but will begin to be evident in tasks outside the industrial environment. Thus, robots in firefighting, underseas exploration, mining, and construction will appear. However, the big push may be in military applications with its actively hostile environments. In the 1990s, robots with intelligence and sensory capabilities will appear in the service industries — in everything from food service to household robots. It is also anticipated that in the 1990s, intelligent robots will enter the space arena, for such tasks as the construction and assembly of large space structures, space manufacture, extra-terrestrial mining and exploration, and operation and maintenance of space installations.

Industrial Applications

In addition to more intelligent robots, AI will influence virtually every aspect of the future industrial plant. Integrated plants that make use of automated planning, scheduling, process control, warehousing, and the operation of automated robot carts, robots, and manufacturing machines, will appear in a few years and will become widespread within the next 10 years.

Computers for Future Automation

Computers and special purpose chips designed to incorporate parallel processing are being developed at several universities and computer organizations. MIT has been developing a parallel machine using VLSI techniques to break problems into subproblems and distribute them among its processors. Another chip will utilize parallel processing to rapidly search through the branches of a semantic network.

The most prominent future system is Japan's Fifth Generation Computer that could store and retrieve some 20,000 rules, incorporate a knowledge base of 100 million data items and help make Japan an AI leader before the end of this century. To help maintain U.S. competitiveness, a dozen of the largest U.S. electronics and computer companies have recently set up the Microelectronics and Computer Technology Corp. (MCC). This well-funded cooperative research venture is designed to develop a broad base of fundamental technologies. Among them is a 10-year program to develop advanced computer architectures and artificial intelligence.

Computer Aided Instruction (CAI)

CAI systems may produce one of the most dramatic changes of all. Education consumes some 10% of the U.S. gross national product today. Systems that will enable students to ask questions and receive insightful answers may begin to overcome the barriers of instruction by machines. Computer systems that model the student based on his or her response can gear instruction to the student's level of ability and interest, something not easily done in a conventional classroom.

To truly learn is to digest and make the material one's own by updating one's internal models and using them in new applications. Real time interaction with a computer providing immediate feedback and individual guidance is particularly appropriate to this goal.

Thus, as computer hardware costs continue to tumble, the nature of the entire present educational system may be radically changed. For adults and members of the armed forces, CAI will probably rapidly become the standard form of instruction.

Learning by Computers

The real breakthrough may come when machine learning is achieved. Already several learning systems, currently in the research stage, have been able to produce very interesting results. Someday machines will able to learn throughout their lifetime, building up the knowledge base needed for advanced reasoning. This will open up spectacular new applications in offices, factories and homes.

Machines may update their knowledge by reading natural language material, as well as learning by experience from the problems the computers are called upon to solve. Computers also may be able to form conclusions from examination of multiple data bases, thereby building new knowledge from existing knowledge.

The Social Impacts

The U.S. Defense Science Board has ranked AI as one of the top 10 military technologies of the 80's. Not only will human-level expertise and decision making capabilities show up in machines, but the task of achieving these results will help us understand how our minds work as well.

Combining expert systems and computer graphics will enable people to "see" the results of the computer actions. This will not only clarify and simplify the interaction, but will greatly speed human learning and decision making. The result may be to compress months of research and engineering experience gained the old way into insights gathered from just a few hours interaction with intelligent computer programs.

AI's effects on society may be slow at first, but by the end of the century the results should be revolutionary. The shift in employment away from manufacturing may be as dramatic as the shift away from agriculture. There will also be a revolution in white collar work—service, research, leisure. How to restructure society to take advantage of a potential abundance of goods and services, or to adapt to new work opportunities and leisure activities, may be the question of the century. This may give society another chance to pursue the social and mental goals so often deferred. It also may at last free us from the monetary and technical bonds to Earth. Perhaps, we can at last "reach for the stars."

SOURCES FOR FURTHER INFORMATION

Journals
- *SIGART Newsletter* — ACM (Association for Computing Machinery).
- *Artificial Intelligence*
- *Cognitive Science* — Cognitive Science Society
- *AI Magazine* — American Association for AI (AAAI)
- *Pattern Analysis and Machine Intelligence* — IEEE
- *International Journal on Robotics Research*
- *IEEE Transactions on Systems, Man and Cybernetics*

Conferences
- International Joint Conference on AI (IJCAI) - biannual. Current one: Aug. 1983 in Germany.
- AAAI Annual Conference
- IEEE Systems, Man & Cybernetics Annual Conference

Recent Books
- Barr, A. and Feigenbaum, E.A., *The Handbook of Artificial Intelligence,* Vols. I, II, Los Altos, CA, W. Kaufmann, 1981, 1982.
- Clocksin, W.F. and Mellish, C.S., *Programming in Prolog,* New York, Springer-Verlag, 1981.
- Cohen, P.R. and Feigenbaum, E.A., (Eds.), *The Handbook of Artificial Intelligence,* Vol. III, Los Altos, CA, W. Kaufmann, 1982.
- Davis, R., and Lenat, D.B., *Knowledge-Based Systems in Artificial Intelligence,* New York, McGraw-Hill, 1982.
- Feigenbaum, E.A. and McCorduck, P. *The Fifth Generation,* Reading, Mass, Addison-Wesley, 1983.
- Hayes-Roth, F. (Ed.), *Building Expert Systems,* Reading, Mass., Addison-Wesley, 1983.
- Michalski, R.S., Carbonell, J.G. and Mitchell, T.M. (Eds.), *Machine Learning — An Artificial Intelligence Approach,* Palo Alto, Tioga, 1983.
- Nilsson, N.J., *Principles of Artificial Intelligence,* Palo Alto, CA, Tioga, 1980.
- Rich, E., *Artificial Intelligence,* New York, McGraw Hill, 1983.
- Simon, H.A., *The Sciences of the Artificial, 2nd Ed.*, Cambridge, Mass, M.I.T. Press, 1981.
- Sowa, J.F., *Conceptual Structures, Information Processing in Mind and Machine,* Reading Mass, Addison-Wesley, 1983.
- Szolovits, P. (Ed.), *Artificial Intelligence in Medicine,* Boulder, CO, Westview Press, 1982.
- Wilensky, R. *Planning and Understanding,* Reading, MA, Addison-Wesley, 1982.
- Winston, P.H. and Horn, B.K.P., *LISP,* Reading, Mass., Addison-Wesley, 1981.

GLOSSARY

A

Activation Mechanism: The situation required to invoke a procedure—usually a match of the system state to the preconditions required to exercise a production rule.

AI Handbook: The Handbook of Artificial Intelligence, E. A. Feigenbaum, A. Barr and P. R. Cohen (Eds.). Published by W. Kaufmann, Los Altos, CA in 1981 and 1982. This important project was supported by DARPA and NIH.

Algorithm: A procedure for solving a problem in a finite number of steps.

AND/OR Graph: A generalized representation for problem reduction situations and two person games. A tree-like structure with two types of nodes. Those for which several successors of a node have to be accomplished (or considered) are AND nodes. Those for which only one of several of the node successors are necessary are OR nodes. (In about half the literature the labeling of AND and OR nodes is reversed from this definition.)

Antecedent: The lefthand side of a production rule. The pattern needed to make the rule applicable.

Argument Form: A reasoning procedure in logic.

ARPANET: A network of computers and computational resources used by the U.S. AI community and sponsored by DARPA (Defense Advanced Research Projects Agency).

Artificial Intelligence (AI): A discipline devoted to developing and applying computational approaches to intelligent behavior. Also referred to as machine intelligence or heuristic programming.

Artificial Intelligence (AI) Approach: An approach that has its emphasis on symbolic processes for representing and manipulating knowledge in a problem solving mode.

Atom: An individual. A proposition in logic that cannot be broken down into other propositions. An indivisible element.

Autonomous: A system capable of independent action.

B

Backtracking: Returning (usually due to depth-first search failure) to an earlier point in a search space. Also a name given to depth-first backward reasoning.

Backward Chaining: A form of reasoning starting with a goal and recursively chaining backwards to its antecedent goals or states by applying applicable operators until an appropriate earlier state is reached or the system backtracks. This is a form of depth-first search. When the application of operators changes a single goal or state into multiple goals or states, the approach is referred to as problem reduction.

Blackboard Approach: A problem-solving approach whereby the various system elements communicate with each other via a common working data storage called the blackboard.

Blind Search: An ordered approach that does not rely on knowledge for searching for a solution.

Blocks World: A small artificial world, consisting of blocks and pyramids, used to develop ideas in computer vision, robotics, and natural language interfaces.

Bottom-Up Control Structure: A problem-solving approach that employs forward reasoning from current or initial conditions. Also referred to as an event-driven or data-driven control structure.

Breadth-First Search: An approach in which, starting with the root node, the nodes in the search tree are generated and examined level by level (before proceeding deeper). This approach is guaranteed to find an optimal solution if it exists.

C

Clause: A syntactic construction containing a subject and a predicate and forming part of a statement in logic or part of a sentence in a grammar.

Cognition: An intellectual process by which knowledge is gained about perceptions or ideas.

Combinatorial Explosion: The rapid growth of possibilities as the search space expands. If each branch point (decision point) has an average of n branches, the search space tends to expand as n^d, as the depth of search, d, increases.

Common Sense: The ability to act appropriately in everyday situations based on one's lifetime accumulation of experiential knowledge.

Common Sense Reasoning: Low level reasoning based on a wealth of experience.

Compile: The act of translating a computer program written in a high level language (such as LISP) into the machine language which controls the basic operations of the computer.

Computational Logic: A science designed to make use of computers in logic calculus.

Computer Architecture: The manner in which various computational elements are interconnected to achieve a computational function.

Computer Graphics: Visual representations generated by a computer (usually observed on a monitoring screen).

Computer Network: An interconnected set of communicating computers.

Computer Vision (Computational or Machine Vision): Perception by a computer, based on visual sensory input, in which a symbolic description is developed of a scene depicted in an image. It is often a knowledge-based, expectation-guided process that uses models to interpret sensory data. Used somewhat synonymously with image understanding and scene analysis.

Conceptual Dependency: An approach to natural language understanding in which sentences are translated into basic concepts expressed as a small set of semantic primitives.

Conflict Resolution: Selecting a procedure from a conflict set of applicable competing procedures or rules.

Conflict Set: The set of rules which matches some data or pattern in the global data base.

Conjunct: One of several subproblems. Each of the component formulas in a logical conjunction.

Conjunction: A problem composed of several subproblems. A logical formula built by connecting other formulas by logical ANDs.

Connectives: Operators (e.g., AND, OR) connecting statements in logic so that the truth-value of the composite is determined by the truth-value of the components.

Consequent: The right side of a production rule. The result of applying a procedure.

Constraint Propagation: A method for limiting search by requiring that certain constraints be satisified. It can also be viewed as a mechanism for moving information between subproblems.

Context: The set of circumstances or facts that define a particular situation, event, etc. The portion of the situation that remains the same when an operator is applied in a problem-solving situation.

Control Structure: Reasoning strategy. The strategy for manipulating the domain knowledge to arrive at a problem solution.

D

Data Base: An organized collection of data about some subject.

Data Base Management System: A computer system for the storage and retrieval of information about some domain.

Data-Driven: A forward reasoning, bottom-up problem solving approach.

Data Structure: The form in which data is stored in a computer.

Debugging: Correcting errors in a plan.

DEC: Digital Equipment Company.

Declarative Knowledge Representation: Representation of facts and assertions.

Deduction: A process of reasoning in which the conclusion follows from the premises given.

Default Value: A value to be used when the actual value is unknown.

Depth-First Search: A search that proceeds from the root node to one of the successor nodes and then to one of that node's successor nodes, etc., until a solution is reached or the search is forced to backtrack.

Difference Reduction: "Means-Ends" analysis. An approach to problem solving that tries to solve a problem by iteratively applying operators that will reduce the difference between the current state and the goal state.

Directed Graph: A knowledge representation structure consisting of nodes (representing, e.g., objects) and directed connecting arcs (labeled edges, representing, e.g., relations).

Disproving: An attempt to prove the impossibility of a hypothesized conclusion (theorem) or goal.

Domain: The problem area of interest, e.g., bacterial infections, prospecting, VLSI design.

E

Editor: A software tool to aid in modifying a software program.

Embed: To write a computer language on top of (embedded in) another computer language (such as LISP).

Emulate: To perform like another system.

Equivalent: Has the same truth value (in logic).

Evaluation Function: A function (usually heuristic) used to evaluate the merit of the various paths emanating from a node in a search tree.

Event-Driven: A forward-chaining problem-solving approach based on the current problem status.

Expectation-Driven: Processing approaches that proceed by trying to confirm models, situations, states or concepts anticipated by the system.

Expert System: A computer program that uses knowledge and reasoning techniques to solve problems normally requiring the abilities of human experts.

F

Fault Diagnosis: Determining the trouble source in an electro-mechanical system.

Fifth Generation Computer: A non-Von Neumann, intelligent, parallel-processing form of computer now being pursued by Japan.

First Order Predicate Logic: A popular form of logic used by the AI community for representing knowledge and performing logical inference. First Order Predicate Logic permits assertions to be made about variables in a proposition.

Forward Chaining: Event-driven or data-driven reasoning.

Frame: A data structure for representing stereotyped objects or situations. A frame has slots to be filled for objects and relations appropriate to the situation.

FRANZLISP: The dialect of LISP developed at the U. of CA, Berkeley.

Functional Application: The generic task or function performed in an application.

Fuzzy Set: A generalization of set theory that allows for various degrees of set membership, rather than all or none.

G

Garbage Collection: A technique for recycling computer memory cells no longer in use.

General Problem Solver (GPS): The first problem solver (1957) to separate its problem-solving methods from knowledge of the specific task being considered. The GPS problem-solving approach employed was "means-ends analysis."

Generate and Test: A common form of state space search based on reasoning by elimination. The system generates possible solutions and the tester prunes those solutions that fail to meet appropriate criteria.

Global Data Base: Complete data base describing the specific problem, its status and that of the solution process.

Goal Driven: A problem-solving approach that works backward from the goal.

Goal Regression: A technique for constructing a plan by solving one conjunctive subgoal at a time, checking to see that each solution does not interfere with the other subgoals that have already been achieved. If interferences occur, the offending subgoal is moved to an earlier non-interfering point in the sequence of subgoal accomplishments.

Graph: A set of nodes connected by arcs.

H

Heuristics: Rules of thumb or empirical knowledge used to help guide a problem solution.

Heuristic Search Techniques: Graph searching methods that use heuristic knowledge about the domain to help focus the search. They operate by generating and testing intermediate states along potential solution paths.

Hierarchical Planning: A planning approach in which first a high level plan is formulated considering only the important (or major) aspects. Then the major steps of the plan are refined into more detailed subplans.

Hierarchy: A system of things ranked one above the other.

Higher Order Language (HOL): A computer language (such as FORTRAN or LISP) requiring fewer statements than machine language and usually substantially easier to use and read.

Horn Clause: A set of statements joined by logical AND's. Used in PROLOG.

I

Identity: Two propositions (in logic) that have the same truth value.

Image Understanding (IU): Visual perception by a computer employing geometric modeling and the AI techniques of knowledge representation and cognitive processing to develop scene interpretations from image data. IU has dealt extensively with 3D objects.

Implies: A connective in logic that indicates that if the first statement is true, the statement following is also true.

Individual: A non-variable element (or atom) in logic that cannot be broken down further.

Infer: To derive by reasoning. To conclude or judge from premises or evidence.

Inference: The process of reaching a conclusion based on an initial set of propositons, the truths of which are known or assumed.

Inference Engine: Another name given to the control structure of an AI problem solver in which the control is separate from the knowledge.

Instantiation: Replacing a variable by an instance (an individual) that satisfies the system (or satisfies the statement in which the variable appears).

Intelligence: The degree to which an individual can successfully respond to new situations or problems. It is based on the individual's knowledge level and the ability to appropriately manipulate and reformulate that knowledge (and incoming data) as required by the situation or problem.

Intelligent Assistant: An AI computer program (usually an expert system) that aids a person in the performance of a task.

Interactive Environment: A computational system in which the user interacts (dialogues) with the system (in real time) during the process of developing or running a computer program.

Interface: The system by which the user interacts with the computer. In general, the junction between two components.

INTERLISP: A dialect of LISP (used at Stanford U.) developed at BBN and XEROX-PARC.

Invoke: To place into action (usually by satisfying a precondition).

K

Knowledge Base: AI databases that are not merely files of uniform content, but are collections of facts, inferences and procedures, corresponding to the types of information needed for problem solution.

Knowledge Base Management: Management of a knowledge base in terms of storing, accessing and reasoning with the knowledge.

Knowledge Engineering: The AI approach focusing on the use of knowledge (e.g., as in expert systems) to solve problems.

Knowledge Representation (KR): The form of the data-structure used to organize the knowledge required for a problem.

Knowledge Source: An expert system component that deals with a specific area or activity.

L

Leaf: A terminal node in a tree representaton.

Least Commitment: A technique for coordinating decision making with the availability of information, so that problem-solving decisions are not made arbitrarily or prematurely, but are postponed until there is enough information.

List: A sequence of zero or more elements enclosed in a pair of parentheses, where each element is either an atom (an indivisible element) or a list.

List Processing Language (LISP): The basic AI programming language.

Logical Operation: Execution of a single computer instruction.

Logical Representation: Knowledge representation by a collection of logical formulas (usually in First Order Predicate Logic) that provide a partial description of the world.

M

MACLISP: A dialect of LISP developed at M.I.T.

Means-Ends Analysis: A problem-solving approach (used by GPS) in which problem-solving operators are chosen in an iterative fashion to reduce the difference between the current problem-solving state and the goal state.

Meta-Rule: A higher level rule used to reason about lower level rules.

Microcode: A computer program at the basic machine level.

Model Driven: A top-down approach to problem-solving in which the inferences to be verified are based on the domain model used by the problem-solver.

Modus Ponens: A mathematical form of argument in deductive logic. It has the form:

If A is true, then B is true.
A is true
Therefore B is true.

N

Natural Deduction: Informal reasoning.

Natural Language Interface (NLI): A system for communicating with a computer by using a natural language.

Natural Language Processing (NLP): Processing of natural language (e.g., English) by a computer to facilitate communication with the computer, or for other purposes such as language translation.

Natural Language Understanding (NLU): Response by a computer based on the meaning of a natural language input.

Negate: To change a proposition into its opposite.

Node: A point (representing such aspects as the system state or an object) in a graph connected to other points in the graph by arcs (usually representing relations).

Non-Monotonic Logic: A logic in which results are subject to revision as more information is gathered.

O

Object-Oriented Programming: A programming approach focused on objects which communicate by message passing. An object is considered to be a package of information and descriptions of procedures that can manipulate that information.

Operators: Procedures or generalized actions that can be used for changing situatons.

P

Parallel Processing: Simultaneous processing, as opposed to the sequential processing in a conventional (Von Neumann) type of computer architecture.

Path: A particular track through a state graph.

Pattern Directed Invocation: The activation of procedures by matching their antecedent parts to patterns present in the global data base (the system status).

Pattern Matching: Matching patterns in a statement or image against patterns in a global data base, templates or models.

Pattern Recognition: The process of classifying data into predetermined categories.

Perception: An active process in which hypotheses are formed about the nature of the environment, or sensory information is sought to confirm or refute hypotheses.

Personal AI Computer: New, small, interactive, stand-alone computers for use by an AI researcher in developing AI programs. Usually specifically designed to run an AI language such as LISP.

Plan: A sequence of actions to transform an initial situation into a situation satisfying the goal conditions.

Portability: The ease with which a computer program developed in one programming environment can be transferred to another.

Predicate: That part of a proposition that makes an assertion (e.g., states a relation or attribute) about individuals.

Predicate Logic: A modification of Propositional Logic to allow the use of variables and functions of variables.

Prefix Notation: A list representation (used in LISP programming) in which the connective, function or predicate is given before the arguments.

Premise: A first proposition on which subsequent reasoning rests.

Problem Reduction: A problem-solving approach in which operators are used to change a single problem into several subproblems (which are usually easier to solve).

Problem-Solving: A procedure using a control strategy to apply operators to a situation to try to achieve a goal.

Problem State: The condition of the problem at a particular instant.

Procedural Knowledge Representation: A representation of knowledge about the world by a set of procedures - small programs that know how do specific things (how to proceed in well-specified situations).

Production Rule: A modular knowledge structure representing a single chunk of knowledge, usually in If-Then or Antecedent-Consequent form. Popular in Expert Systems.

Programming Environment: The total programming set-up that includes the interface, the languages, the editors and other programming tools.

Programming in Logic (PROLOG): A logic-oriented AI language developed in France and popular in Europe and Japan.

Property List: A knowledge representation technique by which the state of the world is described by objects in the world via lists of their pertinent properties.

Proposition: A statement (in logic) that can be true or false.

Propositional Logic: An elementary logic that uses argument forms to deduce the truth or falsehood of a new proposition from known propositions.

Prototype: An initial model or system that is used as a base for constructing future models or systems.

Pseudo-Reduction: An approach to solving the difficult problem case where multiple goals must be satisfied simultaneously. Plans are found to achieve each goal independently and then integrated using knowledge of how plan segments can be intertwined without destroying their important effects.

R

Recursive Operations: Operations defined in terms of themselves.

Relaxation Approach: An iterative problem-solving approach in which initial conditions are propagated utilizing constraints until all goal conditions are adequately satisfied.

Relevant Backtracking (Dependency-Directed or Non-Chronological Backtracking): Backtracking (during a search) not to the most recent choice point, but to the most relevant choice point.

Resolution: A general, automatic, syntactic method for determining if a hypothesized conclusion (theorem) follows from a given set of premises (axioms).

Root Node: The initial (apex) node in a tree representation.

Rule-Interpreter: The control structure for a production rule system.

S

Satisficing: Developing a satisfactory, but not necessarily optimum, solution.

Scheduling: Developing a time sequence of things to be done.

Scripts: Frame-like structures for representing sequences of events.

Search Space: The implicit graph representing all the possible states of the system which may have to be searched to find a solution. In many cases the search space is infinite. The term search space is also used for non-state-space representations.

Semantic: Of or relating to meaning.

Semantic Network: A knowledge representation for describing the properties and relations of objects, events, concepts, situations or actions, by a directed graph consisting of nodes and labeled edges (arcs connecting nodes).

Semantic Primitives: Basic conceptual units in which concepts, ideas or events can be represented.

S-Expression: A symbolic expression. In LISP, a sequence of zero or more atoms or S-expressions enclosed in parentheses.

Slot: An element in a frame representation to be filled with designated information about the particular situation.

Software: A computer program.

Solution Path: A successful path through a search space.

Speech Recognition: Recognition by a computer (primarily by pattern-matching) of spoken words or sentences.

Speech Synthesis: Developing spoken speech from text or other representations.

Speech Understanding: Speech perception by a computer.

SRI Vision Module: An important object recognition, inspection, orientation and location research vision system developed at SRI. This system converted the scene into a binary image and extracted the calculated needed vision parameters in real time, as it sequentially scanned the image line by line.

State Graph: A graph in which the nodes represent the system state and the connecting arcs represent the operators which can be used to transform the state from which the arcs emanate to the state at which they arrive.

Stereotyped Situation: A generic, recurrent situation such as "eating at a restaurant" or "driving to work."

Subgoals: Goals that must be achieved to achieve the original goal.

Subplan: A plan to solve a portion of the problem.

Subproblems: The set of secondary problems that must be solved to solve the original problem.

Syllogism: A deductive argument in logic whose conclusion is supported by two premises.

Symbolic: Relating to the substitution of abstract representations (symbols) for concrete objects.

Syntax: The order or arrangement (e.g., the grammar of a language).

T

Terminal Node (Leaf Node): The final node emanating from a branch in a tree or graph representation.

Theorem: A proposition, or statement, to be proved based on a given set of premises.

Theorem Proving: A problem-solving approach in which a hypothesized conclusion (theorem) is validated using deductive logic.

Time-Sharing: A computer environment in which multiple users can use the computer virtually simultaneously via a program that time-allocates the use of computer resources among the users in a near-optimum manner.

Top-Down Approach: An approach to problem-solving that is goal-directed or expectation-guided based on models or other knowledge. Sometimes referred to as "Hypothesize and Test."

Top-Down Logic: A problem-solving approach used in production systems, where production rules are employed to find a solution path by chaining backwards from the goal.

Tree Structure: A graph in which one node, the root, has no predecessor node, and all other nodes have exactly one predecessor. For a state space representation, the tree starts with a root node (representing the initial problem situation). Each of the new states that can be produced from this initial state by application of a single operator is represented by a successor node of the root node. Each successor node branches in a similar way until no further states can be generated or a solution is reached. Operators are represented by the directed arcs from the nodes to their successor nodes.

Truth-Maintenance: A method of keeping track of beliefs (and their justifications) developed during problem-solving, so that if contradictions occur, the incorrect beliefs or lines of reasoning, and all conclusions resulting from them, can be retracted.

Truth Value: One of the two possible values—True or False—associated with a proposition in logic.

U

Unification: The name for the procedure for carrying out instantiations. In unification, the attempt is to find substitutions for variables that will make two atoms identical.

V

Variable: A quantity or function that may assume any given value or set of values.

Von-Neuman Architecture: The current standard computer architecture that uses sequential processing.

W

World Knowledge: Knowledge about the world (or domain of interest).

World Model: A representation of the current situation.

PART B

APPLICATIONS—EXPERT SYSTEMS, COMPUTER VISION, NATURAL LANGUAGE PROCESSING, ETC.

The information in Part B is from *An Overview of Artificial Intelligence and Robotics. Volume I—Artificial Intelligence, Part B—Applications,* by William B. Gevarter, Office of Aeronautics and Space Technology, National Aeronautics and Space Administration, October 1983.

ACKNOWLEDGMENTS

I wish to thank the many people and organizations who have contributed to this report, both in providing information, and in reviewing the report and suggesting corrections, modifications and additions. I particularly would like to thank Terry Cronin of U.S. Army Signal Warfare Lab., Dave Pallett and Jim Hieronymus of NBS, Ed Zenker of NASA Goddard Space Flight Center, Dave Gilblom, Carl Berney and Gabe Groner of Speech Plus, Jude Franklin of the U.S. Navy Center for Applied Research in AI, and David R. Brown of SRI International for their review of various portions of this report and their many helpful suggestions. However, the responsibility of any remaining errors or inaccuracies must remain with the author.

I. EXPERT SYSTEMS

A. Introduction

Expert Systems is probably the "hottest" topic in Artificial Intelligence (AI) today. Prior to the last decade, in trying to find solutions to problems, AI researchers tended to rely on non-knowledge-guided search techniques or computational logic. These techniques were successfully used to solve elementary problems or very well structured problems such as games. However, real complex problems are prone to have the characteristics that their search space tends to expand exponentially with the number of parameters involved. For such problems, these older techniques have generally proved to be inadequate and a new approach was needed. This new approach emphasized knowledge rather than search and has led to the field of Knowledge Engineering and Expert Systems. The resultant expert systems technology, limited to academic laboratories in the 70's, is now becoming cost-effective and is beginning to enter into commercial applications.

B. What is an Expert System?

Feigenbaum, a pioneer in expert systems, (1982, p.1) states:

> An "expert system" is an intelligent computer program that uses knowledge and inference procedures to solve problems that are difficult enough to require significant human expertise for their solution. The knowledge necessary to perform at such a level, plus the inference procedures used, can be thought of as a model of the expertise of the best practitioners of the field.
>
> The knowledge of an expert system consists of facts and heuristics. The "facts" constitute a body of information that is widely shared, publicly available, and generally agreed upon by experts in a field. The "heuristics" are mostly private, little-discussed rules of good judgement (rules of plausible reasoning, rules of good guessing) that characterize expert-level decision making in the field. The performance level of an expert system is primarily a function of the size and quality of the knowledge base that it possesses.

It has become fashionable today to characterize any large, complex AI system that uses large bodies of domain knowledge as an expert system. Thus, nearly all AI applications to real-world problems can be considered in this category, though the designation "knowledge-based systems" is more appropriate.

C. The Basic Structure of an Expert System

An expert system consists of:
(1) a knowledge base (or knowledge source) of domain facts and heuristics associated with the problem;
(2) an inference procedure (or control structure) for utilizing the knowledge base in the solution of the problem;
(3) a working memory — "global data base" — for keeping track of the problem status, the input data for the particular problem, and the relevant history of what has thus far been done.

A human "domain expert" usually collaborates to help develop the knowledge base. Once the system has been developed, in addition to solving problems, it can also be used to help instruct others in developing their own expertise.

It is desirable, though not yet common, to have a user-friendly natural language interface to facilitate the use of the system in all three modes: development, problem solving, instruction. In some sophisticated systems, an explanation module is also included, allowing the user to challenge and examine the reasoning process underlying the system's answers. Figure I-1 is a diagram of an idealized expert system. When the domain knowledge is stored as production rules, the knowledge base is often referred to as the "rule base," and the inference engine as the "rule interpreter."

An expert system differs from more conventional computer programs in several important respects. Duda (1981, p. 242) observes that, in an expert system ". . . there is a clear separation of general knowledge about the problem (the rules forming a knowledge base) from information about the current problem (the input data) and the methods for applying the general knowledge to the problem (the rule interpreter)." In a conventional computer program, knowledge pertinent to the problem and methods for utilizing this knowledge are all intermixed, so that it is difficult to change the program. In an expert system, ". . . the program itself is only an interpreter (or

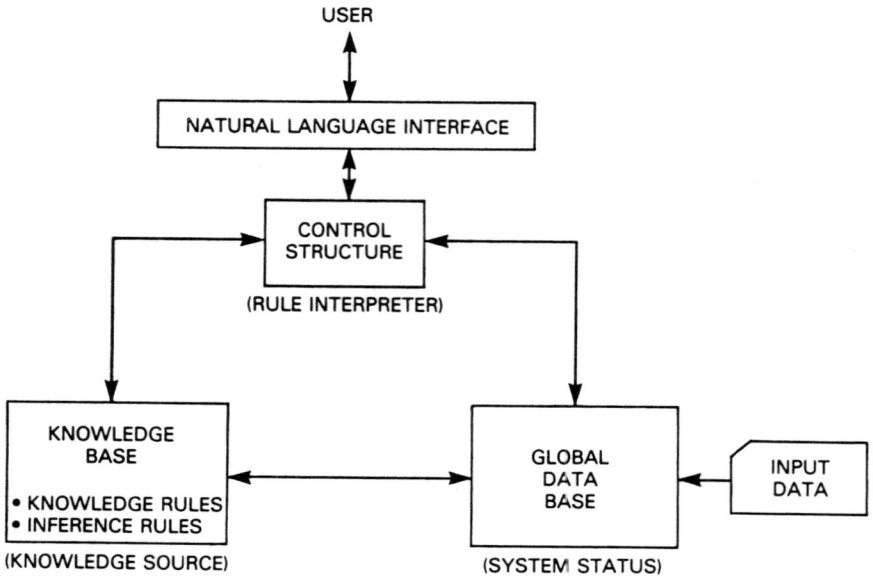

Figure I-1. Basic Structure of an Expert System.

general reasoning mechanism) and (ideally) the system can be changed by simply adding or subtracting rules in the knowledge base."

D. The Knowledge Base

The most popular approach to representing the domain knowledge (both facts and heuristics) needed for an expert system is by production rules (also referred to as "SITUATION-ACTION rules" or "IF-THEN rules").* Thus, often a knowledge base is made up mostly of rules which are invoked by pattern matching with features of the task environment as they currently appear in the global data base.

E. The Control Structure

In an expert system a problem-solving paradigm must be chosen to organize and control the steps taken to solve the problem. A common, but powerful approach involves the chaining of IF-THEN rules to form a line of reasoning. The rules are actuated by patterns (which, depending on the strategy, match either the IF or the THEN side of the rules) in the global data base. The application of the rule changes the system status and therefore the data base, enabling some rules and disabling others. The rule interpreter uses a control strategy for finding the enabled rules and for deciding which of the enabled rules to apply. The basic control strategies used may be top-down (goal driven), bottom-up (data driven), or a combination of the two that uses a relaxation-like convergence process to join these opposite lines of reasoning together at some intermediate point to yield a problem solution. However, virtually all the heuristic search and problem solving techniques that the AI community has devised have appeared in the various expert systems.

F. Uses of Expert Systems

The uses of expert systems are virtually limitless. They can be used to: diagnose, repair, monitor, analyse, interpret, consult, plan, design, instruct, explain, learn, and conceptualize.

G. Architecture of Expert Systems

One way to classify expert systems is by function (e.g. diagnosis, planning, etc). However, examination of existing expert systems indicates that there is little commonality in detailed system architecture that can be detected from this classification. A more fruitful approach appears to be to look at problem complexity and problem structure and deduce what data and control structures might be appropriate to handle these factors.

The Knowledge Engineering community has evolved a number of techniques (presented in the excellent tutorial by Stefik et al. (1982) and summarized in Gevarter (1982)) which can be utilized in devising suitable expert system architectures.

The use of these techniques in four existing expert systems is illustrated in Table I-1-1 thru I-1-4. Table I-1-1 thru I-1-4 outlines the basic approach taken by each of these expert systems and

---

*Not all expert systems are rule-based. The network-based expert systems MACSYMA, INTERNIST/CADUCEUS, Digitalis Therapy Advisor, HARPY and PROSPECTOR are examples which are not. Buchanan and Duda (1982) state that the basic requirements in the choice of an expert system knowledge representation scheme are extendibility, simplicity and explicitness. Thus, rule-based systems are particularly attractive.

TABLE I-1-1. *Characteristics of Example Expert Systems.*

SYSTEM: DENDRAL
INSTITUTION: Stanford University
AUTHORS: Feigenbaum & Lederberg
FUNCTION: Data Interpretation

Purpose	Approach	Key Elements of		
		Knowledge Base	Global Data Base	Control Structure
Generate plausible structural representations of organic molecules from mass spectrogram data	1. Derive constraints from the data. 2. Generate candidate structures. 3. Predict mass spectrographs for candidates. 4. Compare with data.	Rules for deriving constraints on molecular structure from experimental data. Procedure for generating candidate structures to satisfy constraints. Rules for predicting spectrographs from structures	Mass spectrogram data Constraints Candidate structures	Forward chaining Plan, generate and test.

TABLE 1-1-2. *Characteristics of Example Expert Systems.*

SYSTEM: AM
INSTITUTION: Stanford University
AUTHORS: Lenat
FUNCTION: Concept Formation

Purpose	Approach	Key Elements of		
		Knowledge Base	Global Data Base	Control Structure
Discovery of mathematical concepts	Start with elementary ideas in set theory. Search a space of possible conjectures that can be generated from these elementary ideas. Choose the most interesting conjectures and pursue that line of reasoning.	Elementary ideas in finite set theory. Heuristics for generating new mathematical concepts by modifying and combining elementary ideas. Heuristics of "interestingness" for discarding bad ideas.	Plausible candidate concepts.	Plan, generate, and test.

76   Artificial Intelligence

TABLE 1-1-3. *Characteristics of Example Expert Systems.*

SYSTEM: R1
INSTITUTION: CMU
AUTHORS: McDermott
FUNCTION: Design

Purpose	Approach	Knowledge Base	Key Elements of Global Data Base	Control Structure
Configure VAX computer systems (from a customer's order of components).	Break problem up into the following ordered subtasks: 1. Correct mistakes in order. 2. Put components into CPU cabinets. 3. Put boxes into unibus cabinets and put components in boxes. 4. Put panels in unibus cabinets. 5. Lay out system on floor. 6. Do the cabling. Solve each subtask and move on to the next one in the fixed order.	Properties of (roughly 500) VAX components. Rules for determining when to move to next subtask based on system state. Rules for carrying out subtasks (to extend partial configuration). (Approximately 1200 rules total)	Customer order. Current task. Partial configuration (System state).	"MATCH" (data driven) (no backtracking)

TABLE 1-1-4. *Characteristics of Example Expert Systems.*

SYSTEM: MYCIN
INSTITUTION: Stanford University
AUTHORS: Shortliffe
FUNCTION: Diagnosis

Purpose	Approach	Knowledge Base	Key Elements of Global Data Base	Control Structure
Diagnosis of bacterial infections and recommendations for antibiotic therapy.	Represent expert judgmental reasoning as condition-conclusion rules together with the expert's "certainty" estimate for each rule.	Rules linking patient data to infection hypotheses.	Patient history and diagnostic tests.	Backward chaining thru the rules.
	Chain backwards from hypothesized diagnoses to see if the evidence supports it.	Rules for combining certainty factors.	Current hypothesis. Status.	Exhaustive search.
	Exhaustively evaluate all hypotheses.			
	Match treatments to all diagnoses which have high certainty values.	Rules for treatment.	Conclusions reached thus, far, and rule numbers justifying them.	

shows how the approach translates into key elements of the Knowledge Base, Global Data Base and Control Structure. An indication of the basic control structures of the systems in Table I-1-1 thru I-1-4, and some of the other well known expert systems, is given in Table I-2.

Table I-2 represents expert system control structures in terms of the search direction, the control techniques utilized, and the search space transformations employed. The approaches used in the various expert systems are different implementations of two basic ideas for overcoming the combinatorial explosion associated with search in real complex problems. These two ideas are:
(1) Find ways to efficiently search a space,
(2) Find ways to transform a large search space into smaller manageable chunks that can be searched efficiently.

It will be observed from Table I-2 that there is little architectural commonality based either on function or domain of expertise. Instead, expert system design may best be considered as an art form, like custom home architecture, in which the chosen design can be implemented from the collection of available AI techniques in heuristic search and problem solving.

In addition to the techniques indicated in Table I-2, also emerging are distributed knowledge and problem solving approaches exemplified by the MDX expert system (Chandrasekaran, 1983) and the object-oriented programming language, LOOPS (Stefik et al., 1983).

H. Existing Expert Systems

Table I-3 is a list, classified by function and domain of use, of most of the existing major expert systems. It will be observed that there is a predominance of systems in the Medical and Chemistry domains following from the pioneering efforts at Stanford University. From the list, it is also apparent that Stanford University dominates in number of systems, followed by M.I.T., CMU, BBN and SRI, with several dozen scattered efforts elsewhere.

The list indicates that thus far the major areas of expert systems development have been in diagnosis, data analysis and interpretation, planning, computer-aided instruction, analysis, and automatic programming. However, the list also indicates that a number of pioneering expert systems already exist in quite a number of other functional areas. In addition, a substantial effort is under way to build expert systems as tools for constructing expert systems.

I. Constructing an Expert System

Duda (1981, p. 262) states that to construct a successful expert system, the following prerequisites must be met:
- there must be at least one human expert acknowledged to perform the task well.
- the primary source of the expert's exceptional performance must be special knowledge, judgment, and experience.
- the expert must be able to explain the special knowledge and experience and the methods used to apply them to particular problems.
- the task must have a well-bounded domain of application.

Using present techniques and programming tools, the effort required to develop an expert system appears to be converging towards five man-years, with most endeavors employing two to five people in the construction.

TABLE 1-2. *Control Structures of Some Well Known Expert Systems.*

System	Function	Domain	Search Direction				Control								Search Space Transformations				
			Forward	Backward	Forward and Backward	Event Driven	Exhaustive Search	Generate and Test	Guessing	Relevant Backtracking	Least Commitment	Multilines of Reasoning	Network Editor	Beam Search	Multiple Models	Break into Sub-Problems	Hierarchical Refinement	Hierarchical Resolution	Meta Rules
MYCIN	Diagnosis	Medicine		x															
DENDRAL	Data Interpr.	Chemistry	x					x											
EL	Analysis	Elec. Circuits	x							x									
GUIDON	C.A.I.	Medicine				x													
KAS	Knowl. Acquis.	Geology	x										x						
META-DENDRAL	Learning	Chemistry	x					x											
AM	Concept Formation	Math	x					x											
VM	Monitoring	Medicine				x	x												
GA1	Data Interpr.	Chemistry	x				x	x											
R1	Design	Computers	x																
ABSTRIPS	Planning	Robots		x												x	x		
NOAH	Planning	Robots		x					x	x	x					x	x		
MOLGEN	Design	Genetics			x						x				x				
SYN	Design	Elec. Circuits	x								x	x							x
HEARSAY II	Signal Interpr.	Speech Unders.			x									x				x	
HARPY	Signal Interpr.	Speech Unders.	x																
CRYSALIS	Data Interpr.	Crystallography				x		x											x

TABLE I-3. Existing Expert Systems by Function.

Function	Domain	System*	Institution
Diagnosis	Medicine	PIP	M.I.T.
	Medicine	CASNET	Rutgers U.
	Medicine	INTERNIST/CADUCEUS	U. of Pittsburgh
	Medicine	MYCIN	Stanford U.
	Medicine	PUFF	Stanford U.
	Medicine	MDX	Ohio State U.
	Computer Faults	DART	Stanford U./IBM
	Computer Faults	IDT	DEC
	Nuclear Reactor Accidents	REACTOR	E G & G Idaho Inc.
Data Analysis and Interpretation	Geology	DIPMETER ADVISOR	M.I.T./Schlumberger
	Chemistry	DENDRAL	Stanford U.
	Chemistry	GA1	Stanford U.
	Geology	PROSPECTOR	SRI
	Protein Crystallography	CRYSALIS	Stanford U.
	Determination of Causal Relationships in Medicine	RX	Stanford U.
	Determination of Causal Relationships in Medicine	ABEL	M.I.T.
	Oil Well Logs	ELAS	AMOCO
Analysis	Electrical Circuits	EL	M.I.T.
	Symbolic Mathematics	MACSYMA	M.I.T.
	Mechanics Problems	MECHO	Edinburgh
	Naval Task Force Threat Analysis	TECH	Rand/NOSC
	Earthquake Damage Assessment for Structures	SPERIL	Purdue U.
	Digital Circuits	CRITTER	Rutgers U.
Design	Computer System Configurations	R1/XCON	C.M.U./DEC
	Circuit Synthesis	SYN	M.I.T.
	Chemical Synthesis	SYNCHEM	SUNY Stonybrook

*References to these systems can be found in Duda (1981), Stefik, et al. (1982), Buchanan (1981), Buchanan and Duda (1982), Barr and Feigenbaum (1982), IJCAI-81, and AAAI-82.

TABLE I-3. *Existing Expert Systems by Function. (cont.)*

Function	Domain	System*	Institution
Planning	Chemical Synthesis	SECHS	U. of Cal. Santa Cruz
	Robotics	NOAH	SRI
	Robotics	ABSTRIPS	SRI
	Planetary Flybys	DEVISER	JPL
	Errand Planning	OP-PLANNER	Rand
	Molecular Genetics	MOLGEN	Stanford U.
	Mission Planning	KNOBS	MITRE
	Job Shop Scheduling	ISIS-II	CMU
	Design of Molecular Genetics Experiments	SPEX	Stanford U.
	Medical Diagnosis	HODGKINS	M.I.T.
	Naval Aircraft Ops	AIRPLAN	CMU
	Tactical Targeting	TATR	RAND
Learning from Experience	Chemistry	METADENDRAL	Stanford U.
	Heuristics	EURISKO	Stanford U.
Concept Formation	Mathematics	AM	CMU
Signal Interpretation	Speech Understanding	HEARSAY II	CMU
	Speech Understanding	HARPY	CMU
	Machine Acoustics	SU/X	Stanford U.
	Ocean Surveillance	HASP	System Controls Inc.
	Sensors On Board Naval Vessels	STAMMER-2	NOSC, San Diego/SDC
	Medicine—Left Ventrical Performance	ALVEN	U. of Toronto
	Military Situation Determination	ANALYST	MITRE
Monitoring	Patient Respiration	VM	Stanford U.
Use Advisor	Structural Analysis	SACON	Stanford U.
	Computer Program		
Computer Aided Instruction	Electronic Troubleshooting	SOPHIE	B.B.N.
	Medical Diagnosis	GUIDON	Stanford U.
	Mathematics	EXCHECK	Stanford U.
	Steam Propulsion Plant Operation	STEAMER	BBN
	Diagnostic Skills	BUGGY	BBN
	Causes of Rainfall	WHY	BBN
	Coaching of a Game	WEST	BBN
	Coaching of a Game	WUMPUS	M.I.T.
		SCHOLAR	BBN

82   Artificial Intelligence

TABLE 1-3. Existing Expert Systems by Function. (cont.)

Function	Domain	System*	Institution
Knowledge Acquisition	Medical Diagnosis	TEIRESIAS	Stanford U.
	Medical Consultation	EXPERT	Rutgers
	Geology	KAS	SRI
Expert System Construction		ROSIE	Rand
		AGE	Stanford U.
		HEARSAY III	USC/ISI
		EMYCIN	Stanford U.
		OPS 5	CMU
		RAINBOW	IBM
	Medical Diagnosis	KMS	U. of MD
	Medical Consultation	EXPERT	Rutgers
	Electronic Systems Diagnosis	ARBY	Smart Sys. Tech.
	Medical Consultation Using Time-Oriented Data	MECS-AI	Tokyo U.
Consultation/Intelligent Assistant	Battlefield Weapons Assignments	BATTLE	NRL AI Lab
	Medicine	Digitalis Therapy Advisor	M.I.T.
	Radiology	RAYDEX	Rutgers U.
	Computer Sales	XCEL	CMU/DEC
	Medical Treatment	ONCOCIN	Stanford U.
	Nuclear Power Plants	CSA Model-Based Nuclear Power Plant Consultant	GA Tech
	Diagnostic Prompting in Medicine	RECONSIDER	U. of CA, S.F.
Management	Automated Factory	IMS	CMU
	Project Management	CALLISTO	DEC
Automatic Programming	Modelling of Oil Well Logs	ΦNIX	Schlumberger-Doll Res.
		CHI	Kestrel Inst.
		PECOS	Stanford U.
		LIBRA	Stanford U.
		SAFE	USC/ISI
		DEDALUS	SRI
		Programmer's Apprentice	M.I.T.
Image Understanding		VISIONS	U. of Mass.
		ACRONYM	Stanford U.

J. Summary of the State-of-the-Art

Buchanan (1981, pp. 6-7) indicates that the current state of the art in expert systems is characterized by:

- *Narrow domain of expertise*

Because of the difficulty in building and maintaining a large knowledge base, the typical domain of expertise is narrow. The principal exception is INTERNIST, for which the knowledge base covers 500 disease diagnoses. However, this broad coverage is achieved by using a relatively shallow set of relationships between diseases and associated symptoms. (INTERNIST is now being replaced by CADUCEUS, which uses causal relationships to help diagnose simultaneous unrelated diseases.)

- *Limited knowledge representation languages for facts and relations*

- *Relatively inflexible and stylized input-output languages*

- *Stylized and limited explanations by the systems*

- *Laborious construction*

At present, it requires a knowledge engineer to work with a human expert to laboriously extract and structure the information to build the knowledge base. However, once the basic system has been built, in a few cases it has been possible to write knowledge acquisition systems to help extend the knowledge base by direct interaction with a human expert, without the aid of a knowledge engineer.

- *Single expert as a "knowledge czar."*

We are currently limited in our ability to maintain consistency among overlapping items in the knowledge base. Therefore, though it is desirable for several experts to contribute, one expert must maintain control to insure the quality of the data base.

- *Fragile behavior*

In addition, most systems exhibit fragile behavior at the boundaries of their capabilities. Thus, even some of the best systems come up with wrong answers for problems just outside their domain of coverage. Even within their domain, systems can be misled by complex or unusual cases, or for cases for which they do not yet have the needed knowledge or for which even the human experts have difficulty.

- *Requires Knowledge Engineer to Operate*

Another limitation is that for most current systems only their builders or other knowledge engineers can successfully operate them - a friendly interface not having yet been constructed.

Nevertheless, Randy Davis (1982) observes that there have been notable successes. A methodology has been developed for explicating informal knowledge. Representing and using empirical associations, five systems have been routinely solving difficult problems — DENDRAL, MACSYMA, MOLGEN, R1 and PUFF — and are in regular use. The first three all have serious users who are only loosely coupled to the system designers. DENDRAL, which analyzes chemical instrument data to determine the underlying molecular structure, has been the most widely used program (see Lindsay et al., 1980). R1, which is used to configure VAX computer systems, has been reported to be saving DEC twenty million dollars per year, and is now being followed up with XCON. In addition, as indicated in Table I-3, dozens of systems have been constructed and are being experimented with.

K. Future Trends

Figure I-2 lists some of the expert systems applications currently under development.

It will be observed that there appear to be few domain or functional limitations in the ultimate use of expert systems. However, the nature of expert systems is changing. The limitations of rule-based systems are becoming apparent. Not all knowledge can be readily structured in the form of empirical associations. Empirical associations tend to hide causal relations (present only implicitly in such associations). Empirical associations are also inappropriate for highlighting structure and function.

Thus, the newer expert systems are adding deep knowledge having to do with causality and structure. These systems will be less fragile, thereby holding the promise of yielding correct answers often enough to be considered for use in autonomous systems, not just as intelligent assistants.

The other change is a trend towards an increasing number of non-rule based systems. These systems, utilizing semantic networks, frames and other knowledge representations, are often better suited for causal modeling and representing structure. They also tend to simplify the reasoning required by providing knowledge representations more appropriate for the specific problem domain.

- Medical diagnosis and prescription
- Medical knowledge automation
- Chemical data interpretation
- Chemical and biological synthesis
- Mineral and oil exploration
- Planning/scheduling
- Signal interpretation
- Signal fusion—situation interpretation from multiple sensors
- Military threat assessment
- Tactical targeting
- Space defense

- Air traffic control
- Circuit diagnosis
- VLSI design
- Equipment fault diagnosis
- Computer configuration selection
- Speech understanding
- Intelligent Computer-Aided Instruction
- Automatic Programming
- Intelligent knowledge base access and management
- Tools for building expert systems

Figure I-2. Expert System Applications Now Under Development.

Figure I-3 (based largely on Hayes-Roth IJCAI-81 Expert system tutorial and on Feigenbaum, 1982) indicates some of the future opportunities for expert systems. Again no limitation is apparent.

It thus appears that expert systems will eventually find use in most endeavors which require symbolic reasoning with detailed professional knowledge — which includes much of the world's work. In the process, there will be exposure and refinement of the previously private knowledge in the various fields of applications.

On a more near-term scale, in the next few years we can expect to see expert systems with thousands of rules. In addition to the increasing number of rule-based systems we can also expect to see an increasing number of non-rule based systems. Also anticipated are much improved ex-

- *Building and Construction*
    Design, planning, scheduling, control
- *Equipment*
    Design, monitoring, control, diagnosis, maintenance, repair, instruction.
- *Command and Control*
    Intelligence analysis, planning, targeting, communication
- *Weapon Systems*
    Target identification, adaptive control, electronic warfare
- *Professions*
    (Medicine, law, accounting, management, real estate, financial, engineering)
        Consulting, instruction, analysis
- *Education*
    Instruction, testing, diagnosis, concept formation and new knowledge development from experience.
- *Imagery*
    Photo interpretation, mapping, geographic problem-solving.
- *Software*
    Instruction, specification, design, production, verification, maintenance
- *Home Entertainment and Advice-giving*
    Intelligent games, investment and finances, purchasing, shopping, intelligent information retrieval
- *Intelligent Agents*
    To assist in the use of computer-based systems
- *Office Automation*
    Intelligent systems
- *Process Control*
    Factory and plant automation
- *Exploration*
    Space, prospecting, etc.

Figure I-3. Future Opportunities for Expert Systems.

planation systems that can explain (make "transparent") why an expert system did what it did and what things are of importance.

By the late 80's, we can expect to see intelligent, friendly and robust human interfaces and much better system building tools.

Somewhere around the year 2000, we can expect to see the beginnings of systems which semi-autonomously develop knowledge bases from text. The result of these developments may very well herald a maturing information society where expert systems put experts at everyone's disposal. In the process, production and information costs should greatly diminish, opening up major new opportunities for societal betterment.

REFERENCES

- Barr, A., and Feigenbaum, E. A., *The Handbook of Artificial Intelligence,* Vol: 2, Los Altos, CA: W. Kaufman, 1982.
- Buchanan, B. G., "Research on Expert Systems," Stanford University Computer Science Department, Report No. STAN-CS-81-837, 1981.
- Buchanan, B. G. and Duda, R. O., "Principles of Rule-Based Expert Systems," Heuristic Programming Project Report No. HPP 82-14, Dept. of Computer Science, Stanford, CA, Aug. 1982. (To appear in *Advances in Computers, Vol. 22,* M. Yorit. (ed.), New York: Academic Press)
- Chandrasekaran, B., "Towards a Taxonomy of Problem Solving Types," *The AI Magazine,* Vol 4, No. 1, Winter-Spring 1983, pp 9-17.
- Davis, R., "Expert Systems: Where Are We: and Where Do We Go From Here?" *AI Magazine,* Vol. 3. No. 2, Spring 82, pp. 3-25.
- Duda, R. O. "Knowledge-Based Expert Systems Come of Age," *Byte,* Vol. 6, No. 9, Sept. '81 pp. 238-281.
- Feigenbaum, E. A., "Knowledge Engineering for the 1980's," Computer Science Dept., Stanford University, 1982.
- Gevarter, W. B., *An Overview of Expert Systems,* NBSIR 82-2505, National Bureau of Standards, Washington, D.C., May 1982 (Revised October 1982).
- Lindsay, R. K., Buchanan, B. G., Feigenbaum, E. A., and Lederberg, J., *Applications of Artificial Intelligence for Organic Chemistry: The DENDRAL Project,* New York: McGraw-Hill, 1980.
- Stefik, M., Alkins, J., Balzer, R., Benoit, J., Birnbaum, L. Hayes-Roth, R., Sacerdoti, E., "The Organization of Expert Systems, A Tutorial, *"Artificial Intelligence,* Vol. 18, 1982, pp. 135-173.
- Stefik, M., Bobrow, D. G., Mittal, S., and Conway, L., "Knowledge Programming in LOOPS," *The AI Magazine,* Vol 4, No. 3, Fall 1983, pp 3-13.
- *IJCAI-81* — *Proc. of The International Joint Conference on AI,* Vancouver, Aug. 1981.
- *AAAI-82* — *Proc. of the National Conference on AI,* CMU & U. of Pittsburgh, Pittsburgh, PA, Aug. 18-22, 1982.
- *IJCAI-83* — *Proc. of The Eighth International Joint Conference on AI,* Karlsruhe, W. Germany, Aug. 1983.
- *AAAJ-83* — *Proc. of The National Conference on AAAI,* Wash, D.C., Aug. 1983.

II. COMPUTER VISION

A. Introduction

Computer Vision — visual perception employing computers — shares with "Expert Systems" the role of being one of the most popular topics in Artificial Intelligence today. The computer vision field is multifaceted, having many participants with diverse viewpoints, with many papers having been written. However, the field is still in the early stages of development — organizing principles have not yet fully crystalized, and the associated technology has not yet been completely rationalized. However, commercial vision systems have already begun to be used in manufacturing and robotic systems for inspection and guidance tasks, and other systems (at various stages of development) are beginning to be employed in military, cartographic and image interpretation applications.

B. Definition

Computer (computational or machine) vision can be defined as perception by a computer based on visual sensory input. Barrow and Tenenbaum (1981, p. 573) state:

> Vision is an information-processing task with well-defined input and output. The input consists of arrays of brightness values, representing projections of a three-dimensional scene recorded by a camera or comparable imaging device. Several input arrays may provide information in several spectral bands (color) or from multiple viewpoints (stereo or time sequence). The desired output is a concise description of the three-dimensional scene depicted in the image, the exact nature of which depends upon the goals and expectations of the observer. It generally involves a description of objects and their interrelationships, but may also include such information as the three-dimensional structures of surfaces, their physical characteristics (shape, texture, color, material), and the locations of shadows and light sources . . .

C. Relation to Human Vision

MIT's Marr and Nishihara (1978, p. 42) take the view that "Artificial Intelligence is (or ought to be) the study of information processing problems that characteristically have their roots in some aspects of biological information processing." They developed a computational theory of vision based on their study of human vision. Figure II-1 represents the transition from the raw image through the primal sketch to the 2-1/2D sketch (exemplified by Figure II-2), which contains information on local surface orientations, boundaries, and depths.

The primal sketch, reminiscent of an artist's hurried drawing, is a primitive but rich description of the way the intensities change over the visual field. It can be represented by a set of short line segments separating regions of different brightnesses. A list of the properties of the lines segments, such as location, length, and orientation for each segment can be used to represent the primal sketch.

The late Dr. Marr and his associates' development of a human visual information processing theory (Marr, 1982) has had a substantial impact on computational vision.

There are strong indications (see, e.g., Gevarter, 1977) that the interpretative planning areas of the human brain set up a context for processing the input data. (This viewpoint is captured by

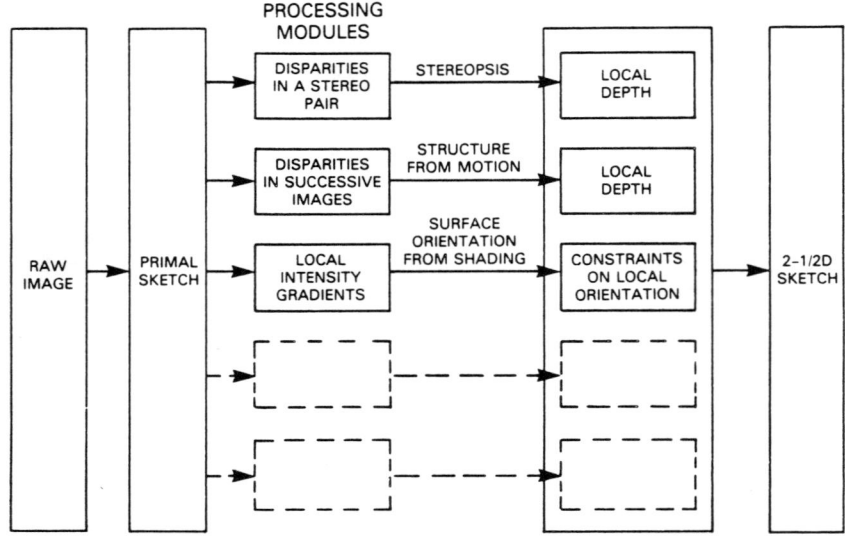

The computations begin with representations of the intensities in an image—first the image itself, (e.g., the gray-level intensity array) and then the primal sketch, a representation of spatial variations in intensity. Next comes the operation of a set of modules, each employing certain aspects of the information contained in the image to derive information about local orientation, local depth, and the boundaries of surfaces. From this is constructed the so-called 2-1/2 dimensional sketch. Note that no "high-level" information is yet brought to bear: the computations proceed by utilizing only what is available in the image itself.

After: Marr and Nishihara, 1978, p. 42.

Figure II-1. A Framework for Early and Intermediate States in A Theory of Visual Information Processing.

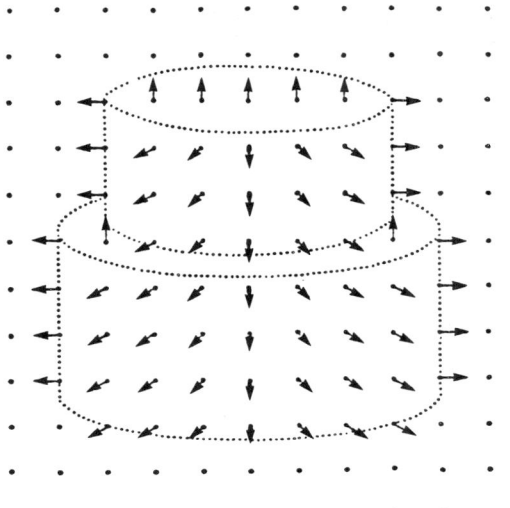

A candidate for the so-called 2-½-dimensional sketch, which encompasses local determinations of the depth and orientation of surfaces in an image, as derived from processes that operate upon the primal sketch or some other representation of changes in gray-level intensity. The lengths of the needles represent the degree of tilt at various points in the surface; the orientations of the needles represent the directions of tilt... Dotted lines show contours of surface discontinuity. No explicit representation of depth appears in this figure.

Source: Marr and Nishihara, 1978, p. 41.

Figure II-2. An Example of a 2-1/2D Sketch.

Minsky's (1975) AI "frame" concept for knowledge representation.) The brain then uses visual and other cues from the environment to draw in past knowledge to generate an internal representation and interpretation of the scene. This knowledge-based expectation-guided approach to vision is now appearing in advanced AI computer vision systems.

D. Basis for a General Purpose Image Understanding System

Barrow and Tenenbaum (1981, p. 573) observe that in going from a scene to an image (an array of brightness values) that the image encodes much information about the scene, but the information is confounded in the single brightness value at each point. In projecting onto the two-dimensional image, information about the three-dimensional structure of the scene is lost. In order to decode brightness values and recover a scene description, it is necessary to employ a priori knowledge embodied in models of the scene domain, the illumination, and the imaging process.

As indicated by Figure II-3, computer vision is an active process that uses these models to interpret the sensory data. To accommodate the diversity of appearance found in real imagery, a high-performance, general-purpose system must embody a great deal of knowledge in its models.

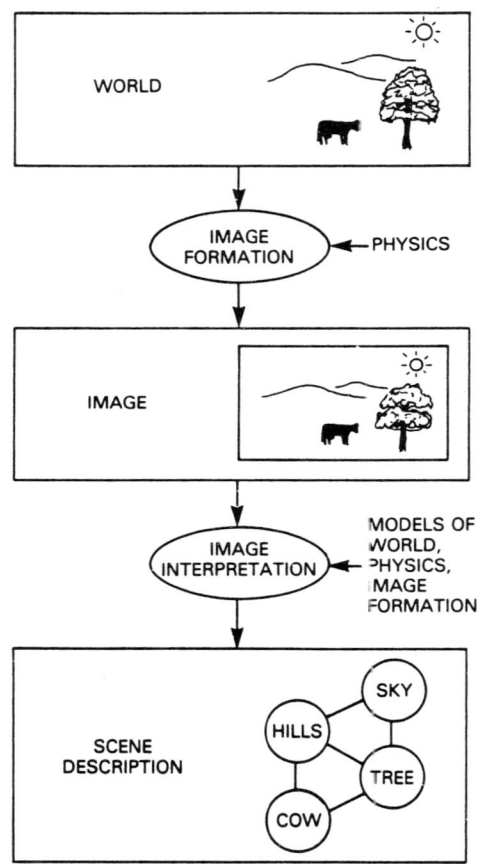

Source: Barrow and Tenenbaum, 1981, p. 573.

Figure II-3. Model-based Interpretation of Images.

E. Basic Paradigms for Computer Vision*

In broad terms, an image understanding system starts with the array of pixel amplitudes that define the computer image, and using stored models (either specific or generic) determines the content of a scene. Typically, various symbolic features such as lines and areas are first determined from the image. These are then compared with similar features associated with stored models to find a match, when specific objects are being sought. In more generic cases, it is necessary to determine various characteristics of the scene, and using generic models determine from geometric shapes and other factors (such as allowable relationships between objects) the nature of the scene content.

A variety of paradigms have been proposed to accomplish these tasks in image understanding systems. These paradigms are based on a common set of broadly defined processing and manipulating elements: feature extraction, symbolic representation, and semantic interpretation. The paradigms differ primarily in how these elements (defined below) are organized and controlled, and the degree of artificial intelligence and knowledge employed.

1. *Hierarchical Bottom-up Approach*

Figure II-4A is a block diagram of a hierarchical paradigm of an image understanding system that employs a bottom-up processing approach. The hierarchical bottom-up approach can be developed successfully for domains with simple scenes made up of only a limited number of previously known objects.

2. *Hierarchical Top-down Approach*

This approach (usually called hypothesize and test), shown in Figure II-4B, is goal directed, the interpretation stage being guided in its analysis by trial or test descriptions of a scene. An example would be using template matching — matched filtering — to search for a specific object or structure within the scene. Matched filtering is normally performed at the pixel level by cross correlation of an object template with an observed image field. It is often computationally advantageous, because of the reduced dimensionality, to perform the interpretation at a higher level in the chain by correlating image features or symbols rather than pixels.

3. *Heterarchical Approach*

Hierarchical image understanding systems are normally designed for specific applications. They thus tend to lack adaptability. A large amount of processing is also usually required. Pratt (1978) (pp. 572-573) observes that often much of this processing is wasted in the generation of features and symbols not required for the analysis of a particular scene. A technique to avoid this problem is to establish a central monitor to observe the overall performance of the image understanding system and then issue commands to the various system elements to modify their operation to maximize system performance and efficiency.

Figure II-4C is a block diagram of an image understanding system that achieves heterarchical operation by distributed feedback control.

---

*This section is primarily based on Pratt, 1978, pp. 570-574.

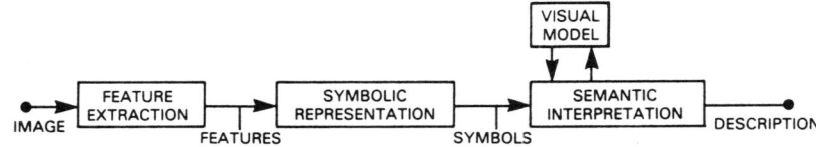

A. HIERARCHICAL BOTTOM-UP APPROACH

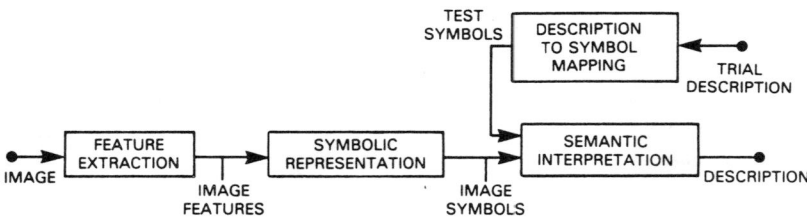

B. HIERARCHICAL TOP-DOWN APPROACH

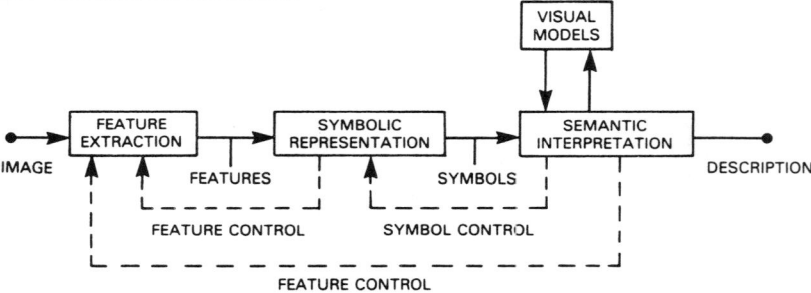

C. HETERARCHICAL APPROACH

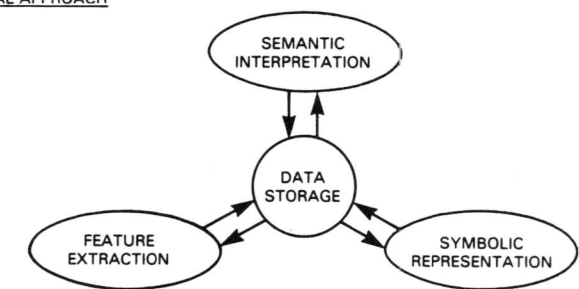

D. BLACKBOARD APPROACH

Source: Pratt, 1978, pp. 570-574.

Figure II-4. Basic Image Understanding Paradigms.

4. Blackboard Approach

Another image understanding system configuration called the blackboard model has been proposed by Reddy and Newell (1975). Figure II-4D is a simplified representation of this approach in which the various system elements communicate with each other via a common working data storage called the blackboard. Whenever any element performs a task, its output is put into the common data storage, which is independently accessible by all other elements. The individual elements can be designed to act autonomously to further the common system goal as required. The blackboard system is particularly attractive in cases where several hypotheses must be considered simultaneously and their components need to be kept track of at various levels of representation.

F. Levels of Representation

A computer vision system, like human vision is, commonly considered to be naturally structured as a succession of levels of representation.

Tenenbaum, et al. (1979, pp. 254-255), sketch in Figure II-5, a way in which to view an organization of a general-purpose vision system. They divide the figure into two parts. The first is

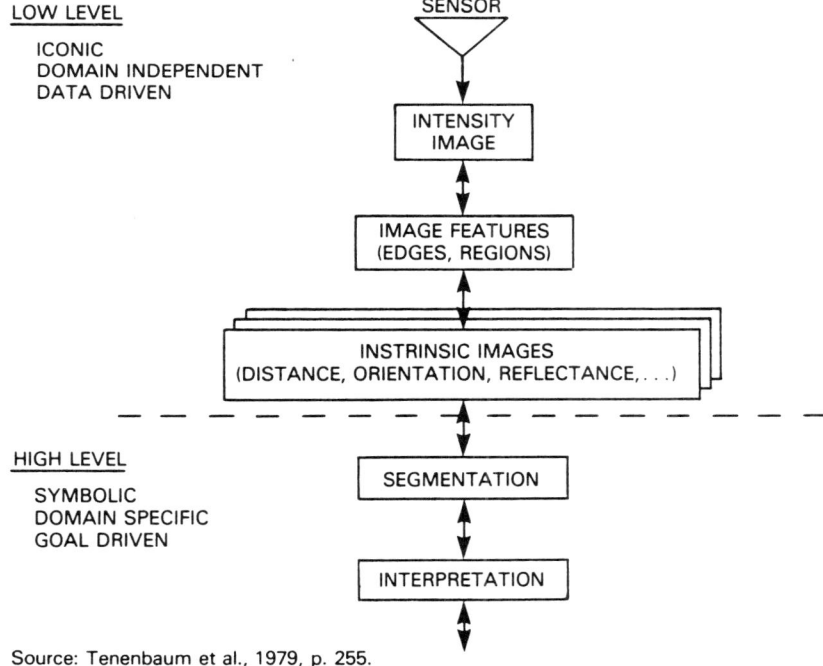

Source: Tenenbaum et al., 1979, p. 255.

Figure II-5. Organization of a Visual System.

image oriented (iconic), domain independent, and based on the image data (data driven). The second part of the figure is symbolic, dependent on the domain and the particular goal of the vision process.

The first portion takes the image, which consists of an intensity array of picture elements ("pixels," e.g., 1000 × 1000), and converts it into image features such as edges and regions. These are then converted into a set of parallel "intrinsic images," one each for distance (range), surface orientation, reflectance,* etc.

The second part of the system segments these into volumes and surfaces dependent on our knowledge of the domain and the goal of the computation. Using domain knowledge and the constraints associated with the relations among objects in this domain, objects are identified and the scene analyzed consistent with the system goal.

G. Research in Model-Based Vision Systems

Most research efforts in vision have been directed at exploring various aspects of vision, or toward generating particular processing modules for a step in the vision process rather than in devising general purpose vision systems. However, there are currently two major U.S. efforts in general purpose vision systems. The ACRONYM system at Stanford University under the leadership of T. Binford, and the VISIONS system at the University of Massachusetts at Amherst under A. Hanson and E. Riseman.

The ACRONYM system, outlined in Table II-1-1, is designed to be a general purpose, model-based system that does its major reasoning at the level of volumes rather than images. The system basically takes a hierarchical top-down approach as in Figure II-4B. ACRONYM has four essential parts: modeling, prediction, description and interpretation. The user provides ACRONYM with models of objects (modeled in terms of volume primitives called generalized cones) and their spatial relationships; as well as generic models and their subclass relationships. These are both stored in graph form. The program automatically predicts which image features to expect. Description is a bottom-up process that generates a model-independent description of the image. Interpretation relates this description to the prediction to produce a three-dimensional understanding of the scene.

The VISIONS system outlined in Table II-1-2, can be considered to be a working tool to test various image understanding modules and approaches. Rather than using specific models, its high level knowledge is in the form of framelike "schemas" which represent expectations and expected relationships in particular scene situations. VISIONS is based on monocular images and does its reasoning at the level of images rather than volumes.

Other research efforts in model-based vision systems are summarized in TABLES III in Appendix I of Gevarter (1982A). All the research computer vision systems are individually crafted by the developers — reflecting the developers' backgrounds, interests and domain requirements. All, except ACRONYM (and to an extent, 3-D Mosaic, Kanade, 1981), use image (2-D) models and are viewpoint dependent. Models are mostly described by semantic networks though feature vectors are also utilized. The systems, capitalizing on their choice to limit their observations to only a few

---

*Fraction of normal incident illumination reflected.

Computer Vision

TABLE II-1-1. Model-Based Vision Systems.

Developer: Brooks et al. (1979), Brooks (1981)
System: ACRONYM
Purpose: General Purpose Vision System
Example Domains: Identifying Airplanes on a Runway in Aerial Images
Simulation for Robot Systems and for Automated Grasping of Objects

Approach	Modeling	Image Feature Extraction & Representation	Search & Matching	Remarks
Hierarchical top down approach.	Represents object classes from which subclasses and specific objects are represented by numeric constraints.	Ribbons and curves obtained from an edge mapper.	Matcher does an interpretation matching by mapping the Observability Graph into the Picture Graph.	Aims to be a general vision system.
Reasons between different levels of representation based on a hierarchy of representations.		Surfaces obtained from a stereo mapper.		Insensitive to viewpoint.
High level modeler provides a high level language to manipulate models using symbolic names.	Models 3-D objects using volume primitives: generalized cones and ribbons.	Nodes of the Picture Graph (symbolic version of image) correspond to ribbons, surfaces and curves.	Matcher works in a coarse to fine order.	A goal is to make use of total information for interpretation.
Predictor and Planner Module is a rule-based system to generate an Observability Graph from the Object Graph (3-D object representation consisting of nodes and relational arcs).	Spatial relations of volume elements within an object defined hierarchically.	Arcs and relations indicate spatial relations between nodes.	Combines local matches of ribbons into clusters.	Feature extraction (e.g., finding lines and regions) still weak.
	Can model both specific and generic volume elements and relations between them.		Searches for maximal subgraph matches in the Observability graph.	
Makes predictions (which are viewpoint insensitive) in the form of symbolic constraint expressions with variables.	Models are part/whole graphs.		Performs major interpretation at the level of volumes rather than at the level of images.	Interpretation is limited to scenes with few objects.
Makes a projective transformation from models.	Volume primitives have local rather than viewer-centered primitives.			Substantial progress has been achieved in past few years.
Predicts appearances of models in images in terms of ribbons and ellipses.				

TABLE II-1-1. *Model-Based Vision Systems (cont.)*

Approach	Modeling	Image Feature Extraction & Representation	Search & Matching	Remarks
Incorporates translation and rotation into observable representations.				
Searches for instances of models in images. It employs geometric reasoning in the form of a rule based problem-solving system.				
It interprets (matches) in 3-D by enforcing constraints of the 3-D model.				

TABLE II-1-2. *Model-Based Vision Systems.*

Developer: Hanson & Riseman (1978a,b)
Systems: VISIONS
Purpose: Interpreting static monocular scenes
 Can be considered to be a working tool to test various image understanding modules and approaches
Example Domains: House scenes from ground level
 Road scenes from ground level

Approach	Modeling	Image Feature Extraction & Representation	Search & Matching	Remarks
Uses hierarchical modular approach to representation and control.	Hierarchical structure	Uses both edge finding and region growing to segment the image into a layered directed graph of regions, line segments and vertices	Generates and stores partial models in "contexts" (of the CONNIVER programming language) which provide a history of decisions to be used when backtracking is necessary	System (Parma, 1980) did reasonably well in making a crude segmentation of a house scene
Tries to be as general as possible to allow both bottom-up and top-down solution hypotheses as well as various intermediate combinations	Scene schemas (like frames) are the highest representation			Viewpoint dependent
	Hierarchy is: —schemas —objects —volumes —surfaces	Uses a hierarchical processing cone (pyramid) to be able to handle image data at various levels of resolution		Schema used depends on specific scene.
Incorporates the flexibility to utilize various feature extraction modules and multiple knowledge sources as required		Uses a relaxation approach to organize edges into boundaries, and pixel clusters into regions, using high-level system guidance (interpretation guided segmentation)	Uses a multiple knowledge source heterarchical approach which generates partial models in the search space of models. Attempts, using top-down and bottom-up relaxation techniques, to converge on a most probable solution.	
Allows for the possibility of generating and verifying hypotheses along many paths	Proposed representations of 3D surfaces and volumes include: —generalized cylinders —surface patches with cubic B-splines to represent boundary and blending functions		Uses rules for *focusing* on an element of a task, *expanding* that element by generating new hypotheses and *verifying* new hypotheses.	
	Employs semantic networks —nodes represent primitive entities (objects, concepts situations, etc.) —Labeled arcs represent relationships between them			

objects, use predominantly the top-down interpretation of images approach, relying heavily on prediction.

H. Industrial Vision Systems
1. General Characteristics

The prominent aspect of industrial vision systems, in distinction to more general vision systems, is that they operate in a relatively known and structured environment. In addition, the situation (such as placement of cameras and lighting) can be configured to simplify the computer vision problem. Usually, the number and nature of possible objects will tend to be restricted, and the visual system will be tailored to the function performed. Thus many of them are based on a pattern recognition, rather than an image understanding, approach. Industrial vision systems are characteristically used for such activities as inspection, manipulation and assembly.

A popular organization for industrial computer vision is a two-stage hierarchy with a bottom-up control flow. The lower level segments the image into regions corresponding to object surfaces. The higher level used this segmentation to identify objects from their surface descriptions.

In practice, most successful systems incorporate aspects of both bottom-up and top-down control. The bottom-up processing is used to extract prominent features of a part to determine its position. Then, top-down control is used to direct a search to determine if the part satisfies an inspection criterion.

Industrial inspection and assembly operations are well suited to model-based analysis, because of the well-defined geometric descriptions associated with manufactured items. CAD/CAM technology allows the specification of objects using either volumetric or surface-based models. These geometrically based models are particularly appropriate to the hypothesis-verify approach, in which low-level image features are extracted and matched to an appropriate computer-generated 2-D representation.

In addition to geometric models, objects may also be represented by graphs. In this case, recognition becomes a graph-matching process.

More commonly at present, rather than using geometric models or graphs, industrial vision systems are taught by being presented sample parts to be recognized in each of their expected stable states. Aspects of the resulting images are typically stored as templates, and recognition becomes template matching. The objects can also be represented in terms of their characteristic features, such as area, number of holes, etc., and the resulting feature vector stored to be matched (via a search process) to the corresponding extracted feature vector of the image during system operation.

To simplify industrial vision systems, the input is usually reduced to a binary (black and white) image, so that objects appear as silhouettes. Simplicity is important in industrial vision systems because the computation time is limited, as most systems are expected to operate in near real time.

2. Examples of Efforts in Industrial Visual Inspection Systems

Kruger and Thompson (1981) discuss some example efforts of vision systems designed for inspection. The systems reviewed are primarily for the inspection of printed circuit boards and IC chips, with template matching being the predominant inspection approach.

Chin (1982) has recently published an extensive bibliography on automated visual inspection techniques and applications.

3. Examples of Efforts in Industrial Visual Recognition and Location Systems

Table II-2 (largely derived from Kruger and Thompson, 1981) lists some example efforts of vision systems designed for industrial part recognition and location. All these systems use a bottom-up approach. It will be observed that (except for Vamos 1979, and Albus, et al., 1982) these systems utilize template or feature vector matching. Vamos does work from a 3D wire frame mode which utilizes computer graphics type techniques to transform a model projection into alignment with observed lines in the image.

Albus' Machine Vision Group in the NBS Industrial Systems Division is using simplified 3D surface models of machined parts to generate expectancy images from needed viewpoints. The group is seeking to achieve real-time, hierarchical, multi-sensory, interactive robot guidance.

4. Commercially Available Industrial Vision Systems

Gevarter (1982A) surveys many of the Industrial Vision Systems that are currently commercially available. Most of the systems require special lighting.

Many of the systems designed for verification and inspection use pattern recognition, rather than AI techniques. The systems tend to be bottom-up (see Figure II-4A) because of the speed required to achieve real-time operations. Often unique edge and feature extraction algorithms are programmed in hardware or firmware.

The more sophisticated systems tend to utilize variations and improvements on the SRI Vision Module described in Table II-2.

A few systems make good use of structured light for 3D sensing. A number of efforts in visual guidance of arc welding also utilize this technique.

I. Who Is Doing It

Rosenfeld, at the University of Maryland, issues a yearly bibliography, arranged by subject matter, related to the computer processing of pictorial information. The issue covering 1981 (Rosenfeld, 1982) includes nearly 1000 references.

The following is a list by category of the U.S. "principal players" in computer vision.

1. Research Oriented
  Universities

Funded Under DARPA IU Program	*Other Active Universities*
CMU	U of Texas at Austin
U of MD	VPI
MIT	Purdue
U. of Mass.	U of PA
Stanford U	U of IL
U of Rochester	Wayne State U
USC	JHU
U of Rhode Island	RPI

TABLE II-2. *Example Research Efforts in Industrial Visual Recognition and Location Systems.*

Developer Purpose Sample Domains	Approach	Modeling and Representations
Agin (1980) SRI Vision Module	Bottom-up approach	Blob descriptors include:
Locate, identify and guide manipulation of industrial parts	Uses thresholding to convert to a binary image	—max. and min. x and y values
	Each line is sequentially scanned and edge points (where pixels change from 1 to 0 or 0 to 1 recorded). Each resulting segment on a line is matched to the previous line to determine their overlapping relationships. Using these relationships, the program traces the appearance and disappearance of blobs (regions) as the image is processed from top to bottom.	—Holes
Engine Parts		—Area
SRI		—Moments of inertia
	Using blob descriptors, the system can recognize parts regardless of their position or orientation. The descriptors are matched using either a binary decision tree or a normalized nearest-neighbor method.	—Perimeter length
		—Linked list of coordinates on the perimeter
	The system is trained by repeatedly showing the object to the TV camera resulting in all potentially useful shape descriptions being automatically calculated and stored	
Holland Rossol & Ward (1979) Consight I	Two linear light sources superimpose a line of light on a conveyor belt perpendicular to its direction of motion. The two lines separate, proportional to the part passing by. Point of separation determines part boundary; degree of separation determines part thickness.	Feature vector of part image characteristics
Industrial part location, recognition and manipulation		
Engine parts	The scene is imaged with a linear array camera and a silhouette automatically generated.	
GM	Uses same feature vector approach as SRI Module.	

TABLE II-2. *Example Research Efforts in Industrial Visual Recognition and Location Systems. (cont.)*

Developer Purpose Sample Domains	Approach	Modeling and Representations
NBS: Albus et al. (1982) Visual servoing for robot guidance (real-time location and identification for manipulation) Machined parts	Employs a point light source, a sheets-of-structured-light generator and a camera, all mounted on the wrist of a robot arm. Uses alternate frames of: 1. A regular point source illumination of the entire object, and 2. Two parallel planes of structured light.	Uses quadratic approximations to surfaces of idealized 3-D objects.
National Bureau of Standards	System determines location and orientation based on triangulation associated with relative height of intersection of light sheets with part, and recognition based on shape and size of observed lines that the planes of light make as they intersect part. Uses this information to interpret outline seen in image produced by the point source illumination. Analysis of vision input is performed with a hierarchically organized group of microprocessors. At each level of the hierarchy, an analytic process is guided by an expectancy-generating modeling process. The modeling process is in turn driven by a store of *a priori* knowledge, by knowledge of the robot's movements, and by feedback from the analytic process. Each such level of the hierarchy provides output to guide a corresponding level of the robot's hierarchical control system.	

TABLE II-2. *Example Research Efforts in Industrial Visual Recognition and Location Systems. (cont.)*

Developer Purpose Sample Domains	Approach	Modeling and Representations
Perkins (1978)	Operates on 32 gray levels	Concurve models of sample parts
Industrial parts recognition	Bottom-up scene segmentation approach	
Engine components GM	1. Reduce 256 × 256 pixel image to an "edge gradient" image 2. Link edges with similar gradient magnitudes to form chains 3. Characterize chains as either straight lines or circular arcs. (This reduces 65,000 pixel image to about 50 concurves.)	
	System matches observed concurves with model generated concurves using:	
	1. A preset control structure to select the order in which combinations of model and scene concurves are to be matched.	
	2. Starts by matching one model and one scene concurve	
	3. The stored model is spatially transformed and rotated to fit associated scene concurves	
	System interactively trained by generating concurves of sample parts	
	Can identify parts partially occluded by other parts	

TABLE II-2. *Example Research Efforts in Industrial Visual Recognition and Location Systems. (cont.)*

Developer Purpose Sample Domains	Approach	Modeling and Representations
Yachida and Tsuji (1978) Industrial parts recognition Nonoccluded parts of a small gasoline engine Osaka Univ.	Uses a boundary detection and isolation of parts in a binary image approach similar to SRI Vision Module Recognition system based on a structured step-by-step analysis with the previously stored models Uses a series of special feature detectors —hole detector —line finder —texture detector —small hole detector System training involves interactive man-machine examination of the identification task	Stable orientation models of parts —part name —orientation —list of primitive features —polar coordinate boundary representation
Vamos (1979) Recognition of 3D objects Bearing housings Assembly Sheet metal parts to be painted Neural nets in microscopic-section in neural research Hungarian Acad. of Science	Finds edges using a simplified version of the Hueckel-operator using only two linear templates Lines are then fitted to edges Wire-frame model transformed (and hidden line elimination used) to correspond to image—yielding recognition and part orientation Objects are interactively taught to system either by building a geometric model or by a computer-aided transformation of viewed samples	3D Wire Frame Models

Computer Vision 103

Non-Profits
SRI International, AI Center
JPL
ERIM

U.S. Government
NBS, Industrial Systems Div., Gaithersburg, MD
NOSC (Naval Ocean Systems Center), San Diego
NIH (National Institutes of Health)

2. Commercial Vision Systems Developers

Hundreds of companies are now involved in vision systems, a partial listing being given in Gevarter (1982A).

J. Summary of the State-of-the-Art

1. Human Vision

Human vision is the only available example of a general purpose vision system. However, thus far not many AI researchers have taken an interest in the computations performed by natural visual systems, but this situation is changing.

The MIT vision group (among others) believes that, to a first approximation, the human visual system is subdivided into modules specializing in visual tasks. There is also evidence that people do global processing first and use it to constrain local processing.

Considerable information now exists about lower level visual processing in humans. However, as we progress up the human visual computing hierarchy, the exact nature of the appropriate representations becomes subject to dispute. Thus, overall human visual perception is still very far from being understood.

2. Low and Intermediate Levels of Processing

Though methods for powerful high-level understanding visual analysis are still in the process of being determined, insights into low-level vision are emerging. The basic physics of imaging, and the nature of constraints in vision and their use in computation is fairly well understood. Detailed programs for vision modules, such as "shape from shading" and "optical flow," have begun to appear. Also, the representational issues are now better understood.

However, even for well understood low-level operations such as edge detection, (see, e.g., Ballard, 1982) there has been no convergence among the many techniques proposed, and no method stands out as the best. In general, edge detectors are still unreliable, though Marr and Hilbert's approach, based on the zero crossing of the second derivative of the intensity gradient, appears promising.

In industrial vision, the primary technique for achieving robust edge finding and segmentation is to use special lighting and convert to a silhouette binary image in which edges and regions are readily distinguishable.

At intermediate levels, edge classification and labelling have been very successfully used in the blocks world.

Binford (1982) in reviewing existing research in model-based vision systems observed that most systems first segment regions then describe their shape. None of the systems makes effective use of texture for segmentation and description. In general, shape description is primitive and interpretation systems have not yet made full use of even these limited capabilities.

As yet, the extraction of useful information from color is extremely rudimentary. The perceptual use of motion (optical flow) has been a focus of attention recently, but findings are preliminary.

For low level processing, many recent algorithms take the form of parallel computations involving local interactions. One popular approach having this character is "relaxation," in which local computations are iteratively propagated to try to extract global features. These locally parallel architectures are well suited to rapid parallel processing techniques using special purpose VLSI chips.

3. Industrial Vision Systems

Barrow and Tenenbaum (1981, p. 572) observe that:

Significant progress has been made in recent years on practical applications of machine vision. Systems have been developed that achieve useful levels of performance on complex real imagery in tasks such as inspection of industrial parts, interpretation of aerial imagery, and analysis of chest x-rays. Virtually all such systems are special purpose, being heavily dependent on domain-specific constraints and techniques.

It has been estimated that as of mid-1982, though less than 50 sophisticated industrial vision systems were actually in use in the U.S., approximately 1000 simple line-scan inspection systems were in regular operation. Though special purpose systems have thus far been the most effective, successful vision applications are now becoming commonplace and are expanding. Vision manufacturers are now beginning to provide easier user programming, friendlier user interfaces, and systems engineering support to prospective users. Many firms are now entering the industrial vision field, with technical leap-frogging being common due to rapidly changing technology.

4. General Purpose Vision Systems

Though many practical image recognition systems have been developed, Hiatt (1981, pp. 2, 8) observes that, "In current vision applications, the type of scene to be processed and acted upon is usually carefully defined and limited to the capability of the machine . . . General purpose computer vision has not yet been solved in practice." This domain specificity makes each new application expensive and time consuming to develop.

Binford (1982) in reviewing current model-based research vision systems concludes that most systems have not attempted to be general vision systems, though ACRONYM does demonstrate some progress toward this goal. Existing vision systems performances are strongly limited by the performance of their segmentation modules, their weak use of world knowledge and weak descriptions, making little use of shape.

With the exception of ACRONYM (and to an extent 3-D Mosaic), the systems surveyed depend on image models and relations, and therefore are strongly viewpoint-dependent. To generalize to viewpoint-insensitive interpretations would require three-dimensional modeling and interpretation as in ACRONYM.

Binford concludes that though the results of these and other efforts are encouraging as first demonstrations, nevertheless as general vision systems, they have a long way to go.

K. Applications and Future Trends

Brady (1981, p. 2) states that, "There is currently a surge of interest in image understanding on the part of industry." Examples of current computer vision applications are indicated in Figure II-6.

As the field of computer vision unfolds, we expect to see the following future trends.*

1. Techniques
- Though most industrial vision systems have used binary representations, we can expect increased use of gray scales because of their potential for handling scenes with cluttered backgrounds and uncontrolled lighting.
- Recent theoretical work on monocular shape interpretation from images (shape from shading, texture, etc.) make it appear promising that general mechanisms for generating spatial observations from images will be available within the next 2 to 5 years to support general vision systems.
- Successful techniques (such as stereo and motion parallax) for deriving shape and/or motion from multiple images should also be available within 2 to 5 years.
- The mathematics of Image Understanding will continue to become more sophisticated.
- Enlargement will continue of the links now growing between Image Understanding and Theories of Human Vision.

2. Hardware and Architecture
- We are now seeing hardware and software emerging that enables real-time operation in simple situations. Within the next 2 to 5 years we should see hardware and software that will enable similar real-time operation for robotics and other activities requiring recognition, and position and orientation information.
- Fast raster-based pipeline preprocessing hardware to compute low-level features in local regions of an entire scene are now becoming available and should find general use in commercial vision systems in 2 to 4 years.
- As at virtually all visual levels, processing seems inherently parallel, parallel processing is a wave of the future (but not the entire answer).
- Relaxation and constraint analysis techniques are on the increase and will be increasingly reflected in future architectures.

3. AI and General Vision Systems

Computer vision will be a key factor in achieving many artificial intelligence applications. The goal is to move from special-purpose visual processing to general-purpose computer vision. Work to date in model-based systems has made a tentative beginning. But the long-run goal is to be able

---

*These trends have been largely derived from statements by Brady (1981A, 1981B), Binford (1982), Kruger and Thompson (1981), Agin (1980), Arden (1980), Rosenfeld (1981), Hiatt (1981), and Barrow and Tenenbaum (1981).

AUTOMATION OF INDUSTRIAL PROCESSES

Object acquisition by robot arms, for example, for sorting or packing items arriving on conveyor belts.
Automatic guidance of seam welders and cutting tools.
VLSI-related processes, such as lead bonding, chip alignment and packaging.
Monitoring, filtering, and thereby containing the flood of data from oil drill sites or from seismographs.
Providing visual feedback for automatic assembly and repair.

INSPECTION TASKS

The inspection of printed circuit boards for spurs, shorts, and bad connections.
Checking the results of casting processes for impurities and fractures.
Screening medical images such as chromosome slides, cancer smears, x-ray and ultrasound images, tomography.
Routine screening of plant samples.
Inspection of alpha-numerics on labels and manufactured items.
Checking packaging and contents in pharmaceutical and food industries.
Inspection of glass items for cracks, bubbles, etc.

REMOTE SENSING

Cartography, the automatic generation of hill-shaded maps, and the registration of satellite images with terrain maps.
Monitoring traffic along roads, docks, and at airfields.
Management of land resources such as water, forestry, soil erosion, and crop growth.
Detecting mineral ore deposits.

MAKING COMPUTER POWER MORE ACCESSIBLE

Management information systems that have a communication channel considerably wider than current systems that are addressed by typing or pointing.
Document readers (for those who still use paper).
Design aids for architects and mechanical engineers.

MILITARY APPLICATIONS

Tracking moving objects.
Automatic navigation based on passive sensing.
Target acquisition and range finding.

AIDS FOR THE PARTIALLY SIGHTED

Systems that read a document and speak what they read.
Automatic "guide dog" navigation systems.

Figure II-6. Examples of Applications of Computer Vision Now Underway.

to deal with unfamiliar or unexpected input.* Reasoning in terms of generic models and reasoning by analogy are two approaches being pursued. However, it is anticipated that it will be a decade or more before substantial progress will be made.

4. *Modeling and Programming*
   - Now emerging is 3D modeling, arising largely from CAD/CAM technology. 3D CAD/CAM data bases will be integrated with industrial vision systems to realistically generate synthesized images for matching with visual inputs.
   - Illumination models, shading and surface property models will be increasingly incorporated into visual systems.
   - Volumetric models which allow prediction and interpretation at the levels of volumes, rather than images, will see greater utilization.
   - High level vision programming languages (such as Automatix's RAIL) that can be integrated with robot and industrial manufacturing languages are now beginning to appear and will become commonplace within 5 years.
   - Generic representations for amorphous objects (such as trees) have been experimentally utilized and should become generally available within 5 years.

5. *Knowledge Acquisition*
   - Strategies for indexing into a large database of models should be available within the next 2 to 5 years.
   - "Training by being told" will supplement "training by example" as computer graphics techniques and vision programming languages become more common.

6. *Sensing*
   - An important area of development is 3D sensing. Several current industrial vision systems are already employing structured light for 3D sensing. A number of new innovative techniques in this area are expected to appear in the next 5 years.
   - More active vision sensors such as lidar are now being explored, but are unlikely to find substantial industrial application until the last half of this decade.

7. *Industrial Vision Systems*
   - We will see increased use of advanced vision techniques in industrial vision systems, including gray scale imagery.
   - We are now observing a shortening time lag between research advances and their applications in industry. It is anticipated that in the future this lag may be as little as one to two years.
   - Advanced electronics hardware at reduced cost is increasing the capabilities and speed of industrial vision, while simultaneously reducing costs.

---

*As computer vision systems move toward this goal, they will increasingly incorporate Expert System components using multiple knowledge sources. Gevarter (1982B) provides An Overview of Expert Systems, in which ACRONYM and VISIONS are considered to be examples of Expert Systems.

- It is anticipated that special lighting and active sensing will play an increasing role in industrial vision.
- Common programming languages and improved interface standards will within the next 3 to 10 years enable easier integration of vision to robots and into the industrial environment.

8. Future Applications

- It is anticipated that about one quarter of all industrial robots will be equipped with some form of vision system by 1990.
- It is likely that in the order of 90% of all industrial inspection activities requiring vision will be done with computer vision systems within the next decade.
- New vision system applications in a wide variety of areas, as yet unexplored, will begin to appear within this decade. An example of such a system might be visual traffic monitors at intersections that could perceive cars, pedestrians, etc., in motion, and control the flow of traffic accordingly.
- Computer vision will play a large role in future military applications. The Defense Mapping Agency intends to achieve fully automated production for mapping, charting and geodesy by 1995, utilizing "expert system"-guided computer vision facilities.

L. Conclusion

In conclusion, the amount of activity and the many researchers in the computer vision field suggest that within the next 5 to 10 years, we should see some startling advances in practical computer vision, though the availability of practical general vision systems still remains a long way off.

REFERENCES

- Albus, J., Kent, E., Nashman, M., Mansbach, P., and Palombo, L., "A 6-D Vision System," *Proceedings of SPIE Technical Symposium East '82,* Arlington, VA, May 3-7, 1982.
- Agin, G. J., "Computer Vision Systems for Industrial Inspection and Assembly," *Computer,* May 1980.
- Arden, B. W., (eds.), *What Can Be Automated?* Cambridge: M.I.T., 1980, pp. 482-487.
- Ballard, D. H. and Brown, C. M., *Computer Vision,* Englewood Cliffs: Prentice Hall, 1982
- Barrow, H. G. and Tenenbaum, J. M., "Computational Vision," *Proceedings of the IEEE,* Vol. 69, No. 5, May 1981, pp. 572-595.
- Binford, T. O., "Survey of Model-based Image Analysis Systems," *Robotics Research,* Vol. 1, No. 1, Spring 1982.
- Brady, M., "Computational Approaches to Image Understanding," M.I.T. A.I. Memo No. 653, October 1981A. (Also in Computing Survey, Vol. 14, No. 1, Mar. 1982, pp. 3-71).
- Brady, M., "The Changing Shape of Computer Vision,"*Artificial Intelligence,* 17 (1-3), 1981B, pp. 1-15.
- Brooks, R., Greiner, R. and Binford, T.O., The ACRONYM Model-Based Vision System, *Proc. Int. Jt, Conf. Artificial Intelligence 1979,* 6, 105-113.
- Brooks, R., "Symbolic Reasoning Among 3-D Models and 2-D Images," *AI* 17, 1981, pp. 285-348.
- Chin, R. T., "Automated Visual Inspection Techniques and Applications: A Bibliography," Pattern Recognition, Vol. 15 (4), 1982, pp. 343-357.

- Cohen, P. R., and Feigenbaum, E. A., Chap. XIII, Vision, *The Handbook of Artificial Intelligence,* Vol. III, Los Altos, CA: Kaufmann, 1982, pp. 125-321.
- Gevarter, W. B., "A Wiring Diagram of the Human Brain as a Model for Artificial Intelligence," *Proc. of the IEEE Inter. Conf. on Cyb. and Society,* Wash., D.C., Sept. 1977, pp. 694-698.
- Gevarter, W. B., *An Overview of Computer Vision,* NSIR 82-2582, National Bureau of Standards, Wash., D.C., Sept. 1982A.
- Gevarter, W. B., *An Overview of Expert Systems,* NBSIR 82-2505, National Bureau of Standards, Wash., D.C., May 1982B.
- Hanson, A. R. and Riseman, E. M., (eds) *Computer Vision Systems,* New York: Academic Press, 1978a.
- Hanson, A. R. and Riseman, E. M. (1978b), "Segmentation of Natural Scenes," in Hanson and Riseman (1978a) pp. 129-163.
- Hiatt, B., "Toward Machines that See," *Mosaic,* Nov/Dec 1981, pp. 2-8.
- Holland, S. W., Rossol, L. and Ward, M. R., "Consight-I: A Vision Controlled Robot System for Transferring Parts from Belt Conveyors," *Computer Vision and Sensor-Based Robots,* G. G. Dodd, and L. Rossol, Eds. New York: Plenum Press, 1979, pp. 81-100.
- Kanade, T., "Model Representation and Control Structures in Image Understanding," *Proc. of IJCAI-77,* Cambridge, Aug. 1977, 1074-1082.
- Kashioka, S. Fjiri, M., and Sakamoto, Y., "A Transistor Wire Bonding System Utilizing Multiple Local Pattern Machine," *IEEE Trans. Syst. Mar. Cybern.,* vol. SMC-6 1976.
- Kruger, R. P. and Thompson, W. B., "A Technical and Economic Assessment of Computer Vision for Industrial Inspection and Robotic Assembly," *Proceedings of the IEEE,* Vol. 69, No. 12, Dec. 1981, pp. 1524-1538.
- Marr, D. C., *Vision,* San Francisco: W. H. Freeman, 1982.
- Marr, D., and Nishihara, H., "Visual Information Processing: Artificial Intelligence and the Sensorium of Sight," *Technology Review,* October 1978, pp. 28-47.
- Minsky, M. L., "A Framework for Representing Knowledge," In P. H. Winston (Ed), *The Psychology of Computer Vision,* New York: McGraw-Hill, 1975, pp. 211-277.
- Parma, C. C., Hanson, A. M., Riseman, E. M., "Experiments in Schema-Driven Interpretation of a Natural Scene," U. of Mass., COINS Tech. Rept 80-10, 1980.
- Perkins, W. A. "Model-Based Vision System for Industrial Parts," *IEEE, Trans. Comput.,* vol. C-27, 1978.
- Pratt, W. K., *Digital Image Processing,* New York: Wiley, 1978, pp. 568-587.
- Rosenfeld, A. "Picture Processing, 1981," Computer Vision Lab Rept. TR-1134, U of MD, College Park, Jan 1982. (Also in *CGIP,* May 1982).
- Tenenbaum, et al., "Prospects for Industrial Vision," in *Computer Vision and Sensor-Based Robots,"* G. G. Dodd and L. Rossol (Eds.), NY: Plenum Press, 1979, pp. 239-259.
- Vamos, T., Bathor, M., and Mero, L., "A Knowledge-Based Interactive Robot-Vision System," *6IJCAI,* 1979, pp. 920-922.
- Yachida, M. and Tsuji, S., "A Versatile Machine Vision System for Complex Industrial Parts," *IEEE Trans. Comput.,* vol. C-26, 1977.
- DARPA Image Understanding Workshops (Annual).
- IEEE Computer Society Conferences on Computer Vision and Pattern Recognition (Annual).

III. NATURAL LANGUAGE PROCESSING (NLP)*

A. Introduction

One major goal of Artificial Intelligence (AI) research has been to develop the means to interact with machines in natural language (in contrast to a computer language). The interaction may be typed, printed or spoken. The complementary goal has been to understand how humans communicate. The scientific endeavor aimed at achieving these goals has been referred to as computational linguistics (or more broadly as cognitive science), an effort at the intersection of AI, linguistics, philosophy and psychology.

Human communication in natural language is an activity of the whole intellect. AI researchers, in trying to formalize what is required to properly address natural language, find themselves involved in the long term endeavor of having to come to grips with this whole activity. (Formal linguists tend to restrict themselves to the structure of language.) The current AI approach is to conceptualize language as a knowledge-based system for processing communications and to create computer programs to model that process.

Communication acts can serve many purposes, depending on the goals, intentions and strategies of the communicator. One goal of the communication is to change some aspect of the recipient's mental state. Thus, communication endeavors to add or modify knowledge, change a mood, elicit a response or establish a new goal for the recipients.

For a computer program to interpret a relatively unrestricted natural language communication, a great deal of knowledge is required. Knowledge is needed of:
— the structure of sentences
— the meaning of words
— the morphology of words
— a model of the beliefs of the sender
— the rules of conversation, and
— an extensive shared body of general information about the world.

This body of knowledge can enable a computer (like a human) to use expectation-driven processing in which knowledge about the usual properties of known objects, concepts, and what typically happens in situations, can be used to understand incomplete or ungrammatical sentences in appropriate contexts.

B. Applications

There are many applications for computer-based natural language understanding systems. Some of these are listed in Table III-1.

---

*A more complete treatment of NLP is given in Gevarter (1983).

TABLE III-1. Some Applications of Natural Language Processing.

Discourse	Interaction with Intelligent Programs
Speech Understanding	Expert Systems Interfaces
Story Understanding	Decision Support Systems
Information Access	Explanation Modules for Computer Actions
	Interactive Interfaces to Computer Programs
Information Retrieval	**Interacting with Machines**
Question Answering Systems	
Computer-Aided Instruction	Control of Complex Machines
Information Acquisition or Transformation	**Language Generation**
Machine Translation	Document or Text Generation
Document or Text Understanding	Speech Output
Automatic Paraphrasing	Writing Aids: e.g., grammar checking
Knowledge Compilation	
Knowledge Acquisition	

C. Approach

Natural Language Processing (NLP) systems utilize both linguistic knowledge and domain knowledge to interpret the input. As domain knowledge (knowledge about the subject area of communication) is so important to understanding, it is usual to classify the various systems based on their representation and utilization of domain knowledge. On this basis, Hendrix and Sacerdoti (1981) classify systems as Types A, B, or C,* with Type A being the simplest, least capable and correspondingly least costly systems.

1. Type A: No World Models

a. Key Words or Patterns

The simplest systems utilize ad hoc data structures to store facts about a limited domain. Input sentences are scanned by the programs for predeclared key words, or patterns, that indicate known objects or relationships.

b. Limited Logic Systems

In limited logic systems, information in their data base was stored in some formal notation, and language mechanisms were utilized to translate the input into the internal form. The internal form chosen was such as to facilitate performing logical inferences on information in the data base.

---

*Other system classifications are possible, e.g., those based on the range cf syntactic coverage.

2. Type B: Systems That Use Explicit World Models

In these systems, knowledge about the domain is explicitly encoded, usually in frame or network representations (discussed in a later section) that allow the system to understand input in terms of context and expectations. Cullingford's work (see Schank and Ableson, 1977) on SAM (Script Applier Mechanism) is a good example of this approach.

3. Type C: Systems that Include Information about the Goals and Beliefs of Intelligent Entities.

These advanced systems (still in the research stage) attempt to include in their knowledge base information about the beliefs and intentions of the participants in the communication. If the goal of the communication is known, it is much easier to interpret the message. Schank and Abelson's (1977) work on plans and themes reflects this approach.

D. The Parsing Problem

For more complex systems than those based on key words and pattern matching, language knowledge is required to interpret the sentences. The system usually begins by "parsing" the input (processing an input sentence to produce a more useful representation for further analysis). This representation is normally a structural description of the sentence indicating the relationship of the component aparts. To address the parsing problem and to interpret the result, the computational linguistic community has studied syntax, semantics, and pragmatics. Syntax is the study of the structure of phrases and sentences. Semantics is the study of meaning. Pragmatics is the study of the use of language in context.

E. Grammars

Barr and Feigenbaum (1981, p. 229) state, "A grammar of a language is a scheme for specifying the sentences allowed in the language, indicating the syntactic rules for combining words into well-formed phrases and clauses." The following grammars are some of the most important.*

1. Phrase Structure Grammar — Context Free Grammar

Chomsky (see, e.g., Winograd, 1983) had a major impact on linguistic research by devising a mathematical approach to language. He defined a series of grammars based on rules for rewriting sentences into their component parts. He designated these as 0, 1, 2, or 3, based on the restrictions associated with the rewrite rules, with 3 being the most restrictive.

Type 2 — Context-Free (CF) or Phrase Structure Grammar (PSG) — has been one of the most useful in natural-language processing. It has the advantage that all sentence structure derivations can be represented as a tree and practical parsing algorithms exist. Though it is a relatively natural grammar, it is unable to capture all the sentence constructions found in most natural languages such as English. Gazder (1981) has recently broadened the applicability of CF PSG by adding augmentations to handle situations that do not fit the basic grammar. This generalized Phrase Structure Grammar is now being developed by Hewlett Packard (Gawron et al., 1982).

---

*Charniak and Wilks (1976) provide a good overview of the various approaches.

2. Transformational Grammar

Tennant (1981, p. 89) observes that "The goal of a language analysis program is recognizing grammatical sentences and representing them in a canonical structure (the underlying structure)." A transformational grammar (Chomsky, 1957) consists of a dictionary, a phrase structure grammar and a set of transformations. In analyzing sentences, using a phrase structure grammar, first a parse tree is produced. This is called the surface structure. The transformational rules are then applied to the parse tree to transform it into a canonical form called the deep (or underlying) structure. As the same thing can be stated in several different ways, there may be many surface structures that translate into a single deep structure.

3. Case Grammar

Case Grammar is a form of Transformational Grammar in which the deep structure is based on cases - semantically relevant syntactic relationships. The central idea is that the deep structure of a simple sentence consists of a verb and one or more noun phrases associated with the verb in a particular relationship. These semantically relevant relationships are called cases. Fillmore (1971) proposed the following cases: Agent, Experiencer, Instrument, Object, Source, Goal, Location, Type and Path.

The cases for each verb form an ordered set referred to as a "case frame." A case frame for the verb "open" would be:

(object (instrument) (agent))

which indicates that open always has an object, but the instrument or agent can be omitted as indicated by their surrounding parentheses. Thus the case frame associated with the verb provides a template which aids in understanding a sentence.

4. Semantic Grammars

For practical systems in limited domains, it is often more useful, instead of using conventional syntactic constituents such as noun phrases, verb phrases and prepositions, to use meaningful semantic components instead. Thus, in place of nouns when dealing with a naval data base, one might use ships, captains, ports and cargos. This approach gives direct access to the semantics of a sentence and substantially simplifies and shortens the processing. Grammars based on this approach are referred to as semantic grammars (see, e.g., Burton, 1976).

5. Other Grammars

A variety of other, but less prominent, grammars have been devised. Still others can be expected to be devised in the future. One example is Montague Grammar (Dowty et al., 1981) which uses a logical functional representation for the grammar and therefore is well suited for the parallel-processing logical approach now being pursued by the Japanese (see Nishida and Doshita, 1982) for their future AI work as embodied is their Fifth Generation Computer research project.

F. Semantics and the Cantankerous Aspects of Language

Semantic processing (as it tries to interpret phrases and sentences) attaches meanings to the words. Unfortunately, English does not make this as simple as looking up the word in the dictionary, but provides many difficulties which require context and other knowledge to resolve. Examples are:

1. Multiple Word Senses

Syntactic analysis can resolve whether a word is used as a noun or a verb, but further analysis is required to select the sense (meaning) of the noun or verb that is actually used. For example, "fly" used as a noun may be a winged insect, a fancy fishhook, a baseball hit high in the air, or several other interpretations as well. The appropriate sense can be determined by context (e.g., for "fly" the appropriate domain of interest could be extermination, fishing or sports), or by matching each noun sense with the senses of other words in the sentence. This latter approach was taken by Reiger and Small (1979) using the (still embryonic) technique of "interacting word experts," and by Finin (1980) and McDonald (1982) as the basis for understanding noun compounds.

2. Pronouns

Pronouns allow a simplified reference to previously used (or implied) nouns, sets or events. Where feasible, using pragmatics, pronoun antecedents are usually identified by reference to the most recent noun phrase having the same context as the pronoun.

3. Ellipsis and Substitution

Ellipsis is the phenomenon of not stating explicitly some words in a sentence, but leaving it to the reader or listener to fill them in. Substitution is similar — using a dummy word in place of the omitted words. Employing pragmatics, ellipses and substitutions are usually resolved by matching the incomplete statement to the structures of previous recent sentences — finding the best partial match and then filling in the rest from this matching previous structure.

G. Knowledge Representation*

As the AI approach to natural language processing is heavily knowledge based, it is not surprising that a variety of knowledge representation (KR) techniques have found their way into the field. Some of the more important ones are:

1. Procedural Representations — The meanings of words or sentences being expressed as computer programs that reason about their meaning.

---

*More complete presentations on KR can be found in Chapter III of Barr and Feigenbaum (1981), and in Part C of this volume.

2. *Declarative Representations*
   a. Logic — Representation in First Order Predicate Logic, for example.
   b. Semantic Networks — Representations of concepts and relationships between concepts as graph structures consisting of nodes and labeled connecting arcs.

3. *Case Frames* — (covered earlier)

4. *Conceptual Dependency* — This approach (related to case frames) is an attempt to provide a representation of all actions in terms of a small number of semantic primitives into which input sentences are mapped (see, e.g., Schank and Riesbeck, 1981). The system relies on 11 primitive physical, instrumental and mental ACT's (propel, grasp, speak, attend, P trans, A trans, etc.), plus several other categories or concept types.

5. *Frame* — A complex data structure for representing a whole situation, complex object or series of events. A frame has slots for objects and relations appropriate to the situation.

6. *Scripts* — Frame-like data structures for representing stereotyped sequences of events to aid in understanding simple stories.

H. Syntactic Parsing

Parsing assigns structures to sentences. The following types have been developed over the years for NLP. (Barr and Feigenbaum, 1981).

1. Template Matching: Most of the early (and some current) NL programs performed parsing by matching their input sentences against a series of stored templates.

2. Transition Nets:

Phrase structure grammars can be syntactically decomposed using a set of rewrite rules such as indicated in Figure III-1. Observe that a simple sentence can be rewritten as a Noun Phrase and a Verb Phrase as indicated by:

$$S \rightarrow NP\ VP$$

The noun phrase can be rewritten by the rule

$$NP \rightarrow (DET)(ADJ^*)N(PP^*)$$

where the parentheses indicate that the item is optional, while the asterisks (associated with the adjectives and prepositional phrases) indicate that any number of items may occur.

An example of an analyzed noun phrase is shown in Figures III-2 and III-3.

As the transition networks analyze a sentence, they can collect information about the word patterns they recognize and fill slots in a frame associated with each pattern. Thus, they can identify noun phrases as singular or plural, whether the nouns refer to persons and if so their gender, etc., needed to produce a deep structure. A simple approach to collecting this information is to attach subroutines to be called for each transition. A transition network with such subroutines attached is called an "augmented transition network," or ATN. With ATN's, word patterns can be

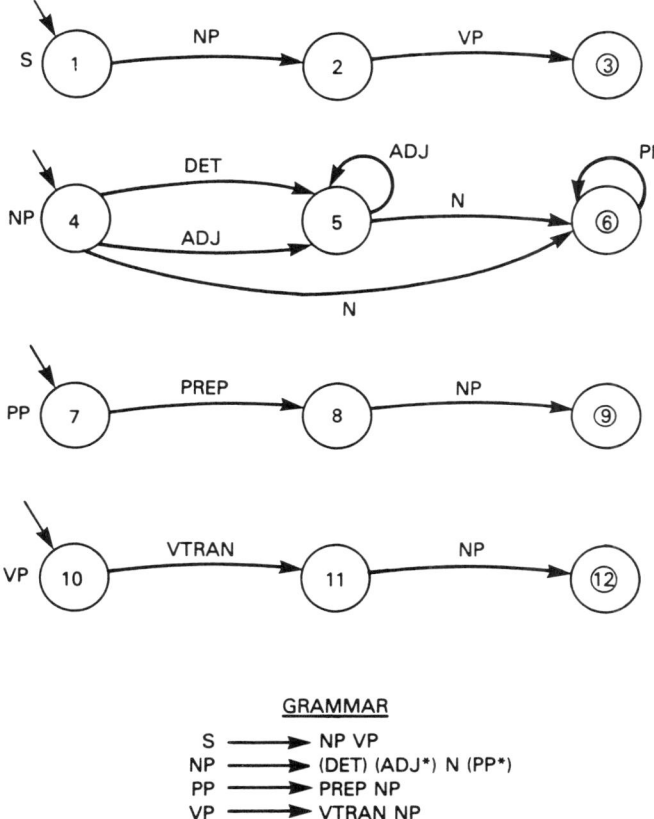

Figure III-1. A Transition Network for a Small Subset of English.

Each diagram represents a rule for finding the corresponding word pattern. Each rule can call on other rules to find needed patterns.

After Graham (1979, p214.)

118   Artificial Intelligence

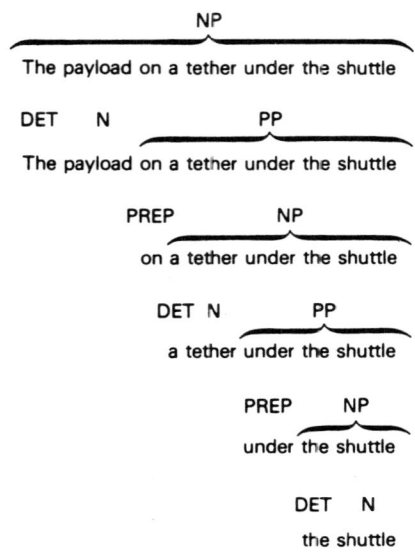

Figure III-2. Example Noun Phrase Decomposition.

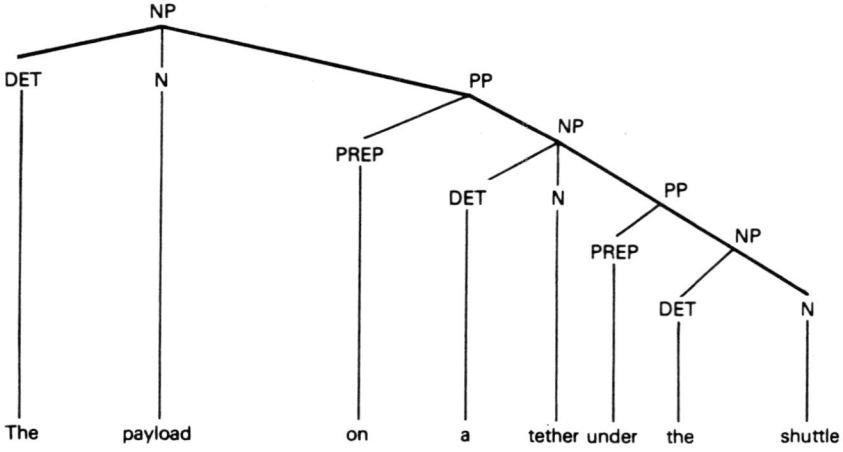

Figure III-3. Parse Tree Representation of the Noun Phrase Surface Structure.

recognized. For each word pattern, we can fill slots in a frame. The resulting filled frames provide a basis for further processing.

3. Other Parsers

Other parsing approaches have been devised, but ATN's remain the most popular syntactic parsers. ATN's are top-down parsers in that the parsing is directed by an anticipated sentence structure. An alternative approach is bottom-up parsing, which examines the input words along the string from left to right, building up all possible structures to the left of the current word as the parser advances. A bottom-up parser could thus build many partial sentence structures that are never used, but the diversity could be an advantage in trying to interpret input word strings that are not clearly delineated sentences or contain ungrammatical constructions or unknown words. There have been recent attempts to combine the top-down with the bottom-up approach for NLP in a similar manner as has been done for Computer Vision.

For a recent overview of parsing approaches see Slocum (1981).

I. Semantics, Parsing and Understanding

The role of syntactic parsing is to construct a parse tree or similar structure of the sentence to indicate the grammatical use of the words and how they are related to each other. The role of the semantic processing is to establish the meaning of the sentence. This requires facing up to all the cantankerous ambiguities discussed earlier.

Charniak (1981) observes that there have been two main lines of attack on word sense ambiguity. One is the use of discrimination nets (Reiger and Small, 1979) that utilize the syntactic parse tree (by observing the grammatical role that the word plays, such as taking a direct object, etc.) in helping to decide the word sense. The other approach is based on the frame/script idea (used, e.g., for story comprehension) that provides a context and the expected sense of the word (see e.g., Schank and Abelson, 1977).

Charniak indicates that the semantics at the level of the word sense is not the end of the parsing process, but what is desired is understanding or comprehension (associated with pragmatics). Here the use of frames, scripts and more advanced topics such as plans, goals, and knowledge structures (see, e.g. Schank and Riesbeck, 1981) play an important role.

J. Natural Language Processing (NLP) Systems

As indicated below, various NLP systems have been developed for a variety of functions.

1. Kinds

a. Question Answering Systems

Question answering natural language systems have perhaps been the most popular of the NLP research systems. They have the advantage that they usually utilize a data-base for a limited domain and that most of the user discourse is limited to questions.

b. Natural Language Interfaces (NLI's)

These systems are designed to provide a painless means of communicating questions or instructions to a complex computer program.

c. Computer-Aided Instruction (CAI)

Arden (1980, p. 465) states:

> One type of interaction that calls for ability in natural languages is the interaction needed for effective teaching machines. Advocates of computer-aided instruction have embraced numerous schemes for putting the computer to use directly in the educational process. It has long been recognized that the ultimate effectiveness of teaching machines is linked to the amount of intelligence embodied in the programs. That is, a more intelligent program would be better able to formulate the questions and presentations that are most appropriate at a given point in a teaching dialogue, and it would be better equipped to understand a student's response, even to analyze and model the knowledge of the student, in order to tailor the teaching to his needs.

d. Discourse

Systems that are designed to understand discourse (extended dialogue) usually employ pragmatics. Pragmatic analysis requires a model of the mutual beliefs and knowledge held by the speaker and listener.

e. Text Understanding

Though Schank (see Schank and Riesbeck, 1981) and others have addressed themselves to this problem, much more remains to be done. Techniques for understanding printed text include scripts and causative approaches.

f. Text Generation

There are two major aspects of text generation: one is the determination of the content and textual shape of the message, the second is transforming it into natural language. There are two approaches for accomplishing this. The first is indexing into canned text and combining it as appropriate. The second is generating the text from basic considerations. McDonald's thesis (1980) provides one of the most sophisticated approaches to text generation.

2. Research NLP Systems

Until recently, virtually all of the NLP systems generated were of a research nature. These NLP systems basically were aimed at serving five functions:

    a. Interfaces to Computer Programs
    b. Data Base Retrieval
    c. Text Understanding
    d. Text Generation
    e. Machine Translation

Gevarter (1983) includes a survey of research NLP systems.

3. Commercial Systems:

The commercial systems available today (together with their approximate price) are listed in Table III-2. Several of these systems are derivatives of past research NLP systems.

TABLE III-2. *Some Commercial Natural Language Systems.*

System	Organization	Purpose	Comments
INTELLECT (Derivative of ROBOT) $50K/System (also distributed as ON-LINE ENGLISH and GRS Executive)	Artificial Intelligence Corp. Waltham, Mass (Culliane) (Information Sciences)	NLI for Data Base Retrieval (Other extensions underway)	• Several hundred systems sold • Takes about 2 weeks to implement for a new data base. • Written in PL-1 • Available for mainframes
PEARL (Based on SAM and PAM) $250K/system	Cognitive Systems New Haven, Conn	Custom NLI's The first system—Explorer—is an interface to an existing map generating system. Others are interfaces to data bases.	• Large start-up cost in building the knowledge base. • Several systems have been, and are being, built. • Written in LISP
Straight Talk (Derivative of LIFER) $660	Dictaphone, Written by Symantec Sunnyvale, CA	Highly portable NLI for DBMS for microcomputers.	• Written in PASCAL. Designed to be very compact and efficient. Available about Nov. 1983. • User customized.
SAVVY $950	SAVVY Marketing International Sunnyvale, CA	System Interface for micro-computers	• Not linguistic. Uses adaptive (best fit) pattern matching to strings of characters. • Released 3/82 • User customized
Weidner System $16K/language direction	Weidner Communications Corp. Provo, UT	Semi-Automatic Natural Language Translation.	• Linguistic approach. Written in FORTRAN IV. • Translation with human editing is approximately 100 words/hr (up to eight times as fast as human alone). • Approx. 20 sold by end of 1982, mainly to large multi-national corporations.
ALPS	ALPS Provo, UT	Interactive Natural Language Translation	• Linguistic Approach • Uses a dictionary that provides the various translations for technical words as a display to human translator, who then selects among the displayed words.

TABLE III-2. *Some Commercial Natural Language Systems (cont.)*

System	Organization	Purpose	Comments
NLMENU	Texas Instruments, Inc. Dallas, TX	NLI to Relational Data Bases	• Menu Driven NL Query System • All queries constructed from menu fall within linguistic and conceptual coverage of the system. Therefore, all queries entered are successful. • Grammars used are semantic grammars written in a context-free grammar formalism. • Producing an interface to any arbitrary set of relations is automated and only requires a 15-30 minute interaction with someone knowledgeable about the relations in question. • System will be available late in 1983 as a software package for a micro-computer.

K. State of the Art

It is now feasible to use computers to deal with natural language input in highly restricted contexts. However, interacting with people in a facile manner is still far off, requiring understanding of where people are coming from — their knowledge, goals and moods.

In today's computing environment, the only systems that perform robustly and efficiently are Type A systems — those that do not use explicit world models, but depend on key word or pattern matching and/or semantic grammars. In actual working systems, both understanding and text generation, ATN-like grammars can be considered the state of the art.

L. Principal U.S. Participants in NLP

*1. Research and Development**

Non-Profit

  SRI
  MITRE

---

*A review of current research in NLP is given in Kaplan (1982).

Universities

Yale U. — Dept. of Computer Science
U. of CA, Berkeley — Computer Science Div., Dept. of EECS.
Carnegie-Mellon U. — Dept. of Computer Science
U. of Illinois, Urbana — Coordinated Science Lab.
Brown U. — Dept. of Computer Science
Stanford U. — Computer Science Dept.
U. of Rochester — Computer Science Dept.
U. of Mass., Amherst — Department of Computer and Information Science
SUNY, Stoneybrook, Dept. of Computer Science
U. of CA, Irvine, Computer Science Dept.
U of PA — Dept. of Computer and Infor. Science
GA Institute of Technology — School of Infor. and Computer Science
USC — Infor. Science Institute.
MIT — AI Lab.
NYU — Computer Science Dept. and Linguistic String Project
U. of Texas at Austin — Dept. of Computer Science
Cal. Inst. of Tech.
Brigham Young U. — Linguistics Dept.
Duke U. — Dept. of Computer Science
N. Carolina State — Dept. of Computer Science
Oregon State U. — Dept. of Computer Science
Purdue U.

Industrial

BBN
TRW Defense Systems
IBM, Yorktown Heights, N.Y.
Burroughs
Sperry Univac
Systems Development Corp., Santa Monica
Hewlett Packard
Martin Marietta, Denver
Texas Instruments, Dallas
Xerox PARC
Bell Labs
Institute of Scientific Information, Phila., PA
GM Research labs, Warren, MI
Honeywell

2. *Principal U.S. Government Agencies Funding NLP Research*
ONR (Office of Naval Research)
NSF (National Science Foundation)
DARPA (Defense Advanced Research Projects Agency)

3. *Commercial NLP Systems*
Artificial Intelligence Corp., Waltham, Mass.
Cognitive Sytems Inc., New Haven, Conn.
Symantec, Sunnyvale, CA
Texas Instruments, Dallas, TX
Weidner Communications, Inc., Provo, Utah
Savvy Marketing International, Sunnyvale, CA
ALPS, Provo, UT

4. *Non-U.S.*
U. of Manchester, England
Kyoto U., Japan
Siemens, Corp., Germany
U. of Strathclyde, Scotland
Centre National de la Recherche Scientifique, Paris
U. di Udine, Italy
U. of Cambridge, England
Phillips Res. Labs, The Netherlands

M. Forecast

Commercial natural language interfaces (NLI's) to computer programs and data base management systems are now becoming available. The imminent advent of NLI's for micro-computers is the precursor for eventually making it possible for virtually anyone to have direct access to powerful computational systems.

As the cost of computing has continued to fall, but the cost of programming hasn't, it has already become cheaper in some applications to create NLI systems (that utilize subsets of English) than to train people in formal programming languages.

Computational linguists and workers in related fields are devoting considerable attention to the problems of NLP systems that understand the goals and beliefs of the individual communicators. Though progress has been made, and feasibility has been demonstrated, more than a decade will be required before useful systems with these capabilities will become available.

One of the problems, in implementing new installations of NLP systems, is gathering information about the applicable vocabulary and the logical structure of the associated data bases. Work is now underway to develop tools to help automate this task. Such tools should be available within 5 years.

For text understanding, experimental programs have been developed that "skim" stylized text such as short disaster stories in newspapers (DeJong, 1982). Despite the practical problems of sufficient world knowledge and the extension of language required, practical tools emerging from these efforts should be available to provide assistance to humans doing text understanding within this decade.

The NRL Computational Linguistic Workshop (1981) concluded that text generation techniques are maturing rapidly and new application possibilities will appear within the next five years.

The NRL workshop also indicated that:

> Machine aids for human translators appear to have a brighter prospect for immediate application than fully automatic translation; however, the Canadian French-English weather bulletin project is a fully automatic system in which only 20% of the translated sentences require minor rewording before public release. An ambitious common market project involving machine translation among six European languages is scheduled to begin shortly. Sixty people will be involved in that undertaking which will be one of the largest projects undertaken in computational linguistics.* The panel was divided in its forecast on the five year perspective of machine translation but the majority were very optimistic.

Nippon Telegram and Telephone Corp. in Tokyo has a machine translation AI project underway. An experimental system for translating from Japanese to English and vice versa is now being demonstrated. In addition, the recently initiated Japanese Fifth Generation Computer effort has computer-based natural language understanding as one of its major goals.

In summary, natural language interfaces using a limited subset of English are now becoming available. Hundreds of specialized systems are already in operation. Major efforts in text understanding and machine translation are underway, and useful (though limited) systems will be available within the next five years. Systems that are heavily knowledge-based and handle more complete sets of English should be available within this decade. However, systems that can handle unrestricted natural discourse and understand the motivation of the communicators remain a distant goal, probably requiring more than a decade before useful systems appear.

REFERENCES

- Arden, B. W. (ed.) *What Can Be Automated*, Cambridge, MA: M.I.T. Press, 1980.
- Barr, A. and Feigenbaum, E. A., Chapter 4, "Understanding Natural Language," *"The Handbook of Artificial Intelligence,* Los Altos, CA: W. Kaufman, 1981, pp. 223-321.
- Burton, R. R., "Semantic Grammar: An Engineering Technique for Constructing Natural Language Understanding Systems," BBN Report 3453, BBN, Cambridge, Dec. 1976.
- Charniak, E. "Six Topics in Search of a Parser: An Overview of AI Language Research," IJCAI-81, pp. 1079-1087.
- Charniak, E. and Wilks, Y., *Computational Semantics,* Amsterdam: North Holland, 1976.
- Chomsky, N., *Syntactic Structures,* The Hague: Mouton, 1957.
- DeJong, G., "An Overview of the FRUMP System," *In Strategies for Natural Language Processing,* W. G. Lehnert and M. H. Ringle (eds.), Hillsdale, N.J.: Lawrence Erlbaum, 1982, pp. 149-176.

---

*EUROTA — A machine translation project sponsored by the European Common Market — 8 countries, over 15 universities, $24 M over several years.

- Dowty, R. et al., *Introduction to Montague Semantics,* Reidel, 1981.
- Fillmore, C., "Some Problems for Case Grammar," In R. J. O'Brien (Ed.), *Report of the Twenty-Second Annual Round Table Meeting on Linguistics and Languages Studies,"* Wash., D.C.: Georgetown U. Press, 1971, pp. 35-56.
- Finin, T. W., "The Semantic Interpretation of Compound Nominals," Ph.D. Thesis, U. of IL, Urbana, 1980.
- Gawron, J. M. et al., "Processing English with a Generalized Phrase Structure Grammar," *Proc. of the 20th Meeting of ACL,* U. of Toronto, Canada, 16-18 June 1982, pp. 74-81.
- Gazdar, G., "Unbounded Dependencies and Coordinate Structure," *Linguistic Inquiry,* 12, 1981, pp. 155-184.
- Gevarter, W. B., *An Overview of Computer-Based Natural Language Processing,* NBSIR 83-2687, National Bureau of Standards, Wash, D.C., April 1983 (also NASA TM 85635).
- Graham, N., *Artificial Intelligence,* Blue Ridge Summit, PA: TAB Books, 1979.
- Hendrix, G. G., Sacerdoti, E. D. Sagalowicz, D. and Slocum, J., "Developing a Natural Language Interface to Complex Data," *ACM Transactions on Database Systems,* Vol. 3, No. 2, June 1978.
- Hendrix, G. G. and Sacerdoti, E. D., "Natural-Language Processing: The Field in Perspective," *Byte,* Sept. 1981, pp. 304-352.
- Kaplan, S. J., (Ed.), "Special Section — Natural Language," *SIGART NEWSLETTER* #79, Jan 1982, pp. 27-109.
- McDonald D. D., "Natural Language Production as a Process of Decision-Making Under Constraints," Ph.D Thesis, M.I.T., Cambridge, 1980.
- Nishida, T. and Doshita, S., "An Application of Montague Grammar to English-Japanese Machine Translation," *Proc. of Conf. on Applied NLP,* Santa Monica, Feb. 1983.
- Reiger, C. and Small, S., "Word Expert Parsing," *Proc. of the Sixth International Joint Conference on Artificial Intelligence,* 1979, pp. 723-728.
- Schank, R. C. and Abelson, R. P., *Scripts, Plans, Goals and Understanding,* Hillsdale, N.J.: Lawrence Erlbaum, 1977.
- Schank, R. C. and Riesbeck, C. K., *Inside Computer Understanding,* Hillsdale, N.J.: Lawrence Erlbaum, 1981.
- Slocum, J., "A Practical Comparison of Parsing Strategies for Machine Translation and Other Natural Language Purposes," Ph.D Thesis, U. of Texas, Austin, 1981.
- Tennant, H., *Natural Language Processing,* New York: Petrocelli, 1981.
- Winograd, T., *Language as a Cognitive Process,* Vol I; Syntax, Reading, Mass: Addison-Wesley, 1983.
- "Applied Computational Linguistics in Perspective," NRL Workshop at Stanford University, 26-27 June 1981. (Proceedings in *Amer. J. of Computational Linguistics,* Vol. 8, No. 2, April-June 1982, pp. 55-83).
- Association for Computational Linguistics (ACL) Annual Conference.
- Computational Linguistics Conferences. (Biannual).

IV. SPEECH RECOGNITION AND SPEECH UNDERSTANDING

A. Introduction

Speech is our fastest means of discourse communication, being about twice as fast as the average typist. It is also nearly effortless: speech doesn't need visual or physical contact and it places few restrictions on the use of the hands or the mobility of the body. Speech is thus well suited to communication with a machine when the individual is engaged in other activities. Its effortlessness also makes it desirable for operating a computer, and it is a long term candidate for direct text preparation (automatic dictation).

Speech understanding systems have all the difficulties of natural language understanding plus the problem of interpreting the speech signal with all its noise and variability. As a result, speech understanding is one of the most difficult AI subjects, being a perception task related to the scene understanding problem in computer vision. Though the constraining aspects of natural language help reduce the magnitude of the task, it remains a major problem area.

Speech systems can be categorized into speech recognition systems and speech understanding systems, the former task being considerably easier. In addition, the systems further divide into those that work with isolated words and those that can handle connected speech, the latter being perhaps an order of magnitude more difficult than the former.

Finally, speech systems are also classified as speaker dependent and speaker independent. The former systems must be trained to recognize the particular speakers using it.

The heart of the speech problem (that gives rise to the above classifications) is the difficulty of recognizing the speech signal, but before we explore that area, let us briefly look at applications for speech devices.

B. Applications

There are many applications emerging for speech recognition and speech understanding systems. Some of these are listed in Tables IV-1 and IV-2.

C. The Nature of Speech Sounds:

It is beginning to be realized that acoustics and phonetics may be the key to speech understanding. Zue (1981) argues that human spectrograph-reading experiments indicate that phonetic recognition in speech systems can be improved substantially, which would result in much more capable speech systems.

Speech recognition is based primarily on the identification of words. An adult speaker may know 100,000 of the 300,000 words in the English language. Each language has a basic set of speech sounds called phonemes. In English there are only about 40 phonemes, compared with some 10,000 for the next largest speech unit, the syllable.

The sounds that make up human speech are generated by the flow of air through the vocal tract in three ways (Levinson and Liberman, 1981):

TABLE IV-1. Speech Recognition Applications.

Manufacturing Processes and Control
- Quality control data entry into computers
- Shipping and receiving — record entry, package sorting
- Maintenance and repair orders — part availability, work needed or under way.
- CAD/CAM

Office Automation
- Executive work station
- Word processing
- Data entry
- Control functions

Technical Data Gathering
- Cartography — inputs when working with maps.
- Working with blueprints
- Medical applications:
    Dental records
    Pathology
    Services for the handicapped
    Operating room logging
    Command/control of medical instrumentation

Security Applications
- Building access
- Computer file access
- Communications security
- Speaker verification/identification

Consumer Products Applications
- Control functions
- Status queries

Equipment Subsystem Operation
- Aircraft
- Spacecraft
- Military equipment

TABLE IV-2. Speech Understanding Applications

- Universal access to large data bases via the telephone network.

- Automatic telephone transaction systems — Airline reservations and inquiries.

- Command and Control

    — Military
    — Business

- Operation of complex machines.

1. The vocal cords can be made to vibrate, resulting in the frequency of the sound referred to as pitch.
2. A constriction can be formed in the vocal tract, narrow enough to cause turbulence, resulting in noise-like sounds, like that used to produce "f".
3. Pressure built up behind a closure (such as the lips) can release a burst of acoustic energy as in the pronunciation of consonants, such as "p", "t" and "k".

These three sources of speech sound are shaped acoustically by the time-varying physical shape of the vocal tract.

One way to characterize the speech signal is by its Fourier transform, which specifies the amplitude and phase of each of the frequencies in the Fourier series of the signal. As the phase makes little perceptual difference, the signal is represented in practice by its amplitude spectrum, in a representation called a spectograph.

D. Isolated Word Recognition

Figure IV-1 indicates a basic paradigm for speech recognition. The signal is first operated upon to emphasize the 2 to 3 kHz frequency range, filtered to chop off high frequencies (>8 kHz), then digitized. The end points of the word are detected, and a set of parameters representing the word are generated. This is then matched with stored parameter sets in the system's vocabulary, and the word with the closest match chosen. For a word, the acoustic signal varies both in duration and amplitude each time the same speaker says it. Thus it may have to be warped to achieve the best comparison with the reference — this task being one of the toughest problems for a speech recognizer. The warping is usually accomplished by dynamic programming.

Doddington and Schalk (1981, p. 28) state that:

The most common means of feature extraction is direct measurement of spectrum amplitude, with, for example, a set of 16 bandpass filters. Another means is measurement of the zero-crossing rate of the signal in several broad frequency bands to give an estimate of the formant [resonant] frequencies in these bands. Yet another means is representing the speech signal in terms of the parameters of a filter whose spectrum best fits that of the input speech signal. This technique known as linear predictive coding (LPC) has gained popularity because it is efficient, accurate, and simple.

130 Artificial Intelligence

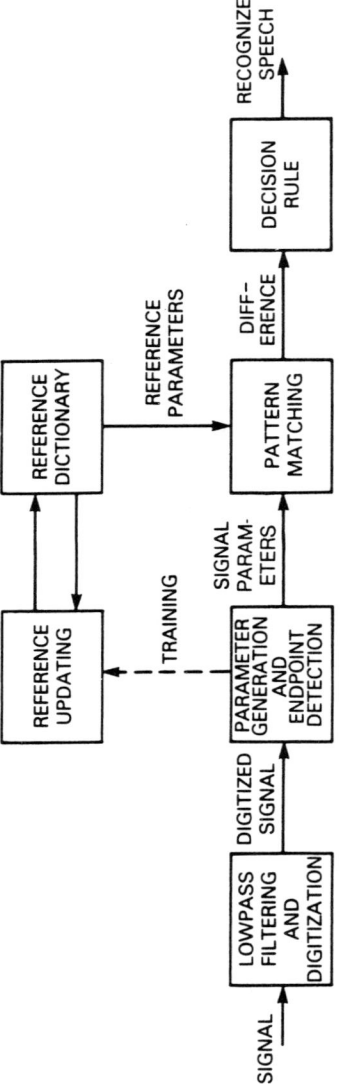

Figure IV-1. Basic Speech-Recognition Paradigm

E. Recognizing Continuous Speech

For continuous speech, rather than attempting to match all possible word patterns, it is often more efficient to work with speech units much smaller than words, particularly phonemes. Breaking down the speech signal into these smaller components and giving them symbols, is referred to as segmentation and labeling. Usually, several phoneme labels are assigned to each segment by a pattern-matching process, which also assigns a probability value representing the goodness of the match. With the appropriate acoustic-phonetic knowledge, it is possible to combine, regroup, and delete segments to form larger phoneme units. The lexical knowledge of word pronunciation can now be used to generate a multiplicity of word hypotheses. For a sufficiently limited vocabulary, and perhaps also employing some syntactic and word boundary knowledge, speech recognition can be achieved.

F. Speech Understanding

Arden (1980, pp. 475, 478) observes that:

> Speech-understanding systems differ somewhat from recognition systems, in that they have access to and make effective use of task-specific knowledge in the analysis and interpretation of speech. Further, the criteria for performance are somewhat relaxed, in that the errors that count are not the errors in speech recognition, but errors in task accomplishment.
>
> To successfully decode the unknown utterance, a speech perception system must effectively use the many diverse sources of knowledge about the language, the environment, and the context. These sources of knowledge include the characteristics of speech sounds (acoustic-phonetic), variability in pronunciation (phonology), the stress and intonation patterns of speech (prosodics), the sound patterns of words and sentences (lexicon), the grammatical structure of language (syntax), the meaning of words and sentences (semantics), and the context of the conversation (pragmatics) . . .
>
> What makes speech perception a challenging and difficult area of A.I. is the fact that error and ambiguity permeate all the levels of the speech-decoding process . . . .
>
> The grammatical structure of sentences can be viewed principally as a mechanism for reducing search by restricting the number of acceptable alternatives . . . .

Barr and Feigenbaum (1981, p. 332) note that the types of knowledge at the various levels in processing spoken knowledge include (from the signal level up):

1. *Phonetics* — representations of the physical characteristics of the sounds in all of the words in the vocabulary.
2. *Phonemics* — rules describing variations in pronunciation that appear when words are spoken together in sentences (coarticulation across word boundaries, "swallowing" of syllables, etc.);
3. *Morphemics* — rules describing how morphemes (units of meaning) are combined to form words (formation of plurals, conjugations of verbs, etc.);
4. *Prosodics* — rules describing fluctuation in stress and intonation across a sentence;
5. *Syntax* — the grammar or rules of sentence formation resulting in important constraints on the number of sentences (not all combinations of words in the vocabulary are legal sentences);
6. *Semantics* — the "meaning" of words and sentences, which can also be viewed as a constraint on the speech understander (not all grammatically legal sentences have a meaning — e.g., The snow was loud); and, finally,
7. *Pragmatics* — rules of conversation (in a dialogue, a speaker's response must not only be a meaningful sentence but also be a reasonable reply to what was said to him). For instance, it is pragmatic knowledge that tells us that the question "Can you tell me what time it is?" requires more than just a Yes or No response.

Using this knowledge, the hierarchical structure leading to speech understanding can be characterized as shown in Figure IV-2.

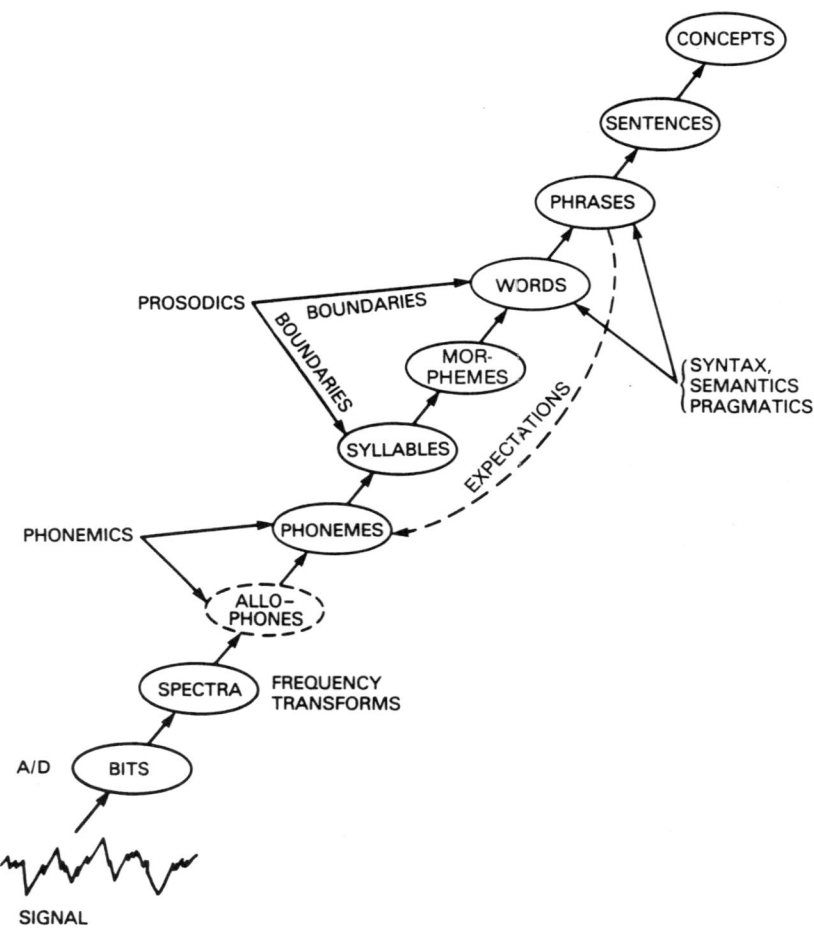

Figure IV-2. The Processing Hierarchy in Speech Understanding

G. The ARPA Speech Understanding Research (SUR) Project

1. Introduction

In 1971, ARPA (The Advanced Research Projects Agency) initiated a five year speech understanding research effort that proved to be one of the most significant projects in AI history. Not only did it greatly advance our knowledge of speech, but it also provided new insights on how to structure and control a complex "expert system."

Lea and Shoup (1979) reported that the ARPA SUR project had the highly ambitious goals of understanding, with 90% accuracy, continuous speech from a 1000 word vocabulary spoken by several cooperative speakers under near ideal conditions of quiet rooms and high-fidelity equipment. It was intended that the processing take no more than several times real-time using large very fast computers.

There were three principal complete systems developed under the project — HEARSAY II and HARPY at Carnegie Mellon University (CMU), and HWIM (Hear What I Mean) at Bolt, Berenek and Newman (BBN). In 1976, the ARPA goals were essentially met at CMU by HARPY exhibiting a 95% accuracy and HEARSAY II achieving a 90% accuracy. HWIM had a substantially lower accuracy, but utilized a more difficult vocabulary. (HWIM's domain was Travel Budget Management. HEARSAY II's and HARPY's was Retrieval of AI Documents.) These three systems were heavily knowledge-based and are now considered to be expert systems.

All the ARPA SUR systems utilized a combination of bottom-up and top-down processing. The lower levels used knowledge about the variable phonetic composition of the words in the vocabulary (lexicon) to interpret pieces of the speech signal by comparing it with prestored patterns. The top level aided in recognition by building expectations about which words the speaker was likely to say, using syntactic and semantic constraints (Barr and Feigenbaum, 1982, pp. 326-327).

2. HEARSAY II

HEARSAY II is characterized by its cooperative problem-solving system architecture (see Figure IV-3) which employs a set of programmed "specialists" (Knowledge Sources: KS's) interacting via a shared common blackboard on which their decisions were recorded. The blackboard can be visualized as a global data structure representing a multi-level network of alternative hypotheses.

HEARSAY has a total of 12 KS's, which at the lower levels created syllable class hypotheses from segments, word hypotheses from syllables, etc. At the higher levels, KS's acted to: predict all possible words that might syntactically precede or follow a phrase, create phrase hypotheses from verified contiguous word-phrase pairs, etc.

The majority of the hypotheses contributed by the KS's at any level did not end up in the final interpretation of the sentence. Instead, only the most likely hypotheses were chosen for expansion. The individual KS's operated somewhat independently and asynchronously through pattern-invoked programs when matching patterns appeared on the blackboard. To economize on computing resources, each hypothesis was rated and (using an appropriate scheduling routine) the most likely patterns were expanded first.

134 Artificial Intelligence

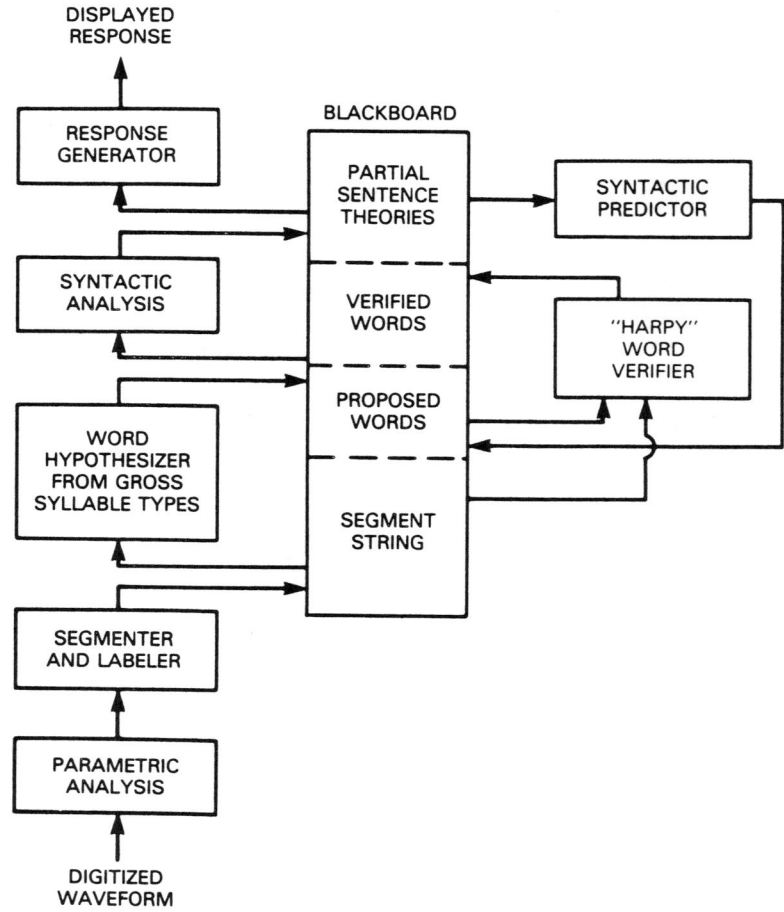

After Klatt (1977)

Figure IV-3. A Block Diagram of the CMU Hearsay-II System Organization

3. HARPY

A crude way of thinking of HARPY is as a compiled version of HEARSAY II. HARPY uses a single precompiled network knowledge structure. Barr and Feigenbaum (1981, p. 349) report:

> The network contains knowledge at all levels: acoustic, phonemic, lexical, syntactic, and semantic. It stores acoustic representations of every possible pronunciation of the words in all of the sentences that HARPY recognizes. The alternative sentences are represented as paths through the network, and each node in the network is a template of allophones (distinctive variations of phonemes, dependent on adjacent phonemes).
>
> The paths through the network can be thought of as "sentence templates," much like the word templates used in isolated-word recognition.

HARPY uses a heuristic method called "beam search" for searching for the sentence in the network that most closely matches the input signal. HARPY proceeds from left to right through the network, matching spoken sounds to allophonic states; and assigning scores based on the goodness of the match. HARPY keeps the paths with the best cumulative scores, pruning away others which fall some threshold amount below the best scoring path (Erman et al, 1980).

4. HWIM

The HWIM (Hear What I Mean) speech understanding system was developed at BBN. HWIM's domain was that of travel budget management. HWIM's organization is shown in Figure IV-4. The lower components digitize the speech signal and generate a parametric representation of it, which is then segmented and labeled into phonemes which are ranked as to the quality of their match. These ranked phonemes are pictured as a segmented lattice, which is a graph that is divided into time segments and read from left to right. This graph is matched against a dictionary of work pronunciations (stored as a network with phonemes for nodes) by lexical retrieval components which generate word hypotheses.

HWIM's higher levels include information about trips (semantics), syntax and word verification. The verification component takes the pronunciation of hypothesized words and generates a synthesized parameter representation that is compared to the parameters generated from the actual signal.

HWIM has a central control which uses the system's knowledge sources as subroutines. The system extends bottom-up theories using the top-down syntactic and semantic components. The system expands its hypotheses about the first recognized word in the sentence.

5. Summary of the ARPA SUR Program

ARPA's program did not result in a useable speech understanding system. The resulting systems were too slow, too restricted and required large computational resources. However, it did discover and elucidate much new information about speech, and developed new architectural insights, particularly the blackboard architecture that has since been used in other AI systems. Performances of the different systems were difficult to compare because of the different vocabularies and domains employed. One critical factor in comparison is the average branching factor (ABF). This refers to the average number of words that might come next after each work in a legal sentence. Table IV-3 summarizes the three major ARPA SUR projects. Note that the ABF is 196 for HWIM's database retrieval task, versus 33 for HEARSAY's and HARPY's document retrieval task.

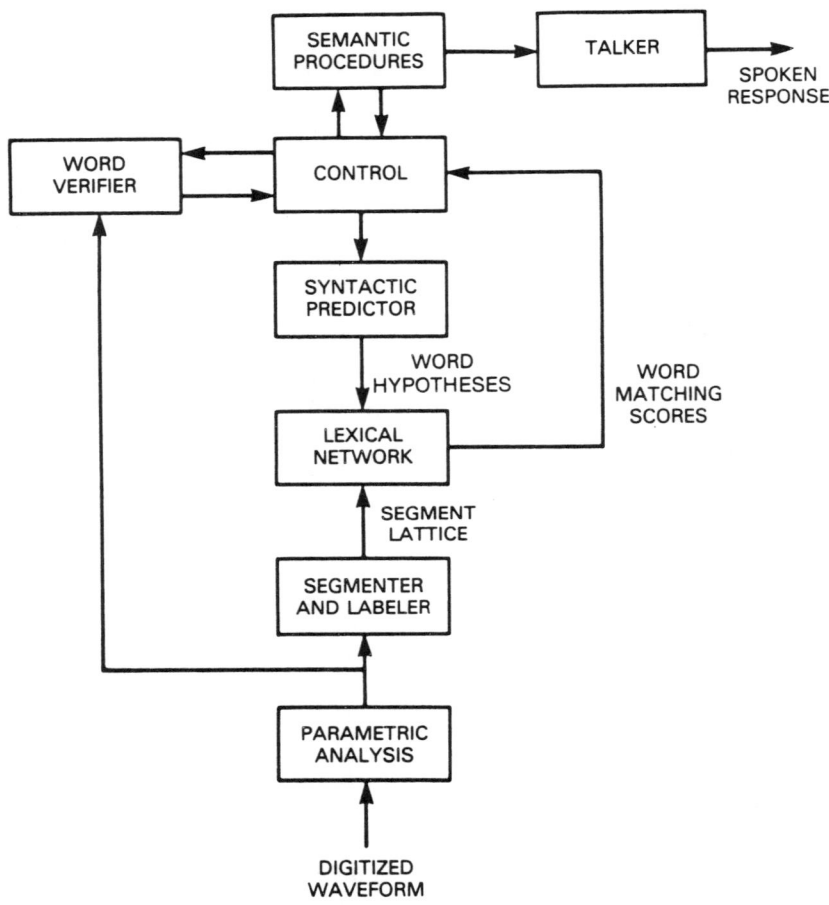

After Klatt (1977)

Figure IV-4. Block Diagram of the BBN HWIM System Organization

Speech Recognition and Speech Understanding 137

TABLE IV-3. Summary of ARPA's Speech Understanding Systems

Name/Org	Domain/Purpose	Approach	Knowledge Rep.	Control	ABF	Accuracy	Comments
HEARSAY II CMU	AI Publications Document Retrieval	Utilizes cooperating independent system experts (Knowledge Sources) that communicate via posting hypotheses on a blackboard.	Independent KS's composed of production rules.	• Asynchronous pattern-invoked knowledge sources • Opportunistic scheduling by first expanding the highest scoring hypothesis	33	90%	• Development of blackboard architecture and use of independent cooperating knowledge sources most significant • A parallel processor version has been built to exploit KS modularity.
HARPY CMU	AI Publications Document Retrieval	Compiled a network of all possible pronunciations of all possible sentences. Paths thru network are "sentence templates."	Precompiled Network. Each node is a template of allophones, which when linked form acoustic representations of every possible pronunciation of words in the domain.	"Beam Search" No backtracking	33	95%	• Approach cannot easily accommodate pragmatics. • Needs a large memory. • Sensitive to missing acoustical segments and missing words.

Artificial Intelligence

TABLE IV-3. Summary of ARPA's Speech Understanding Systems (cont.)

Name/Org	Domain/Purpose	Approach	Knowledge Rep.	Control	ABF	Accuracy	Comments
HWIM BBN	Travel Budget Management	• The system extends bottom-up word theories, using top-down syntactic and semantic components. Verifies hypothesized words by generating a parameter representation that is compared with that from the actual speech input. • Uses an ATN semantic grammar.	Uses networks to represent: 1) trip facts and relations. 2) Lexicon 3) Phoneme hypotheses from signal	• Centralized control using KS's as subroutines. • Expands sentences about the first recognized word in sentence (Island Driving).	196	44%	• Speaker Independent • Very slow • Most difficult domain in SUR project.

H. State of the Art

1. Speech Recognition

Table IV-4 is a summary of a recent Texas Instruments' study of commercial speech recognizers tested on a 20 word vocabulary consisting of the 10 spoken digits "zero" thru "nine" and ten command words: start, stop, yes, no, go, help, erase, rubout, repeat and enter.

In 1982, speaker-dependent connected-word short-string, small vocabulary (approx. 50 words) recognizers were commercially available. These could recognize up to 90 wpm of connected speech compared to a typical person's speaking rate of 150 wpm. The vocabulary size is usually less than 150 words, but is application dependent. Recognition accuracies of 98% or greater are being achieved in factory environments. Current turnkey systems are in the $5K to $75K range. Consumer product speech-recognizer subsystems for toys, personal computers, voice-controlled appliances, etc., cost from $6 to $100.

Voice recognition systems are here, viable, proven, but still somewhat costly. In industry applications, they have demonstrated large increases in productivity. Hundreds of successful installations exist today. Plohar (1983) discusses the human factor considerations associated with successful applications.

2. Speech Understanding

There are no commercial true speech-understanding systems today. However, there are a number of U.S. companies working on future commercial systems.

a. Bell Labs

Has been working on a semantic sentence recognizer and interpreter utilizing a finite state grammar and a small vocabulary. The intent is to produce an interactive speech understanding system for use over the telephone (Levinson and Liberman, 1981).

b. IBM — T.J. Watson Res. Center

IBM has had the largest effort in continuous-speech recognition and understanding, capitalizing on the HARPY "Beam Search" approach.

c. Other organizations involved in developing speech understanding systems include BBN.

I. Who Is Doing Speech Recognition Related Work

1. Commercial Organizations
IBM
TI
Bell Labs
Verbex
Nippon Electric
Threshold Technology
Interstate Electronics
Matsushita
Scott Instruments
Sanyo
INTEL
ITT (San Diego)
Fairchild

TABLE IV-4. T.I.'s Test of Speech Recognizers on Individual Words

Manufacturer	Model*	Nominal Price in 1981	Nominal Price for Comparable 1983 Model	% Substitutions
Verbex	1800	$65K	$19.6K	0.2
Nippon Electric	DP-100	$65K	$27K	1.2
Threshold Technology	T-500	$12K	$5K	1.4
Interstate Electronics	VRM	$2.4K	$2.4K	2.9
Heuristics	7000	$3.3K	NA	5.9
Centigram	MIKE 4725	$3.5K	NA	7.1
Scott Instruments	VET/1 (home computer peripheral)	$ .5K	$ .9K	12.6

*First two systems are capable of connected speech.
Verbex is the only system having speaker-independent capability.

After Doddington and Schalk (1981).

Hewlett Packard
Haskins Lab
Lincoln Labs
Speech Communications Research Lab
Sperry Univac
Votan
Voice Machine Communications
Voice Processing Corp.
General Instrument — Milton Bradley
Voice Control Systems

2. *Universities*
   M.I.T.
   C.M.U.
   V.P.I.
   U of CA at Berkeley

J. Problems and Issues*

- Speech perception at the acoustic level is a critical factor in achieving advanced recognition capability. Current commercial word recognizers have not yet made full use of available knowledge.
- Widespread use of speech recognizers await the availability of low cost connected-speech systems achieving better than a 99% accuracy with limited vocabularies — 100 words.
- Capabilities of a word recognizer depend on:
  (1) Can it recognize connected speech?
  (2) Is it speaker independent?
  (3) How big a vocabulary can it recognize?
- The greatest difficulty that speech recognizers have is determining word end-points — the source of many word-recognition errors for isolated word recognizers.
- A major problem is separating linguistically significant variations in the speech signal from insignificant variations (such as variations in word pronunciations).
- Noise is also a major problem in speech recognition, often resulting from actions of the speaker himself.
- Large vocabulary size is a problem to users, who need to remember what the machine can recognize.
- The two main errors made by speech recognizers are:
  (1) Substitution, and
  (2) Rejection
- Other less common errors are insertion and deletion.
- There are as yet no standards for test or evaluation of systems — a major problem.

*These have been gleaned primarily from Doddington and Schalk (1981).

- It is not the number of words that are the major difficulty, it is how close their sound is to each other. The natural English alphabet is a particularly difficult set of sounds to distinguish.
- Software or hardware may also have idiosyncracies that adversely affect recognition performance.
- As recognizer performance improves, evaluation becomes more difficult, because more testing is required to achieve statistical significance.
- The pronunciation of individual words change depending on the adjacent words in the sentence.
- The hypothesize and test approach needs abundant computer power — a major factor limiting its commercial use.
- Integrating recognizers into an application requires substantial software and human factors considerations. This has limited real-world adoption.

K. Future Trends

It is anticipated that speaker-independent, continuous-speech recognition systems with limited vocabularies (10-20 words), having an accuracy of 98% or better, will be available by the mid-1980's. Automatic dictation will probably not appear before the 1990's, with Japanese language systems being the first to appear. (Japanese language has only on the order of 500 syllables, compared to 10K for English.) Speech understanding is a major part of the Japanese 5th Generation Computer Project (Feigenbaum and McCorduck, 1983).

Due to the advancement in VLSI, it is expected that voice recognition chips for toys will soon be in the $6 range — $50 for a complete system.

A strong expectation is that a speech understanding system using a natural language parser will be introduced by IBM in the mid-80's.

Around 1990, true commercial speech understanding systems, having the capabilities of the ARPA SUR systems but operating in near real-time, are expected to appear.

By 1990, speech recognition and understanding is expected to be a billion dollar a year industry (Elphick, 1982).

REFERENCES

- Arden, B. W., (Ed.), *What Can Be Automated,* Cambridge: M.I.T. Press, 1980.
- Barr, A. and Feigenbaum, E. A. (Eds.), *The Handbook of Artificial Intelligence,* Vols I and II, Los Altos, CA: W. Kaufmann, 1981, 1982.
- Doddington, G. R. and Schalk, T.B., "Speech Recognition: Turning Theory to Practice," *IEEE Spectrum,* Sept. 1981, pp. 26-32.
- Elphick, M., "Unraveling the Mysteries of Speech Recognition," *High Technology,* Vol 2, No. 2, March/April 1982, pp. 71-76.
- Erman, L. D., Hayes-Roth, F., Lesser, V. R. and Reddy, D. R., "The HEARSAY-II Speech-Understanding System: Integrating Knowledge To Resolve Uncertainty." *Computing Surveys,* Vol 12, No. 2, 1980.

- Feigenbaum E. A. and McCorduck, P., *The Fifth Generation,* Reading, Mass: Addison-Wesley, 1983.
- Klatt, D. H., "Review of the ARPA Speech Understanding Project," *J. Acoustical Soc. of America,* Vol 62, No. 6, Dec. 1977, pp. 1345-1366.
- Lea, W. A. and Shoup, J. E., *Review of the ARPA SUR Project and Survey of Current Technology in Speech Understanding,* Speech Communications Research Lab., Los Angeles, Jan. 16, 1979.
- Levinson, S. E. and Liberman, "Speech Recognition by Computer," *Scientific American,* Vol 244, No. 4, April 1981, pp. 64-76.
- Pluhar, K., "Speech Recognition — An Exploding Future for the Man-Machine Interface," *Control Engineering,* Jan. 1983, pp. 70-73.
- Zue, V. W., "Acoustic-Phonetic Knowledge Representation: Implications from Spectrogram Reading Experiments," *Proceedings of the 1981 NATO Advanced Summer Institute on Automatic Speech Analysis and Recognition,* D. Reidel Pub., 1981.

V. SPEECH SYNTHESIS

A. Introduction

Speech synthesis — speech output from a computer — is an emerging technology whose products are already becoming commonplace. Though the present market for these devices is still small, the future looks very bright.

Speech synthesis is not normally considered an AI topic, though it is sure to play an important part in many future AI systems, particularly when coupled with speech understanding. One may very well consider these synthesis systems, which employ rules (often heuristic) for deriving speech from stored speech elements, as an example of an "expert system on a chip."

B. Why Synthesis

One approach to making available speech when needed is to record the speech and play it back as required. The disadvantage is that mechanical devices are often unreliable and the ability to generate new sentences from stored words is quite limited because of access time, and therefore unsuitable for most computer-based applications.

A more reliable approach is to use digital sound recording techniques, enabling speech to be stored in solid-state memories having no moving parts to break down. The disadvantage is that an enormous amount of storage is required — in the order of 50,000 bits per second of digital speech (at the typical speaking rate of 150 words per minute). However, if words are represented by the digital code for their letters, the same information requires only about 100 bits per second of speech. This two to three orders of magnitude difference highlights the importance of speech compression for any digital representation of speech, not only to save storage requirements, but also to vastly reduce the bandwidth required for electronic speech transmission. All speech synthesis methods use some form of speech compression.

Speech synthesis serves three basic purposes:
1) Recreating speech from a compressed speech representation
2) Generating speech from stored speech elements such as by concatenating representations for words, and
3) Generating speech from text.

The first purpose is associated with minimizing storage or transmission bandwidth requirements. The second with creating speech from stored components under microprocessor or computer control. The third with reading machines and computer-human interaction.

An indication of applications of speech synthesis is given in Table V-1.

C. Human Speech

As many speech synthesizers actually employ an approximate simulation of the human speech production mechanism, it is helpful to briefly review human speech and its generation. Human

TABLE V-1. Applications of Speech Synthesis.

Military
- Operation of military equipment
- Warnings
- Reminders
- Service and operation aids
- Trainers and simulators
- Secure communications

Computer
- Communication by computers to users.

Consumer
- Talking appliances
- Teaching devices
- Toys
- Talking typewriters and calculators
- Talking watches
- Automobile warning devices, reminders, and annunciators for instruments
- Devices for the blind
- Communication for the speech handicapped

Telecommunications
- Synthesized telephone messages
- Speech compression for "store and forward," to reduce communication costs
- Vocal delivery of electronic mail

Industrial
- Speaking instruments
- Speaking cash registers
- Alarm systems
- Automated office equipment
- Industrial process control
- Station and floor announcers for trains, buses, elevators, etc.
- Systems operations where the operators have their visual attention elsewhere
- Emergency warning devices for airplanes, machines, etc.
- Control room annunciators for sensors
- Text readers
- Data entry (with vocal verification)

speech consists basically of a combination of vocal sounds such as vowels, fricative sounds—such as f, th or sh, and plosive or stop consonant sounds such as b and d.

The human vocal tract can be considered as an acoustic tube terminated at one end by the vocal cords and at the other end by the lips. This resonant tube has a side branch — the nasal resonator — separated by a flap called the velum.

Voiced sounds are produced by forcing air from the lungs past the tensed vocal cords which are thus forced to vibrate, emitting puffs of air into the vocal tract. (The puff frequency — about 100 hertz in males, 200 hertz in females — is a function of the vocal cord size and tenseness.) These puffs of air excite the vocal tract, stimulating their resonant (formant) frequencies. Most of the resulting sound energy is contained in these resonant responses, the frequency of which can be varied by changing the shape of the vocal tract by moving the lips, jaw or tongue.

Fricative sounds occur when a constriction in the vocal tract leads to turbulent air flows after the constriction.

Plosives are generated by briefly closing the vocal tract until pressure builds up and then releasing the pressure.

D. Electronic Simulation of the Speech Mechanism

The three basic human speech sounds can be electronically simulated as follows — as illustrated by the Computalker Consultants Model CT-1* synthesizer shown schematically in Figure V-1.

Voiced sounds can be simulated by passing energy from a variable periodic source — corresponding to the vocal cord puffs — through a series of variable filters (f_1, f_2, f_3) corresponding to the vocal tract resonances (formants). Plosive sounds are produced the same way, but require rapid changes in the amplitude parameters A_o and A_n. Fricative sounds are produced by passing white noise through a variable filter (f_f). Some sounds, such as v and z, are produced using both the periodic and noise mechanisms.

Using this approach, human speech can be simulated by controlling the frequency parameters (f_i) and the amplitude parameters (A_i) over time. Some variant of this basic method — referred to as parametric coding—is used in all speech synthesizers that simulate human speech production.

E. Synthesis in Speech Compression and Regeneration

Synthesis has the role of regeneration in speech compression schemes (associated with speech storage or minimal bandwidth speech transmission).

There are two basic speech compression techniques — frequency domain analysis (parametric coding as discussed in the previous section on electronic simulation), and time domain analysis. Frequency domain methods tend to dominate commercial speech synthesis, but time domain analysis has become important for limited-vocabulary word synthesis.

The frequency domain approach analyzes the incoming speech to be compressed and generates the parameters needed for regenerating the signal using an electronic simulation of the vocal tract. In some cases, these parameters may be further compressed for reduced storage. Speech is generated by inverting the process as indicated in Figure V-2.

Time domain analysis is characterized by waveform compression techniques. Waveform digitization coding, researched extensively by Bell Labs, takes the original waveform of spoken

---

*No longer in production, but the Phillips speech chip essentially does the same thing.

Speech Synthesis 147

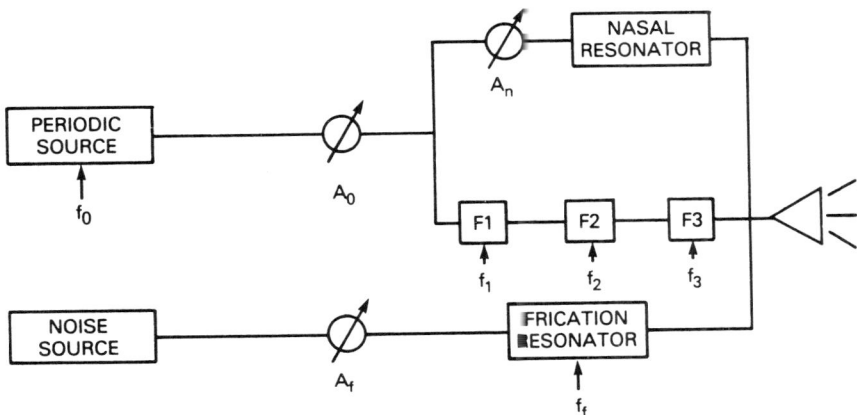

After Sherwood (1979)

Figure V-1. A Simplified Diagram of the Computalker CT-1 Parametric Synthesizer.

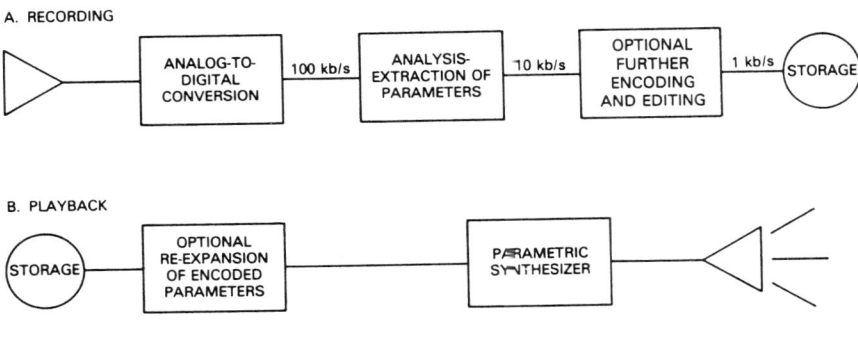

After Sherwood (1979)

Figure V-2. Recording and Reproduction of Speech Using a Compressed-Speech System.

words and compresses them using a complicated algorithm. The final compressed waveform is stored as bits in memory for later reconstruction of the original waveform. Though generally producing better sounding speech than parametric coding, waveform digitization coding requires two to four times as much storage as that needed for parametric coding.

F. Parametric Coding Schemes

1. Introduction:

All frequency domain compression techniques employ some sort of electronic model of the human vocal tract. Thus, all have one or more filters to simulate vocal tract resonances, and periodic and noise energy sources, and are controlled by varying the parameters associated with pitch, loudness, and filter frequencies.

2. Formant Coding

This is a straightforward approach to controlling an electronic model of the vocal tract by controlling the tunable filters using parametric signals that represent the formant (vocal tube resonant) frequencies such as those shown in Figure V-1. As the formant frequencies change relatively slowly, the parameters need to be updated relatively infrequently, thus allowing data compression.

3. Linear Predictive Coding (LPC)

LPC, pioneered by TI for "Speak and Spell," is a form of formant coding which allows further compression of the parameters. As the formant frequencies tend to change slowly, current samples are predicted from weighted linear combinations of previous samples. TI's LPC's clever prediction approach, and the use of an ingenious lattice filter, greatly simplifies the synthesis circuitry. The resulting system can be stored on a single chip and produces high quality natural sounding speech.

4. PARCOR

PARCOR (partial correlation), utilized by Japanese manufacturers, is a variant of LPC. LPC extrapolates from a series of formant samples to predict following formant frequencies. Though most speech patterns change slowly, plosive and fricative sounds involve rapid changes. PARCOR makes LPC more sensitive to sudden changes by giving greater emphasis to the correlation between adjacent parametric samples and less to the longer term patterns. However, there appears to be little resultant subjective differences in observed speech quality between the two approaches.

5. Line Spectrum Pair (LSP)

NTT (Nippon Telephone and Telephone Public Corp.) which developed PARCOR, has come up with LSP, an approach allowing still further compression. LSP defines the boundary conditions for the individual formant frequencies as those corresponding to the open and closed vocal tract. NTT claims that for a complete system, some 40% more compression can be achieved with LSP than with PARCOR, while maintaining nearly the same speech quality.

6. Parametric Waveform Coding (PWC)

PWC is another variant of LPC, as used by Centigram's Voice Ware system to produce vocabularies for the Lisa Speech Board.* PWC uses a variable-length slice of waveform to produce the linear prediction coefficients. Each slice (about 20 milliseconds in length) corresponds to a "glottal event" — the event associated with each puff of air passing through the vocal tract. Voice Ware uses an array processor to determine 13 linear prediction coefficients for each glottal event. To synthesize speech, the Lisa Speech Board uses these coefficients and the lengths of the events to recreate speech waveforms as in other LPC synthesizers. The PWC approach tends to yield more natural speech than the simpler LPC systems, but requires a higher data rate.

G. Waveform Coding Schemes

1. ADPCM

Digitized speech at a 8 kHz sampling rate results in 32,000 bits per second (bps) for a 4 bit sampling size using the adaptive differential pulse code modulation (ADPCM) proposed as the worldwide preferred method of digitized voice telephone signals for long distance transmission. In ADPCM, the digitized speech is encoded in terms of the amplitude differences between adjacent samples. These differences are adaptively encoded in terms of quantization level (a function of the previous quantization level and the previous PCM value). A close relative of ADPCM is CVSD (continuous variable slope delta modulation).

2. Mozer's Waveform Coding

Though ADPCM is suitable for telephone transmission, its high bit rate is unsuitable for stored speech synthesis. A scheme by Dr. Forrest Mozer of the University of California is a variation of ADPCM which provides substantial further compression. This technique has been incorporated into the National Semiconductor's Corporation's Digitalker. Dr. Mozer's approach is to:
1) Analyze the waveform to detect short periods with little change. The waveform for these periods are then replaced with identical waveforms.
2) Fourier analyze the signal and adjust the phase angle of each Fourier component to produce a symmetrical waveform and then discard half.
3) Discard low amplitude portions of the waveform which are not heard by the ear.
4) Employ ADPCM to further reduce data.

The net result of these actions is more than a 40 to one reduction in the data that needs to be stored, as compared with the data in direct digitization. To produce speech the process is inverted. Though these resultant signals look little like the original, the result is very good speech reproduction.

H. Coding the Words To Be Stored

Though the schemes discussed thus far provide a huge amount of reduction in the storage required, generating the required custom vocabulary in terms of the stored parameters requires hand tailoring by an expert. As yet, there is no acceptable automatic mechanism for directly converting speech into satisfactory storage elements for encoding schemes that provide high data

---
*No longer in production.

compression. (ADPCM is automatic. Parametric schemes can be automated with small residual errors.)

Developing the vocabulary for the Mozer Waveform Coding, used in National Semiconductor's Digitalker, takes about one hour of processing per word. It involves working with the data compression and zero phase-encoding algorithms, that produce the stored bit patterns, making it very difficult for users to program their own custom vocabularies (Ciarcia, 1983).

To enable users to develop their own custom vocabularies for their products, when large vocabularies are required, Centigram Corp. has offered as a product their Voice Ware development system. With it, users can input tape recorded voice to a digitizer that supplies a 4800 bps data stream to a microprocessor-based CRT-terminal work station. The station converts the signal into parametric waveform coding (PWC). The user can then edit the messages, combine them into files, and feed them back through the Lisa synthesizer to hear how they sound. If the sound is unsatisfactory, particularly for concatenated phrases, the phrases can be rerecorded to achieve the desired continuity and balance.

In general, for synthesizer users requiring a small custom vocabulary, it is customary for them to contract with the synthesizer manufacturer or other development source for the words required. This cost is in the order of $100 per word for LPC chips.

I. Generating Speech from Text

English has some 40 basic speech sounds called phonemes, corresponding to 16 vowel sounds, 6 stops, 8 fricatives, 3 nasals (such as ng), 4 liquids/glides (such as l in lice) and 3 others (such as ch in church). These sounds vary somewhat depending upon how they are combined into words or used in speech. These phoneme variations are called allophones. (Texas Instruments developed a set of 128 allophones to characterize English speech.) Allophones and the rules to string them together can be stored in computer memory chips. The first text-to-speech system used a phonemic synthesizer (Votrax). Votrax utilized a hard-wired phonemic to parameter converter which then fed a formant synthesizer to create speech. A simplified text-to-speech system schematic is given in Figure V-3.

The highly-intelligible state-of-the-art speech synthesizer, the Speech Plus "Prose 2000," utilizes a generation approach consisting of five serial processes: 1) Text normalization, 2)

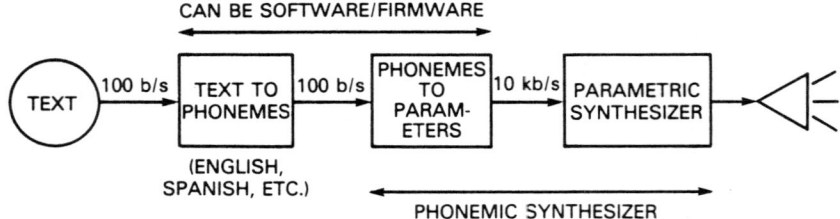

After Sherwood (1979)

Figure V-3. Text to Speech Synthesis.

Phonemics, 3) Allophonics, 4) Prosodics, 5) Parameter generation. For words not in the exceptions lexicon, the phonemics process is implemented as a real-time expert system consisting of a small rule interpreter and an ordered set of about 400 context-sensitive rules.

J. State of the Art

Elphick (1981, p. 42) notes that:

> Most commercial synthesizers, especially low-cost ones used for consumer products, derive their speech elements from recordings of actual human speech. The recorded speech patterns are compressed, and the speech is disassembled into a vocabulary of small elements for later reassembly into messages.

High quality speech by phoneme synthesizers has been achieved in research systems, but not in commercial systems. The most natural commercial speech synthesizers use the waveform approach.

Figure V-4 is an indication of speech quality versus bit storage requirements for the various synthesis techniques.

Thus far, in industrial applications, only short messages are practical, as prolonged listening to synthetic speech tends to fatigue the operators (Andreiev, 1981).

Speech chips with limited vocabularies are available in the range of $10 and up. To construct the initial representations for new words (to be stored in ROMs) runs upward of tens of dollars per word.

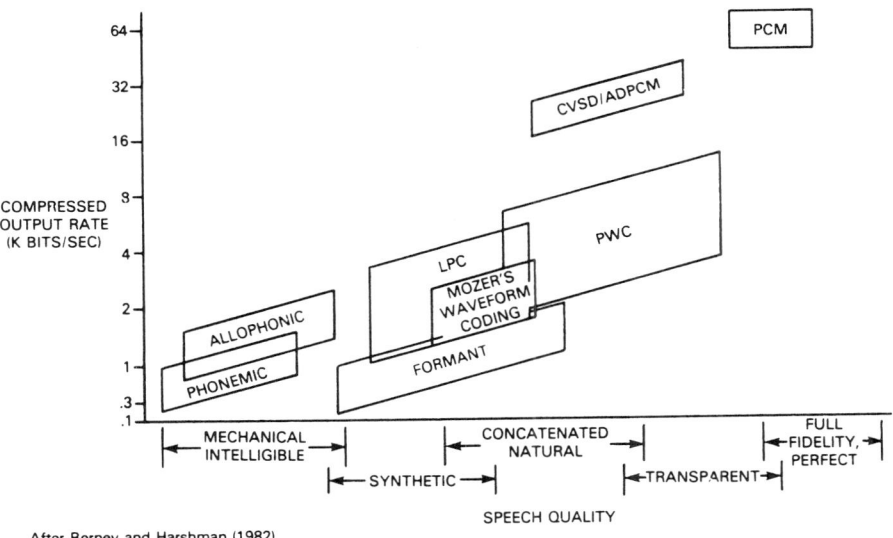

After Berney and Harshman (1982)

Figure V-4. Speech Quality Versus Bit Rate for Various Coding Schemes.

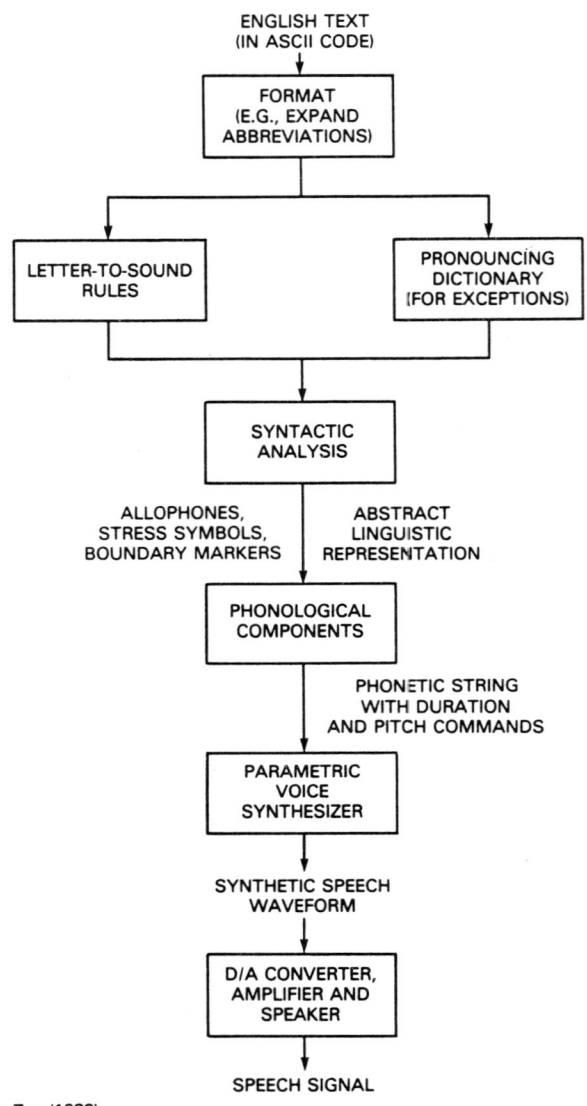

Figure V-5. Text to Speech Conversion.

Programming advanced speech synthesizers, to be used with speech generation from text, is an enormous task. The flow diagram for such a state of the art system is given in Figure V-5. First, the printed text must be converted into phonemes by using a combination of rules and a stored pronouncing dictionary, taking into account pitch, intensity, and duration associated with emphasis, as influenced by word use determined by the syntax of the sentence. The resultant allophones (phonemic variations) are then fed to a phonemic voice synthesizer.

The major commercial application thus far for speech generation from text is reading systems for the blind. These products input text using optical character recognition, and output speech using a text-to-speech synthesizer. Other applications include electronic mail-to-voice, and proofreading.

K. Some Available Commercial Systems

An indication of manufacturers and currently available commercial systems is given by Table V-2.

L. Problems and Issues

- There is a tradeoff in system design between speech quality, vocabulary size, and cost.
- Problem of how to best divide the fundamental units to be used — allophones, syllables, words. The smaller units permit very large vocabularies without excessive storage requirements, while the larger units (such as phrases) provide superior speech quality.
- Memory cost considerations tend to restrict the use of the word synthesis approach.
- As the synthesizer techniques improve, it may be that errors due to low sampling rates, and inadequate consideration of coarticulation and prosodic (speech stress) effects may be the limiting factors.
- Speech compression techniques are crucial to minimize memory requirements in the synthesizer.
- The high cost of generating words for synthesizer vocabularies needs to be reduced.
- Similarly, the high cost of storing words in ROM needs to be addressed.
- Updating stored vocabularies is problematical due to the need to keep the same speaker available.

M. Forecast

Though the market for voice synthesizers is still relatively small, it is estimated that it will be close to one-half billion dollars by 1985 and will reach several billion dollars by 1990. Talking devices will have a big impact on industrial operations, a major effect on learning devices, and will probably be ubiquitous throughout home and consumer products. These devices will be a boon to the handicapped, in everything from talking typewriters and appliances, and reading machines for the blind, to speech prosthetics. It is also anticipated that these devices will be found virtually everywhere in vehicles and transportation systems.

Because of their integration into single chips, the cost of stored vocabulary devices will continue to drop so that basic hardware costs of less than $10, for units having vocabularies of several hundred words, are foreseen by the end of this decade.

TABLE V-2. Some Available Commercial Synthesizer Systems

Manufacturer	Model	Cost	Type	Comments
Votrax (Troy, MI)	VSM/1	$995	Formant	A singleboard complete system incorporating a programmable memory
	SVA		Formant	Singleboard synthesizer for unlimited text to speech (no internal word storage)
	SC-02		Formant	Synthesizer chip with phoneme library
Speech Plus, Inc. (Mt. View, CA)	Prose 2000	$3500	Formant	Singleboard system achieving an unlimited vocabulary capability by using 400 rules and a 3000 word exceptions lexicon. For use with text.
	Speech 1000	$1200	LPC	Synthesizer board with up to 6 minutes stored vocab.
Texas Instruments (TI) (Dallas, TX)	TMS 5220	$5	LPC	Single chip voice synthesizer processor.
	TMS 6100	$5	LPC	Single chip voice synthesizer memory.
	Speech synthesizer for TI 99/4A Personal Computer	$100	LPC	Text to speech implemented in 99/4A.
	TM 990/306		LPC	Speech module (does not have unlimited vocabulary capability of formant systems).
National Semiconductor (Santa Clara, CA)	Digitalker MM 54104		Mozer's Waveform Digitizer	Single chip with 256 possible addressable expressions.
Centigram (Sunnyvale, CA)	GIM	$350	Formant	An SBX module using the GI250 synthesizer chip.
	SYBIL	$495	Formant	A single channel synthesizer for the IBM PC.

TABLE V-2. Some Available Commercial Synthesizer Systems (cont.)

Manufacture	Model	Cost	Type	Comments
Kurzweil Computer Products (Cambridge, MA)	Reading Machine for Blind	$30,000	Formant	Uses Speech Plus Prose 2000 synthesizer.
American Microsystems (Santa Clara, CA)	53610 53620	* *	LPC LPC	
General Instruments (Hicksville, N.Y.)	Allophone Synthesis Module		LPC	Annunciates 64 Allophones
	SP250	*	Formant	Single channel synthesizer
	SP256	*	Formant	Single channel synthesizer, with microprocessor control
Hitachi	HD 38880	*	PARCOR	Uses Partial Autocorrelation (closely related to LPC)
Nippon Electric Corp			PARCOR	
Sanyo	LC 1800	*	PARCOR	
Mitsubishi	M58817	*	PARCOR	
Matsushita (Japan)		*	LPC	
Master Specialties (Costa Mesa, CA)	1650	$500 + Vocabulary at $50/word	Word Synthesis	
Intex Micro Systems (Troy, N.Y.)	Intex-Talker		Text-to-Speech Synthesizer	Uses a text-to-phoneme algorithm and a Votrax SC-01 chip.
Motorola			CVSD	Encoder and Decoder Chips.
Phillips/Signetics	MEA 8000	*	Formant	
	MEA 10000	*	Formant	
OKI Semiconductor			ADPCM	Encoder and Decoder Chips.

*Chip prices range from $3 to $15 depending on model and quantity. Speech Plus provides custom vocabulary generation services for speech synthesizer chips at $100/word.

REFERENCES

• Andreiev, N., "Speech Synthesis: High Technology's Dark Horse in Search of New Pastures," *Control Engineering,* September 1981, pp. 95-98.

• Berney, C. L. and Harshman, C., "Voice Ware Does It Differently, *Mini-Micro Systems,* March 1982, pp. 183-193.

• Brightman, T. and Crook, S., "Exploring Practical Speech I/O," *Mini-Micro Systems,* May 1982, pp. 291-306.

• Ciarca, S., "Use ADPCM for Highly Intelligible Speech Synthesis," *Byte,* June 1983, pp. 35-49.

• Damper, R. I., "Speech Technology — Implications for Biomedical Engineering," *J. of Medical Engineering and Technology,* Vol 6 No. 4 (July/Aug 1982), pp. 135-149.

• Elphick, M. "Talking Machines Aim for Versatility," *High Technology,* Sept/Oct 1981, pp. 41-48.

• Flanagan, J. L., "Talking with Computers: Synthesis and Recognition of Speech by Machines," *IEEE Transactions on Biomedical Engineering,* Vol BME-29, No. 4, April 1982, pp. 223-232.

• Gilblom, D. L., "A High-Quality Real-Time Text-to-Speech Converter," *Electro-82 Professional Program Record, Session 11,* Boston, Mass, May 1982, Paper No. 11/2.

• Lerner, E. J., "Products That Talk," *Spectrum,* July 1982, pp. 32-37.

• Sherwood, B. A., "The Computer Speaks," *Spectrum,* August 1979, pp. 18-25.

• Zue, V. W., *Tutorial on Natural Language Interfaces: Part 2-Speech,* Menlo Park, CA: AAAI, Aug 17, 1982.

VI. PROBLEM SOLVING AND PLANNING

A. Introduction

Nilsson at SRI originally specified problem solving and planning as being one of the four fundamental application areas of AI. However, the "weak methods," employing little domain knowledge, originally used in AI for problem solving and planning, proved inadequate for complex real-world problems. Thus, in seeking solutions in this area, larger amounts of knowledge have since been utilized. The net result has been that the "Knowledge Engineering" methodology used for Expert Systems has been adapted for use in problem-solving and planning. Thus, the boundary between problem-solving and planning and expert systems has faded and it is now common to refer to all these knowledge-based activities as expert systems and are therefore covered in that volume of this series. Nevertheless, this chapter will briefly review some of the earlier less knowledge-intensive systems and several examples of recent systems.

B. Planning Defined

Most of AI applications can be considered as examples of problem-solving, which are well covered in the other AI application areas: Expert Systems, Computer Vision, Language Understanding, etc. In this chapter we will only consider planning systems. Planning can be defined for our purposes as the design process for selecting and stringing together individual actions into sequences in order to achieve desired goals.

C. Basic Planning Paradigm

Wilensky (1983) outlines the basic structure of plans from the viewpoint of common-sense problem solving and natural language understanding. A schematic for Wilensky's basic planning paradigm is given in Figure VI-1. In this paradigm, the planner recognizes from the environment that a new situation has arisen which merits a goal. The planner then retrieves from memory a plan that might be used to achieve this goal, or generates a new trial plan if no existing plan is suitable. This candidate plan is then projected forward (via simulation) to observe the outcome. This outcome is examined to see if there are any conflicts that will arise in achieving other goals if this plan is pursued. If not, this and other candidate plan outcomes are evaluated and the maximum-valued plan is chosen. The plan, when implemented, will modify the current state-of-affairs. This impact, together with any other changes in the environment, results in a new world model with new situations that may merit new goals, so that the cyclic process of planning continues. When candidate plans are being considered, if the candidate plan overlaps existing plans for other goals, these overlapping plans may be merged to conserve resources.

A basic problem in planning is that of conflicting goals. The causes of conflicting goals are indicated in Figure VI-2. (A preservation goal is a goal to preserve an already existing condition, or is a goal not to undo a desirable state or goal resulting from another plan.)

158   Artificial Intelligence

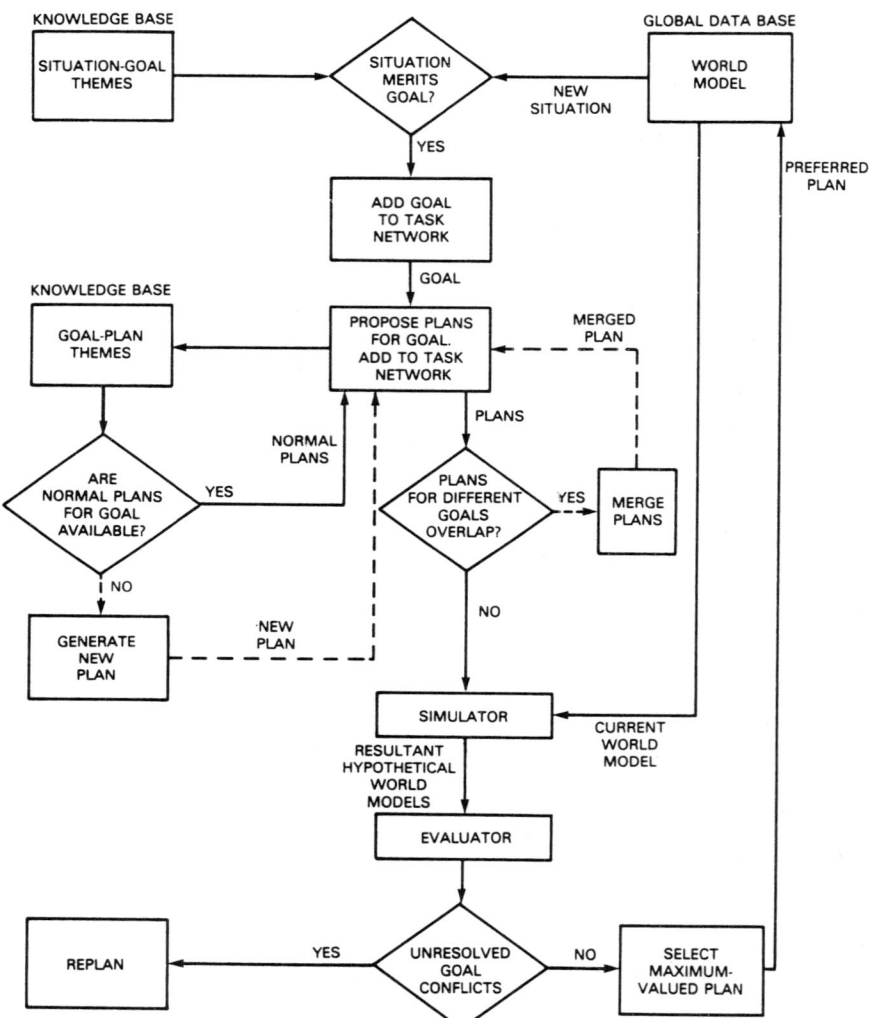

Figure VI-1. Wilensky Planning Paradigm.

Problem Solving and Planning 159

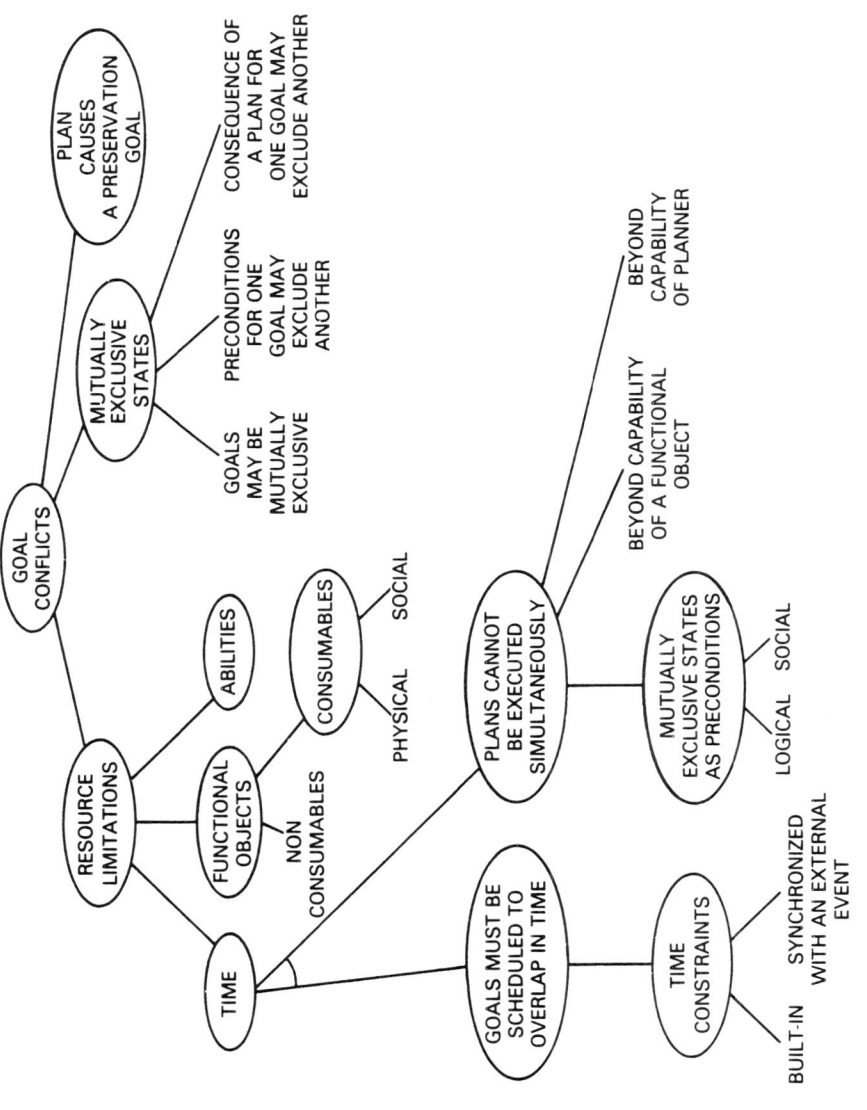

Figure VI-2. Nature of Goal Conflicts.

Problems arising from conflicting goals are dealt with by replanning or by eliminating the factors causing the goal conflicts. A flow diagram for resolving goal conflicts is given in Figure VI-3. If the goal conflicts cannot be completely resolved, then partial fulfillment of goals may be attempted or goals of lesser importance may have to be dropped. The global strategy is to achieve as many goals as possible, maximizing the composite value of the goals achieved, and not waste resources in achieving them.

DEVISER (Vere, 1983) is a good example of a planning program designed to deal with conflicting goals resulting from resource and time constraints.

Wilensky also discusses "competing goals" that arise in competitive situations. The planning strategies given in this case are to:
1) Avoid conflicts
2) Outdo an opponent
3) Hinder an opponent
4) Induce alterations in competitive plans.

D. Paradigms for Generating Plans

The major issue in any planning system is reducing search. The other key issue is how to handle interacting subproblems. The following paradigms are different approaches to addressing these issues.

Cohen and Feigenbaum (1982) discuss four distinct approaches to planning: nonhierarchical, hierarchical, script-based (skeletal) and opportunistic. Virtually all plans, both hierarchical and nonhierarchical, have hierarchical subgoal structures. That is, each goal can be expanded into several subgoals, which themselves can be further expanded, etc. until the bottom level consists of operators needed to achieve the lowest level goals. The distinction between hierarchical and nonhierarchical planners is that ". . . a hierarchical planner generates a hierarchy of representations of a plan in which the highest is a simplification, or abstraction of the plan and the lowest is a detailed plan, sufficient to solve the problem. In contrast, nonhierarchical planners have only one representation of a plan." (pp. 516-517)

1. Nonhierarchical Planning

Nonhierarchical planning does not initially distinguish between important and unimportant actions so that everything is considered in the initial plan, including cumbersome details. For complex problems, this often results in a large search. One way the search can be greatly reduced is by initially assuming subgoals independent and then trying to repair the plan to account for the interactions (as in HACKER, Table VI-1-2).

A knowledge based approach used in ISIS-II (Fox et al., 1982) is to prune the search space prior to search by using constraints, and then narrow the space actually searched by using a "beam search" approach.

2. Hierarchical Planning

In this approach, first a high level plan is formulated considering only the important aspects, then the vague parts of the plan are refined into more detailed subplans. By ignoring the details at

Problem Solving and Planning   161

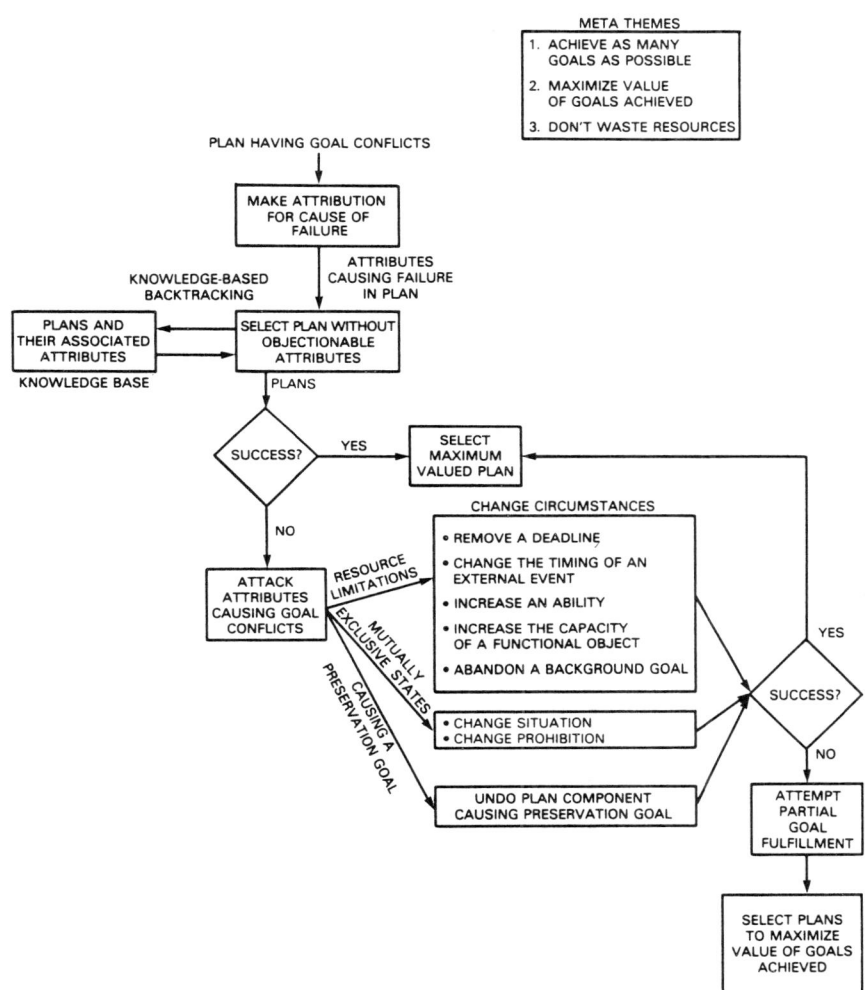

Figure VI-3. *Resolving Conflicting Goals by Replanning (and/or Attacking Factors Causing Conflicts).*

the higher levels, search is vastly reduced. ABSTRIPS (Table VI-1-5) is illustrative of this approach.

3. Utilization of Skeleton Plans

This approach utilizes stored plans which contain the outlines for solving many different kinds of problems. The skeleton plans are then filled in for the particular problem being solved. This technique has similarities to Schank's script-based approach to language understanding. KNOBS (Engelman et al., 1980, Table VI-1-10), a frame-based planning system for tactical air strikes, is an example of a skeletal plan approach.

4. Opportunistic Planning

Opportunistic planning (Hayes Roth and Hayes Roth, 1978) is based on the way that humans often approach planning. In this approach, the plan is developed piecewise, with parts of the plan being developed separately, and then added to, enlarged and linked together as opportunities present themselves. Planning of this sort incorporates both top-down and bottom-up components.

E. Planners

In this section we summarize the characteristics of some of the key AI planning systems that have evolved over the years. Figure VI-4 diagrams the various systems that are reviewed and their relation to the basic paradigms. Tables VI-1 outline the systems shown in Figure VI-4, using the Expert Systems format (Figure I-1) developed in Chapter I. Note that planners evolve by building on past techniques. For example, DEVISER (Table VI-1-9), the first planner to deal explicitly with time, is based on NOAH (Table VI-1-4), with facilities having been added to keep track of event "windows" and durations. Figure VI-5 presents a simplified flow chart of Deviser's core planning component.

Information on current research in planning is given in Robinson (1983).

F. Trends

Automatic Planning is still a difficult task. The current trend is toward the use of knowledge engineering to configure planners as expert systems. Thus, knowledge-based planners are included, and further discussed, in the volume on expert systems.

Another trend is toward increased concern with spatial-temporal planning. This is exemplified by Malik and Binford (1983), Allen and Koomen (1983) and Brooks (1983).

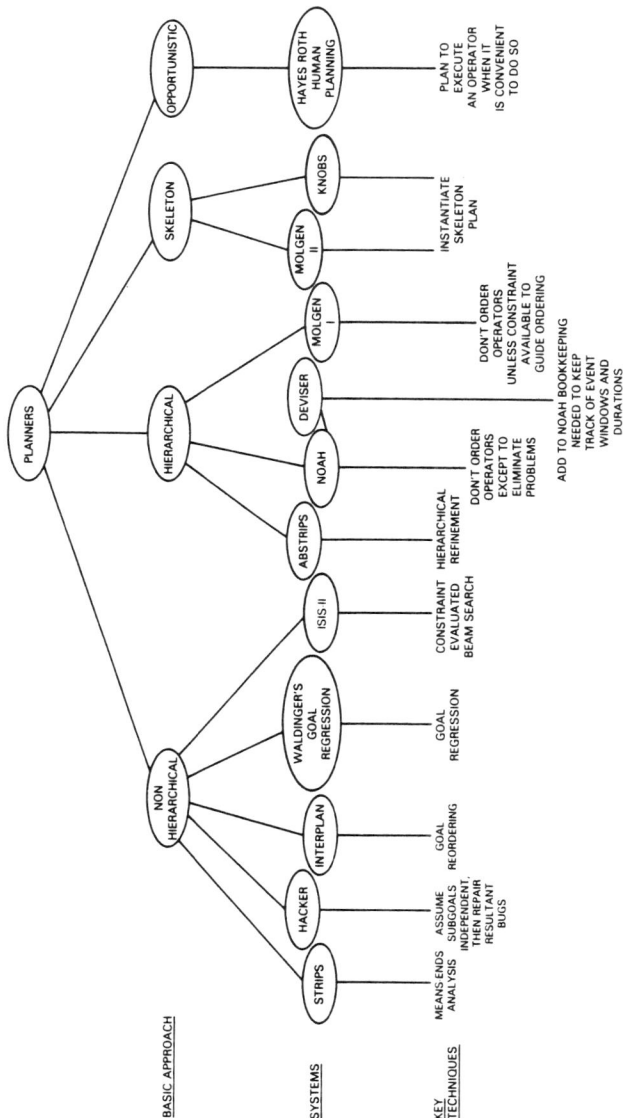

Figure VI-4. Planning Techniques.

TABLE VI-1-1. Planners.

SYSTEM: STRIPS
INSTITUTION: SRI
AUTHORS: Fikes, R.E. and Nilsson, N.J. (1971)

Purpose	Approach	Knowledge Base	Key Elements of Global Data Base (System Status)	Control Structure
• Devises plans for a robot to move objects between rooms.	• Uses Means-Ends analysis (A particular implementation of GPS). • Learns by constructing macro-operators (by saving and generalizing plans).	• Uses a first-order logic representation of facts (world model). • List of problem solving operators, together with their necessary preconditions and the changes they make in the state (what is added and what is deleted from world model when they are applied).	• Goal • Initial state of the system. • Operators used thus far • Current state of the system.	• Means-Ends Analysis • Depth first search using backtracking as required.

TABLE VI-1-2. Planners.

SYSTEM: HACKER
INSTITUTION: M.I.T.
AUTHORS: Sussman, G.J. (1975)

Purpose	Approach	Knowledge Base	Key Elements of Global Data Base	Control Structure
• Skill Acquisition: Devises a skill (set of procedures) to solve a problem. • e.g. plan to reorder blocks to a stack.	• Formulate plans to solve subgoals independently and then patch them up. (e.g., to correct interferences where achieving one subgoal may prevent accomplishment of another). • Solves Problems by: 1) Searching for an appropriate procedure. 2) If procedure does not achieve desired goal, reasons for failure are formalized as bugs. 3) Using library of bug correction procedures, the plan is debugged. • If no procedure is available to solve problem, a new procedure is written using the programming techniques library.	• Answer Library: problem-solving procedures • Knowledge Library: facts about the domain • Programming Techniques Library: to devise new problem-solving procedures • Library of generic bugs • Library of bug correction procedures	• Goals • Procedures used • Bugs	• Search for appropriate procedures to achieve goals and correct bugs. • Write new procedure when no appropriate procedure is found.

TABLE VI-I-3. *Planners.*

SYSTEM: INTERPLAN
INSTITUTION: U. of Edinburgh
AUTHORS: Tate, A. (1975)

Purpose	Approach	Knowledge Base	Key Elements of Global Data Base	Control Structure
Planning in the blocks world, e.g. stacking blocks.	Formulates plans to solve subgoals independently. If achieving one subgoal prevents accomplishment of another and it cannot be repaired with a procedure to achieve its prerequisite (as in HACKER) then it reorders its subgoals. The subgoal at which failure occurs is promoted — moved to an earlier position in the list of subgoals to be achieved.	• Facts about the domain. • Operators to achieve state changes — includes information about preconditions and what changes operators make in world model.	• Goals • Operators used thus far • Interferences noted	• Search for operators to achieve subgoals. • Correct interferences by reordering subgoals.

TABLE VI-1-4. Planners.

SYSTEM: Not Named
INSTITUTION: SRI
AUTHORS: Waldinger, R. (1977)

Purpose	Approach	Knowledge Base	Key Elements of Global Data Base	Control Structure
• Planning • e.g: stack blocks	Construct a plan by solving one conjunctive subgoal at a time. If a subgoal solution interferes with other goals already achieved, rather than reordering the conjunctive subgoals use "goal regression." That is, move the offending subgoal back over previously achieved goals until it finds a place in the plan where the goal will not violate previously achieved goals.	• Facts about the domain • Operators to achieve state changes — together with their preconditions and what changes they make in world model.	• Goals • Operators used thus far • Interferences noted • New subgoals (regressed goals)	• Search for operators to achieve subgoals. • Goal regression

TABLE VI-1-5. *Planners.*

SYSTEM: ABSTRIPS
INSTITUTION: SRI
AUTHORS: Sacerdoti, E. D. (1974)

Purpose	Approach	Knowledge Base	Key Elements of Global Data Base	Control Structure
Devises plans for a robot to move objects between rooms.	Do hierarchical planning by first devising a top level plan based on the key aspects of the problem, then successively refining it by considering less critical aspects of the problem. Recipe: 1. Fix abstraction levels for solutions (plans). 2. Problem solution proceeds top down (most abstract to most specific). 3. Complete solution at one level and then move to next level below.	Criticality assignments of elements in robot planning domain. Configuration of the rooms. Objects and their properties in the domain. Rules for decrementing criticality level. Heuristic search rules for each level.	Goal Initial state of system (criticality at maximum) Plans thus far. Current criticality level	Goal directed (backward chaining at each level). Top down refinement of plans using hierarchical abstract search spaces.

TABLE VI-1-6. *Planners*.

SYSTEM: NOAH
INSTITUTION: SRI
AUTHORS: Sacerdoti, E.D. (1975)

Purpose	Approach	Knowledge Base	Key Elements of Global Data Base	Control Structure
Robot Planning System (assigns an ordering to operators in a plan, e.g., an assembly task)	• Hierarchical planner—develops hierarchy of subgoals by expanding goals. (Lowest level subgoals eventually expanded by problem-solving operators.) • Expands, in parallel, individual plans for interacting subgoals, but initially assigns only a partial ordering to operators. Stops when interference between the partial subgoal plans is observed, and adjusts the ordering of the operators as needed to resolve the interference. • Develops procedural nets to represent plans as they are developed.	• Rules for recognizing interference between plans. • Rules for resolving interferences. • Domain Knowledge —functions that expand goals into subgoals —operators to transform one state to another. Effects of actions are represented explicitly (via add lists and delete lists)	• World Model • Goal • Subgoals • Partial ordering of operators in subgoal plans. • Interference between plans.	• Least commitment. • Backward chaining.

Problem Solving and Planning 169

TABLE VI-1-7. *Planners.*

SYSTEM: MOLGEN I
INSTITUTION: Stanford U.
AUTHORS: Stefik, M.J. (1980)

Purpose	Approach	Knowledge Base	Key Elements of Global Data Base	Control Structure
• Assist molecular geneticists in planning experiments.	• Hierarchical planner using three levels of control —Strategy space: switches between least commitment and heuristic guessing —design space: makes decisions about how plan is to develop (produces goals and constraints). —planning space: contains a hierarchy of operations. Initially plan experiments with abstract operations (merging, amplifying, reacting and sorting) and general objects (gene, organism and plasmel). As specific operators or objects are chosen to replace the abstract ones, constraints are introduced into the plan.	• Explicit meta-level problem-solving operators to reason with constraints. • Problem-solving rules. • Rules for guessing • Rules for discovering interactions between subproblems via constraint propagation. • Domain knowledge	• Goals • Partial solutions • History of guesses and their effects. • Constraints.	Constraint propagation. Least commitment Heuristic guessing Relevant backtracking Use of meta-rules to reason with constraints. Hierarchical refinement. Difference reduction.

TABLE VI-1-7. *Planners. (cont.)*

Purpose	Approach	Key Elements of		
		Knowledge Base	Global Data Base	Control Structure
	• Represent interactions between subproblems as constraints.			
	• Formulate constraints as goals to be solved.			
	• Use constraint propagation to reveal interactions between subproblems.			
	• Suspend problem-solving as necessary, until sufficient information is derived from the interchange of constraints (least commitment, opportunistic expansion).			
	• Use heuristic guessing to make choices when there is otherwise no compelling reason to do so.			
	• Retract guesses as necessary when an unresolvable problem is encountered.			

TABLE VI-1-8. Planners.

SYSTEM: MOLGEN II
INSTITUTION: Stanford U.
AUTHORS: Friedland, P.E. (1979)

Purpose	Approach	Knowledge Base	Key Elements of Global Data Base	Control Structure
Plan molecular genetic experiments	• Start with skeletal plan • Instantiate each of plan steps by a method that will work within the environment of the particular problem. • Plan steps are established by choosing techniques that (in order of priority) satisfy the criteria: 1. It will carry out the specific goal of the step. 2. Be successfully applied to the given molecule. 3. Of the techniques satisfying criteria 1 and 2, it is the best (e.g., with respect to reliability, convenience accuracy, cost, time required).	• Well organized expert domain knowledge—represented using the UNITS package: —skeletal plans classified according to utility. —objective knowledge. —hierarchical organization of about 400 techniques needed to instantiate plans.	• Goal • Skeletal plan chosen • Plan thus far.	• Proceed linearly thru plan matching skeletal steps to techniques by name, synonym, or function, and choosing the most desirable of those that match.

TABLE VI-1-9. Planners.

SYSTEM: DEVISER
INSTITUTION: JPL
AUTHORS: Vere, S. (1983)

Purpose	Approach	Knowledge Base	Key Elements of Global Data Base	Control Structure
General Purpose Automated Planner/Scheduler to generate parallel plans to achieve goals with time constraints. (e.g., Scheduling spacecraft actions during a planetary flyby).	• Backward chaining from unordered subgoals by: 1) Satisfying goals where possible, by linking goal nodes with the same already achieved nodes. 2) If subgoals cannot be met by linking, nodes are expanded in parallel, step by step, into activities which achieve the subgoals. 3) When two parallel expansions produce contradictions, conflicts are resolved by ordering nodes (formerly unordered). 4) If conflicts can't be resolved by ordering, DEVISER backtracks to the last choice point and tries another alternative.	• Rules for recognizing interferences between subgoal expansions. • Rules for reordering subgoal plans to resolve conflicts. • Domain Knowledge: —Operators to transform one state to another. Effects of actions are represented explicitly by add lists and delete lists. —Goal windows and durations —Event schedules	• World Model • Subgoals • Ordering of operators in subgoal plans. • Interferences between subgoal plans. • Node expansion histories. • Current windows.	• Least commitment • Backward chaining • Dynamic maintenance of windows of activities and goals to preserve consistency.

TABLE VI-I-9. Planners. (cont.)

Purpose	Approach	Key Elements of		
		Knowledge Base	Global Data Base	Control Structure
	• A start window for each activity in the plan is updated dynamically during plan generation, in order to maintain consistency with the windows and durations of adjacent goals and activities.			

TABLE VI-1-10. Planners.

SYSTEM: KNOBS
INSTITUTION: MITRE
AUTHORS: Engelman, C. et al. (1980)

Purpose	Approach	Key Elements of		Control Structure
		Knowledge Base	Global Data Base	
Planning Consultant for A.F. Tactical Missions. Other domains include: —Naval "show of flag" missions. —Scheduling of crew activities for the NASA space shuttle.	• Assist a user by interactively accepting mission data and using it to instantiate a stereotypical solution to user's problem—checking input for inconsistencies and oversights. • Represent the stereotypical missions as frames. The checks are constraints among the possible slot values in such frames. • Uses a natural language interface (APE II).	• Targets stored hierarchically in frames —individual targets inherit from generic targets. • Frames representing protypical missions and sub-missions. • Resource data —frames representing static descriptions of object attributes, with inheritances via linkage to more generic frames. • Scripts composed of causally linked chains. • The overall knowledge base network consists of several thousand frames. • Rules for instantiation of frames and slots.	• Target • Airbase from which to fly mission. • Type of Aircraft • Armaments • etc.	• Frame instantiation uses rules and constraints. • Backward chaining of production rules in a MYCIN-like deductive manner to manage such generic choices as aircraft, weapons, support, and electronic countermeasures. • Inference mechanism uses a syntactic pattern matcher with provisions for restrictions on variable instantiations.

Problem Solving and Planning 175

TABLE VI-1-11. Planners.

SYSTEM: ISIS-II
INSTITUTION: CMU
AUTHORS: Fox, Allen & Strom (1982)

Purpose	Approach	Knowledge Base	Key Elements of Global Data Base	Control Structure
Job-Shop Planning/ Scheduling of Parts Production	• Generate schedules by heuristic search using evaluation functions based on constraints associated with costs, process applicability, machine availability, and supervisor preferences. • Set up mechanism to dynamically relax constraints as required. **Sequence for Generating a Schedule** 1. Use constraints to perform a rule-based pre-search analysis to bound search. 2. Do a constraint-directed "beam-search" where only the top-rated "n" partial paths are saved. 3. Perform post-search analysis to determine if search was effective.	• Constraints (and their importance) —Organization goals (associated with profit). —Physical constraints —Gating constraints (preconditions for object applicability or process initiation).	• Preference constraints —queue positions —machine preferences • Partial paths and their evaluations. • Work in progress • Shop status • Goals, due dates, and attributes of parts to be manufactured.	• Pre-search pruning of search space—based on constraints • Beam Search using evaluation functions based on constraints

Problem Solving and Planning 177

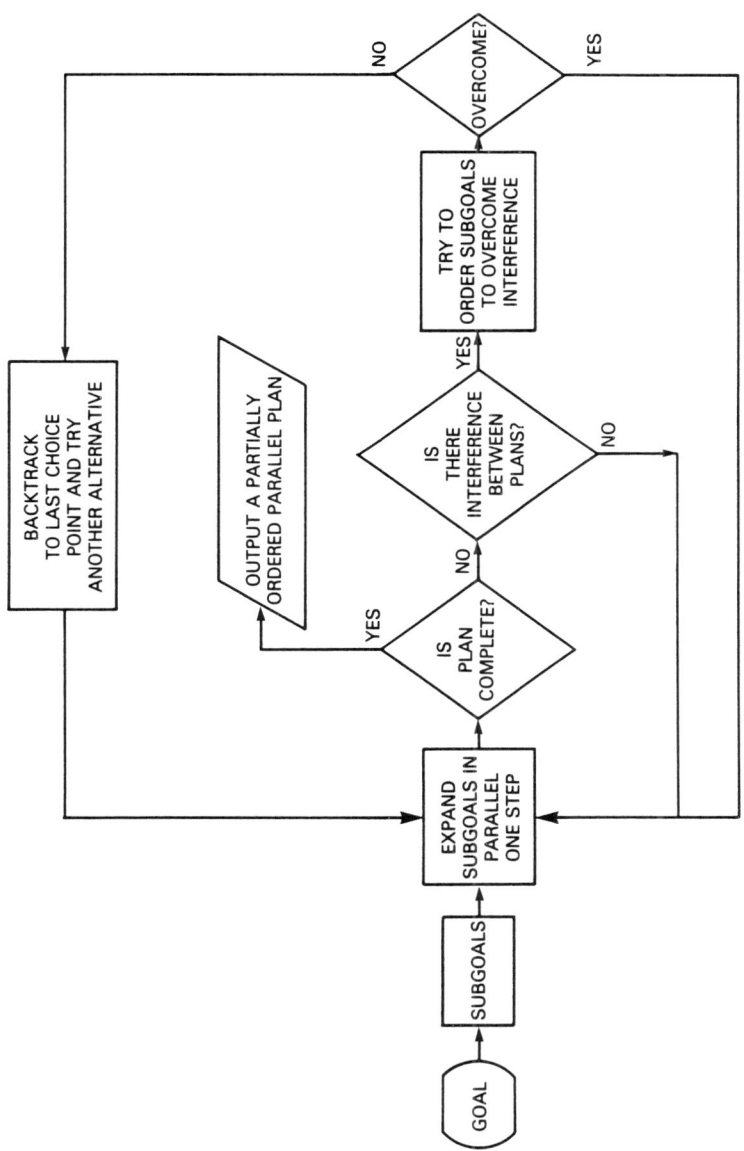

Figure VI-5. Simplified Flow Chart of Deviser's Core Planner.

REFERENCES

- Allen, J. F. and Koomen, J. A., "Planning Using a Temporal World Model," *Proc. of the Eighth International Joint Conference on AI,* Karlsruhe, W. Germany, Aug. 8-12, 1983, Los Altos, CA; W. Kaufmann, 1983, pp 741-747.
- Brooks, R. A., "Find-Path for a PUMA-Class Robot," *Proc. of the National Conference on AI,* Wash, D.C., August 22-26, 1983, Los Altos, CA: W. Kaufmann, 1983, pp 40-44.
- Cohen, P.R. and Feigenbaum, E.A., *The Handbook of Artificial Intelligence,* Vol. III, Los Altos, CA: W. Kaufmann, 1982.
- Engelman, C., Scarl, E. and Berg, C., "Interactive Frame Instantiation," in *Proc. of the First Annual Conference on Artificial Intelligence,* Stanford, 1980.
- Fikes, R.E. and Nilsson, N.J., "STRIPS: A New Approach to the Application of Theorem Proving to Problem Solving," *Artificial Intelligence,* Vol. 2, 1971, pp 189-208.
- Fox, M.S., Allen, B. and Strohm, G., "Job-Shop Scheduling: An Investigation in Constraint-Directed Reasoning," *Proc. Second Annual Nat. Conf. on AI,* Carnegie-Mellon U., August 1982, pp 155-158.
- Friedland, P.E., "Knowledge-Based Experiment Design in Molecular Genetics," Rep. No. 79-771, Computer Science Dept., Stanford U., 1979.
- Hayes Roth, B. and Hayes Roth, F., "Cognitive Processes in Planning," Rep. No. R-2366-ONR, Rand Corp., Santa Monica, CA, 1978.
- Malik, J. and Binford, T. O., "Reasoning in Time and Space," *Proc. of the Eighth International Joint Conference on AI,* Karlsruhe, W. Germany, Aug. 8-12, 1983, Los Altos, CA: W. Kaufmann, 1983, pp 343-345.
- Robinson, A.E., "Research on Planning," *SIGART Newsletter,* No. 83, Jan. 1983, pp 27-36.
- Sacerdoti, E.D., "Planning in a Hierarchy of Abstraction Spaces," *Artificial Intelligence,* Vol. 5, 1974, pp 115-135.
- Sacerdoti, E.D., "A Structure for Plans and Behavior," Tech. Note 109, AI Center, SRI Inter., Menlo Park, CA, 1975.
- Stefik, M.J., "Planning with Constraints," Rep. No. 80-874, Computer Sci. Dept., Stanford U., 1980.
- Sussman, G.J., *A Computer Model of Skill Acquisition,* New York: American Elsevier, 1975.
- Tate, A., "Project Planning Using a Hierarchic Nonlinear Planner," Rep. No. 25, AI Res. Dept., U. of Edinburgh, 1976.
- Vere, S., "Planning in Time: Windows and Durations for Activities and Goals," *Pattern Analysis and Machine Intelligence,* Vol. PAMI-5, No. 3, May 1983, pp. 246-266.
- Waldinger, R., "Achieving Several Goals Simultaneously," In E.W. Elcock and D. Michie (Eds.) *Machine Intelligence 8,* New York: Halstead/Wiley, 1977.
- Wilenksy, R., *Planning and Understanding: A Computational Approach to Human Reasoning,* Reading, MA: Addison-Wesley, 1983.

PART C
BASIC AI TOPICS—
AUTOMATION, SEARCH-ORIENTED PROBLEM SOLVING, KNOWLEDGE REPRESENTATION, COMPUTATIONAL LOGIC

The information in Part C is from *An Overview of Artificial Intelligence and Robotics. Volume I—Artificial Intelligence, Part C—Basic AI Topics,* by William B. Gevarter, Office of Aeronautics and Space Technology, National Aeronautics and Space Administration, October 1983.

ACKNOWLEDGMENTS

I wish to thank the many people and organizations who have contributed to this report, both in providing information, and in reviewing the report and suggesting corrections, modifications and additions. I particularly would like to thank Terry Cronin of the U.S. Army Signal Warfare Lab., Earl Sacerdoti of Machine Intelligence Corporation, Jack Minker of U. of MD, Harry Porta of JPL, Bob Hong and Paul Orlovski at Grumman Aerospace Corp., Jude Franklin and Y.T. Chien of the U.S. Navy Center for Applied Research in AI, Larry Wos of the Argonne Nat. Lab., and David R. Brown of SRI International for their review of portions of this report and their many helpful suggestions. However, the responsibility for any remaining errors or inaccuracies must remain with the author.

I. ARTIFICIAL INTELLIGENCE AND AUTOMATION

A. Mechanization and Automation

To better understand what is meant by Artificial Intelligence (AI) and robotics it is helpful to step back a bit and first look at terms such as mechanization and automation. To do this we will try to synthesize the views of others who have approached this problem.

The original industrial revolution was based on mechanization. Mechanization was the use of machines to take over some of the previous muscle jobs performed by either animals or human beings. Laurie (1979) states:

> When we apply ordinary production techniques — the application of leverage and power — to a process, we are mechanizing it. Automation involves a good deal more...Automated devices are truly automated when feedback information automatically causes the machinery to adjust to reachieve the norm. The internal adjustments of the machine or system are made by servomechanisms (p. 355).
>
> Automation is the achievement of self-directing productive activity as a result of the combination of mechanization and computation...(p. 15).

Peter Marsh (1981, pp. 419-420) elaborates further on mechanized machines, automatic devices and automated devices:

> [The classification of mechanization] depends on whether machines or combinations of animals and people are responsible for the three fundamental elements that occur in every activity (human or otherwise) — power, action and control. [Simple mechanized devices] need a human to control them. If a mechanical device is responsible for control, however, we have a self-acting or automatic device. Automatic devices are not the same as automated ones.... automation equals mechanization plus automatic control plus one (or more) of three extra control features — a "systems" approach, programmability or feedback.
>
> **Extras that make automation**
>
> With a systems approach, factories make parts by passing them through successive stages of a manufacturing process without people intervening. Thus the transfer lines of car factories in the 1930s count as automated systems.
>
> With programmability — the second of the three "extras" that define automation — an automated system can do more than one kind of job. Hence an industrial robot is an automated, not an automatic, device. The computer that controls it can be fed different software to make the machine do different things — for example, spray paint or weld bits of metal together. Finally, [external] feedback makes an automatic machine alter its routine according to changes that take place around it. An automatic lathe with feedback — in which, for instance, a sensor detects that the metal it is cutting is wrongly shaped and so instructs the machine to stop — is thus an automated device. It is clearly more useful than a lathe without this feature.

B. Tools, Machines, Teleoperators, Robots

To extend the concepts of mechanization and automation further, we will consider tools, machines, teleoperators and robots. To do this, we will utilize Marsh's (1981) basic elements — power, action and control.

Tool: A device used to perform an action. If used by a human, the person provides the power and control.

Machine: A device that utilizes non-human power to do an action. For a simple machine the human provides the control.

Teleoperator: A machine capable of action at a distance under the control of a human.

Robot: A flexible machine capable of controlling its own actions for a variety of tasks utilizing stored programs. Basic task flexibility is achieved by its capability of being reprogrammed. More advanced—intelligent—robots would be capable of setting their own goals, planning their own actions and correcting for variations in their environment.

C. Computation and Artificial Intelligence

Laurie (1979, p. 15) defines a computer as "...an electronic device capable of following an intellectual map. We call the map a program." Arden (1980, p. 9) suggests that "...computer science is the study of the design, analysis, and execution of algorithms* in order to better understand and extend the applicability of computer systems."

Though everyone agrees that "Artificial Intelligence" (AI) is difficult to define precisely, the most commonly accepted definition is that "Artificial Intelligence is the branch of computer science devoted to programming computers to carry out tasks that if carried out by human beings would require intelligence."

A slightly different definition is giving by Duda et al. (1979, p. 728):

> Artificial Intelligence (AI) is the subfield of computer science concerned with the use of computers in tasks that are normally considered to require knowledge, perception, reasoning, learning, understanding and similar cognitive abilities. Thus, the goal of AI is a qualitative expansion of computer capabilities.

Nilsson (1980, p. 2) notes that:

> AI has also embraced the larger scientific goal of constructing an information-processing theory of intelligence. If such a science of intelligence could be developed, it would guide the design of intelligent machines as well as explicate intelligent behavior as it occurs in humans and other animals. Since the development of such a general theory is still very much a goal, rather than an accomplishment of AI, we limit our attention here to those principles that are relevant to the engineering goal of building intelligent machines.

More recently, Nilsson (1981/1982) indicated that he would like to narrow the working definition of AI even further to the central processes of intelligence. He thus states:

> With regard to humans, I am inclined to consider as *central* those cognitive processes that are involved in reasoning and planning. Work on automatic methods of deduction, commonsense reasoning, plan synthesis, and natural-language understanding and generation are examples of AI research on central processes.
>
> Perhaps as important as the processes themselves is the "knowledge" they manipulate. In fact, the subject of knowledge representation formalisms is a good starting point for a more detailed explanation of just what I think AI is.

Arden (1980, pp. 22 and 23) states:

> Though "intelligent behavior" is difficult to define, and is currently understood differently by different people, there has been some convergence of views within the AI community as the technical requirements for the computer solution of certain classes of problems becomes better understood. To be sure, the human solution of a complex equation might be classified as intelligent behavior, while the corresponding action by a machine might not be so classified, even though both machine and man had been programmed for (learn) the process. One possible requirement is that there be something unstructured, something nondeterministic, for the solution process to qualify as intelligent. Another is that it depends on the knowledge that must be used in obtaining the solution, or on the methods used...
>
> Another important aspect is the use of heuristic rules** of the kind humans use to solve problems. Although, in general, such rules cannot be proved effective, they often lead to solutions. Some computer scientists argue that heuristic programming better describes the field now called "artificial intelligence."

---

*The Dictionary of Electronics, *(Fort Worth: Radio Shack, 1975) defines algorithm as, "A set of rules or processes for solving a problem in a finite number of steps."*

**Heuristics are "rules-of-thumb" (compiled experience) used to help guide problem solving. They do not guarantee a solution as algorithms do.*

Hayes-Roth (1981, p. 1) notes that:

> AI provides techniques for flexible, non-numerical problem-solving. These techniques include symbolic information processing, heuristic programming, knowledge representation, and automated reasoning. No other fields or alternative technologies exist with comparable capabilities. And nearly all complicated problems require most of these techniques. Many forces combine to identify AI as the central technology for exploitation. Systems that reason and choose appropriate courses of action can be faster, cheaper, and more effective and viable than rigid ones. To make such choices in realistically complex situations, the system needs at least rudimentary understanding of mundane phenomena.

In summary, AI is concerned with intelligent behavior, primarily with non-numeric processes that involve complexity, uncertainty and ambiguity and for which known algorithmic solutions do not usually exist. Unlike conventional computer programming, it is knowledge based, almost invariably involves search, and uses heuristics to guide the solution process.*

Thus AI can be considered to be built upon

1. Knowledge of the domain of interest.
2. Methods for operating on the knowledge.
3. Control structures for choosing the appropriate methods and modifying the data base (system status) as required. This contrasts with conventional computer programs which utilize known algorithms for solution, are primarily numeric (number crunching) in nature rather than symbolic manipulation, and in general do not require knowledge to guide the solution.

D. Relationship of AI to Automation

Artificial Intelligence may be considered to be the top layer of control on the hierarchical road to autonomous machines. This is illustrated in Figure I-1, derived from Marsh (1981).

However, AI includes a large area of activity which is not normally included in automation, e.g.:

natural language processing
perception and pattern recognition
intelligent information storage and retrieval
game playing
automatic programming
computational logic
problem solving
expert systems

Nevertheless, as Computer Integrated Manufacturing and intelligent robots emerge, AI will have a major role to play. AI contributions to perception and object-oriented programming are reviewed by Brady (1984) for this new breed of robots.

E. AI and Other Fields

Duda, et al. (1978, pp. 729-730) state:

> Historically, AI has both borrowed from and contributed to other closely related disciplines concerned with advanced methods for information processing. Thus, links exist between AI and aspects of such theoretical areas as mathematical logic, operations research, decision theory, information theory, pattern recognition and mathematical linguistics. In addition, research in AI has stimulated important developments in software technology, particularly in the area of advanced programming languages. What distinguishes AI from these related fields, however, is its central concern with all of the mechanisms of intelligence.

---

*As AI matures, the expectations associated with it are increasing. Schank (1983) states that it is time to demand learning capability from AI programs. He thus suggests a new definition: "AI is the science of endowing programs with the ability to change themselves for the better as a result of their own experiences."

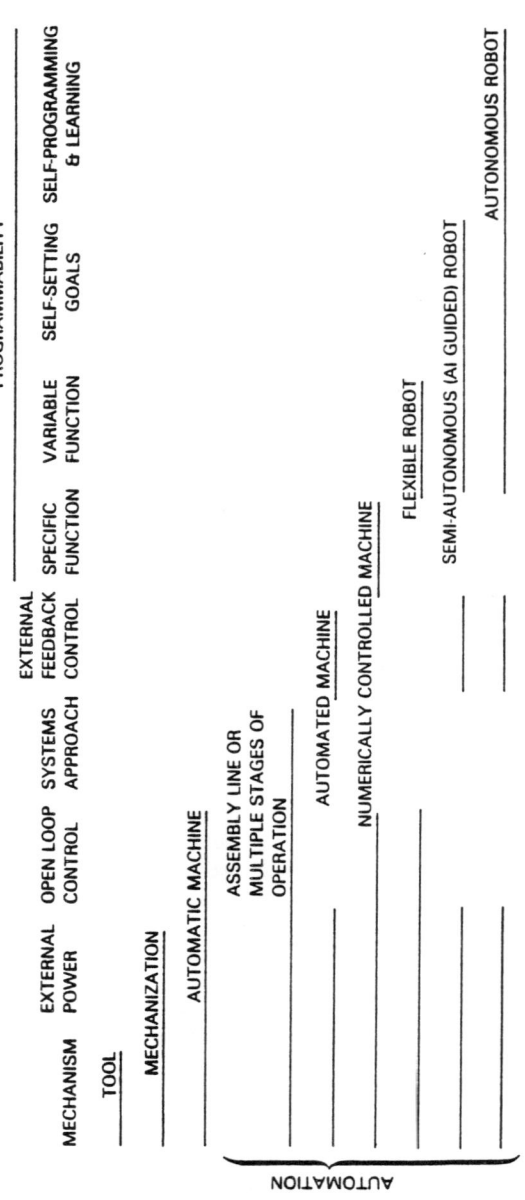

Figure 1-1. *Mechanization, Automation and Artificial Intelligence*

Newell, et al. (1978, pp. 19-20), in referring to AI as Machine Intelligence (MI), note that:

> The aims of research in MI are so broad — nothing less than extending the capabilities of symbol processing machines for intelligent action — that it is not always easy to identify applications as emanating specifically from research in this field.
>
> Consider the important contributions that MI has already made. List processing has become an integral part of programming technology. The abstract theory of programming owes much of its early impetus to LISP. The initiation of verification of programs is likewise due strongly to work in machine intelligence. This is also true of the subfield of symbolic mathematics. Even some of the concepts of structured programming can be traced back to early MI languages — concepts of extensive hierarchization and recursion, for instance. Similarly, fundamental ideas of heuristic search are used widely in operations research programs for domains where powerful optimization techniques are unavailable or inadequate. Heuristic search is especially necessary today for handling large combinatorial problems, such as job-shop scheduling.
>
> As these examples illustrate, MI applications are characterized by helping to initiate fields of application and then becoming freely mixed with independent invention and development from within the field. For example, in operations research, branch-and-bound techniques for limiting search (analogous to alpha-beta procedures in game trees) and optimal scheduling algorithms came not from MI, but from within operations research. Structured programming and symbolic mathematics have run essentially independent courses from work in MI. An extreme example of this "initiation" syndrome in MI applications was the strong effect of MI on the initiation of time sharing, but with little specific technical transfer.
>
> The reported MI research has some ties to specific areas of applications as we note below. However, its ultimate fate is likely to be similar to the examples above, in which most of the applications will not be identified as MI. For instance, work on control structures is of fundamental significance to future applications. Every intelligent system must employ a control structure capable of using partial knowledge, discovering relevant knowledge, coping with pervasive error, etc. But as we discover effective system organizations, they will become assimilated into the application area, their further development being seen as part of the application. Similarly, progress in heuristic search, being of general utility, will diffuse through various applications fields.

Barrow (1979, p. 3) agrees, stating:

> It is probably safe to say that AI seeks to understand and model virtually all human intellectual activity. In doing so, it has drawn from or contributed to many other disciplines, particularly psychology, mathematical linguistics, mathematical logic, operations research, decision theory, pattern recognition, and computer science. It has stimulated important developments in software technology, especially concerning advanced programming languages and systems.

It is interesting to note that no mention is made of an intersection of control theory and AI. As control theory has primarily dealt with analog or numeric computation in relation to servomechanisms, and AI has primarily dealt with symbolic manipulation, this lack of intersection is not too surprising. However, this situation is beginning to change. DeJong (1983) examines the role of AI in control, and Sauers and Walsh (1983) indicate requirements and architectures for future expert systems that can operate in the real-time environment associated with control. A technique for coordinating control and knowledge-based components for an autonomous mobile robot guidance system is proposed by Harmon (1983).

Saridis (1979) lays out a taxonomy of increasingly sophisticated control systems on the path to intelligent controls. The furthest point on the path he identified as AI. Based on Saridis, Figure I-2 indicates the increasing level of sophistication in control.

Saridis (1979, p. 1129) states that, "Intelligent controls should represent the perfect interface between control hardware and a digital computer for higher level decision making according to the principle of increasing intelligence with decreasing precision in a hierarchical control structure." To state it another way, AI can provide the topmost level in a control structure. "Such systems, implemented by the fast large modern digital computer, can solve problems, identify objects, or plan a strategy for a complicated function of a system" (Saridis, 1979, p. 1129).

186   Artificial Intelligence

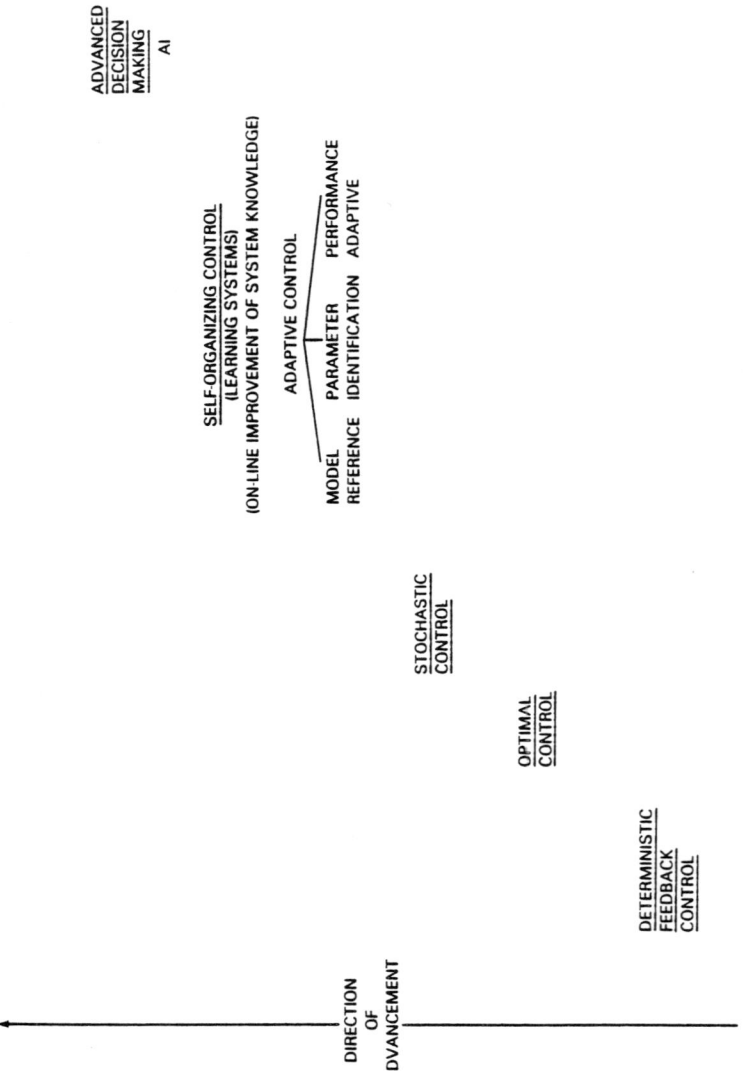

Figure 1-2. Increasing Sophistication on the Path to Intelligent Controls

Albus, et al. (1981, 1983) have developed a theory of hierarchical control that can exhibit learning and thereby provide learned reflex responses to complex situations. It also provides for the problem-solving and planning functions that are normally associated with the highest level of intelligent action that is considered to be the domain of AI, and incorporates expert system rules for error correction at the intermediate levels of the control hierarchy. It therefore appears that AI will not only be a key to the development of intelligent robots and factories of the future, but is destined to become a central ingredient in advanced control systems as well.

REFERENCES

- Albus, J.S., et al., "Theory and Practice of Hierarchical Control," *Proceedings of the Twenty-third IEEE Computer Society International Conference,* Sept. 1981, pp. 18-39.
- Albus, J.S., McLean, C.R., Barbera, A.J. and Fitzgerald, M.L., "Hierarchical Control for Robots in an Automated Factory," *Proc. of 13th Inter. Symp. on Industrial Robots and Robot 7,* Chicago, IL, April 17-21, 1983, pp. 13-29 to 13-43.
- Arden, B.W. (Ed.), *What Can Be Automated,* Cambridge: MIT Press, 1980.
- Barrow, H., "Artificial Intelligence: State-of-the Art," Menlo Park: SRI Intl. Technical Note 198, October 1979.
- Brady, M., "Artificial Intelligence and Robotics," To be published in *Artificial Intelligence,* M. Brady and L. Gerhardt (Eds.), New York: Springer Verlag, 1984.
- DeJong, K., "Intelligent Control: Integrating AI and Control Theory," *Proc. IEEE Trends and Applications 1983,* Gaithersburg, MD, May 25-26, 1983.
- Duda, R.O., et al., "State of Technology in Artificial Intelligence," in *Research Directions in Software Technology,* Wenger, P. (Ed.), Cambridge: MIT Press, 1979, pp. 729-749.
- Graham, N., *Artificial Intelligence,* Blue Ridge Summit, PA: Tab Books, 1979.
- Harmon, S.Y., "Coordination Between Control and Knowledge Based Systems for Autonomous Vehicle Guidance," *Proc of IEEE Trends and Applications 1983,* Gaithersburg, MD, May 25-26, 1983, pp. 8-11.
- Hayes-Roth, F., "AI: The New Wave—A Technical Tutorial for R&D Management," Santa Monica, Rand Corp., 1981 (AIAA-81-0827).
- Laurie, E.J., *Computers, Automation and Society,* Homewood, IL: R.D. Irwin, Inc., 1979.
- Marsh, P., "The Mechanization of Mankind," *New Scientist,* 12 February 1981, pp. 418-421.
- Newell, A., et al., "Research in Information Processing," Pittsburgh: Carnegie-Mellon Univ., AD/A-064 845, Final Report, December 1978.
- Nilsson, N.J., *Principles of Artificial Intelligence,* Palo Alto: Tioga Publishing Co., 1980.
- Nilsson, N.J., "Artificial Intelligence: Engineering Science, or Slogan," *AI Magazine,* Vol. 3, No. 1, Winter 1981/1982 pp. 2-9.
- Sardis, G.N., "Toward the Realization of Intelligent Controls," *Proc. of the IEEE,* Vol. 67, No. 8, Aug. 1979, pp. 1115-1132.
- Sauers, R. and Walsh, R., "On Requirements of Future Expert Systems," *Proc. of the 8th Inter. Joint Conf. on AI: IJCAI-83,* 8-12 Aug 1983, Karlsruhe, W. Germany. Los Altos, CA: W. Kaufmann, 1983.
- Schank, R.C., "The Current State of AI: One Man's Opinion," *AI Magazine,* Vol. 4, No. 1, Winter-Spring 1983, pp. 3-8.

II. SEARCH-ORIENTED AUTOMATED PROBLEM SOLVING AND PLANNING TECHNIQUES

This chapter provides an overview of search-oriented automated problem solving and planning techniques. It endeavors to present the basic approaches to automated problem-solving at a level where the concepts involved can be readily understood. It also provides an indication of the state of the art and current and future research.

A. AI as Problem Solving

One way of viewing intelligent behavior is as problem-solving. Many AI tasks can naturally be viewed this way, and most AI programs draw much of their strength from their problem-solving components. AI applications that have strong problem-solving components include scene analysis, natural language understanding, theorem proving, task planning, expert systems, game playing, and information retrieval and extraction.

Two important types of problem solving tasks are 1) synthesizing a set of actions (a plan) to achieve a goal and 2) deduction. The latter involves deducing (or inferring) conclusions from data or a given set of propositions (applications include theorem proving and information retrieval). In this chapter we will restrict ourselves to action synthesis, leaving a review of deduction for Chapter IV.

Many tasks can be formulated in terms of: given a goal, how do we achieve it? If direct methods are not available for solution, as is the usual case in AI problems, then a search procedure to select from the various possible alternatives is required. Thus, finding efficient search methods is one of the central issues in automated problem solving.

B. Elements of a Problem Solver

All problems have certain common aspects: an initial situation, a goal (desired situation) and certain operators (procedures or generalized actions) that can be used for changing situations. In solving the problem, a control strategy is used to apply the operators to the situations to try to achieve the goal. This is illustrated in Figure II-1, where we observe a control strategy operating on the procedures to generate a sequence of actions (called a plan) to transform the initial conditions in the situation into the goal conditions. Normally, there are also constraints and preconditions (conditions necessary for a specific procedure to be applied) which must be satisfied in generating a solution. In the process of trying to generate a plan, it is necessary for the problem solver to keep track of the actions tried and the effects of these actions on the system state. Figure II-2 is a restatement of Figure II-1 in which we can view the operators as manipulating the data base (representing the problem status) to change the current situation (system state).

C. State Graphs as an Aid to Problem Representation

One easy way to focus on the relationships between the operators and the states is through the use of state graphs. State graphs are networks made up of points (called nodes) connected by lines (called arcs). For our purposes, we let nodes correspond to system states and arcs correspond to operators. Figure II-3 illustrates a state graph for a simple problem (such as finding the simplest route from city A to city D). Note that there are several sequences (of different lengths) that will achieve goal state D, as well as a dead-end F.

The various paths through a state graph can be represented, as shown in Figure II-4, as a hierarchical structure called a tree. The solution paths run from the initial state along the branches and terminate on the leaves (terminal nodes) labelled "goal state." We could have also generated a tree of paths starting from the goal state, as shown in Figure II-5. From Figures II-4 or II-5, it is apparent that the plan with the smallest sequence is to first use operator R, then operator S.

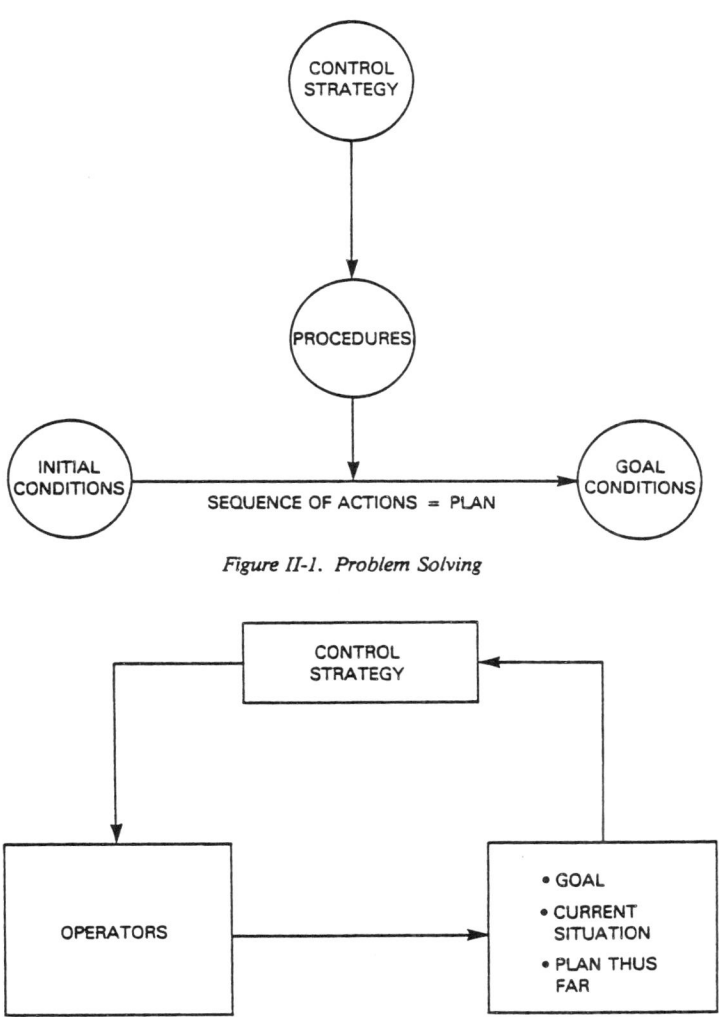

Figure II-1. Problem Solving

Figure II-2. Automated Problem Solving Relationships

190   Artificial Intelligence

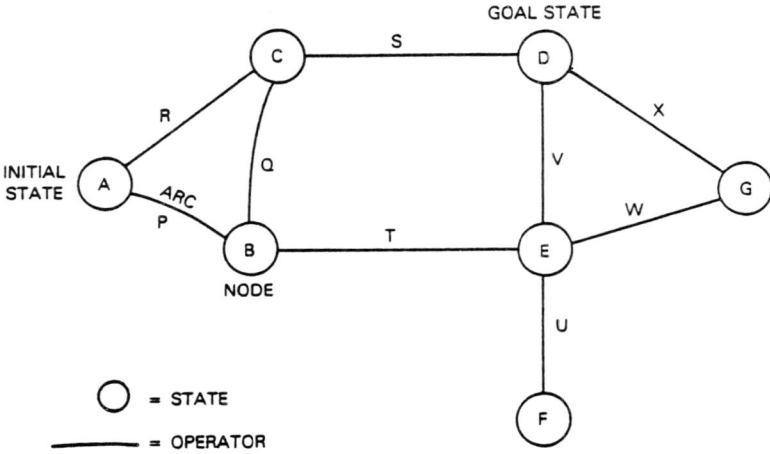

Figure II-3. State Graph for a Simple Problem

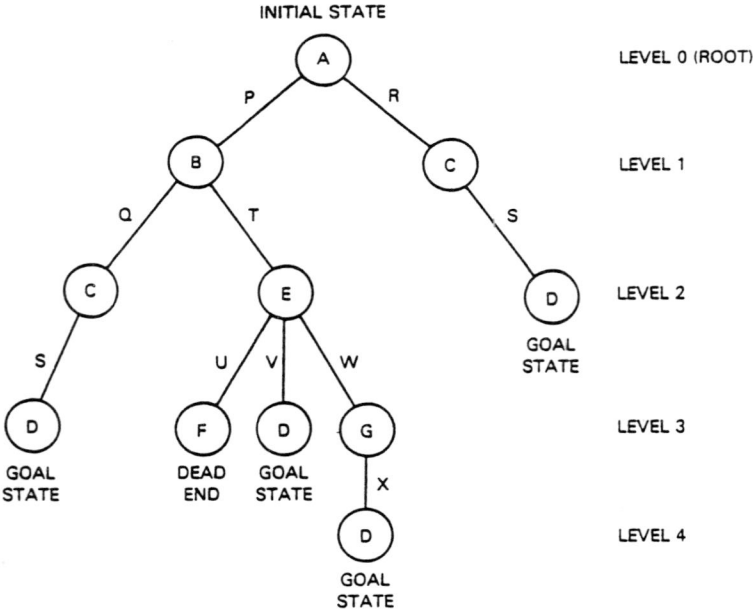

Figure II-4. Tree Representation of Paths Thru the State Graph of Figure II-3

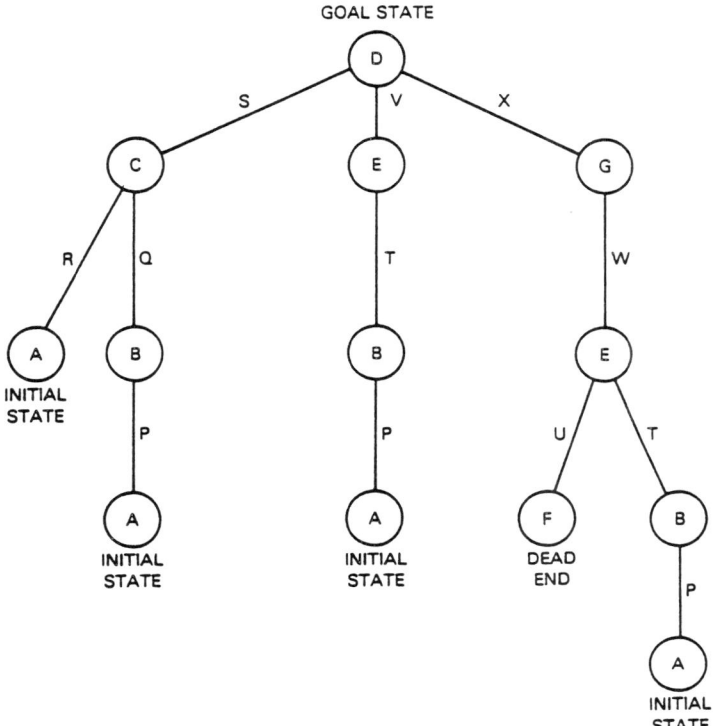

Figure II-5. Working Backwards from the Goal State

For a large complex problem, it is obviously too cumbersome to explicitly draw such trees of all the possibilities and directly examine them for the best solution. Thus, the tree is usually implicit; the computer generating branches and nodes as it searches for a solution.

D. Reasoning Forward and Backward

In searching for a solution we may reason forward from the initial state, as in Figure II-4, or we may reason backward from the goal, as in Figure II-5 (or both). Forward reasoning is said to be data driven or bottom-up. Backward reasoning is said to be goal-directed or top-down.

E. Problem Solving Using Blind Search

If a procedure for successfully generating a solution in a reasonable time (an algorithm) is known, it is applied and the problem is solved. Unfortunately, for many important problems no such algorithm is known and a search procedure is required.

For fairly simple problems, a straightforward, but time-consuming, approach is blind search, where we select some ordering scheme for the search and apply it until the answer is found.

The search proceeds by successively generating and examining the branches emanating from the nodes, starting with the root node and proceeding along generated branches to new nodes. The search tree grows as operators are applied to the nodes and the various paths explored. A node is referred to as "open" if branches have not yet been generated from it.

As indicated in Figure II-4, each node can be assigned a level. The root node is at level 0, its immediate successors at level 1, and so on, with the level number being referred to as the depth.

1. Breadth-First Search

In this approach, the nodes of the search tree are generated and examined level by level starting from the root node. No nodes at a deeper level are examined until all nodes at the previous level have been explored. Breadth-first search always finds the shortest number of steps to the goal. (However, this may not be the most desirable or cheapest solution, because of the different costs associated with applying the various operators. See following discussion on heuristic search.)

2. Depth-First Search

As a search proceeds, new nodes are generated from the node currently being examined. These successor nodes are called children and the generating node is called the parent. A depth-first search is one which always continues in the parent-to-child direction until forced to backtrack. To prevent consideration of paths that are too long, a depth bound is often specified.

A depth-first search does not necessarily find the shortest solution, but often can be programmed to minimize memory requirements by only saving in memory the path currently being explored.

3. Backward Chaining

Backward chaining is a name given to depth-first, backward reasoning—an important search strategy. An operator is chosen that would achieve the goal if selected. If it is applicable in the initial state, it is applied and a solution has been found. If not, operators that would achieve the preconditions required for its applicability are sought and the search continues recursively until a sequence of operators are found that transform the initial state into the goal state. If the search fails, the program backtracks and a new candidate operator is selected that would achieve the goal if applied, and the process is repeated.

For problems requiring only a small amount of search, backward chaining strategies are often perfectly adequate and efficient. For larger problems, it is critical that the correct operator be chosen first almost always, because this strategy follows out a line of action fully before rejecting it, which can result in very lengthy searches.

4. Problem Reduction

A generalization of backward chaining is problem reduction. Very often to satisfy a goal, several subproblems (conjuncts) must be satisfied simultaneously. For this case of backward reasoning, applying an operator may divide the problem into a set of subproblems, each of which may be significantly simpler to solve than the original problem.

A good example of problem reduction is readying a space vehicle for launch, as indicated in Figure II-6. Note that we can represent the goal—spacecraft ready to launch—as a conjunction of subgoals, e.g., spacecraft fueled, all systems checked, power on. These in turn can consist either of a set of simultaneous ("AND") subgoals, or of one of several acceptable alternatives ("OR" subgoals). The AND subgoals are denoted on the graph by horizontal arcs connecting the lines leading to them.

Search-Oriented Automated Problem Solving and Planning Techniques   193

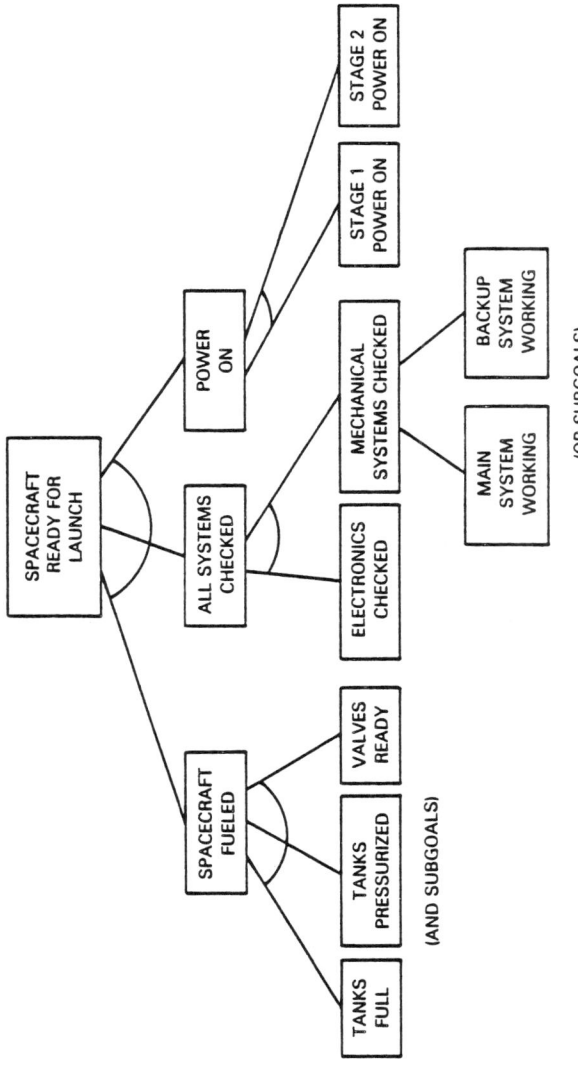

Figure II-6. Simplified AND/OR Graph for Readying a Spacecraft for Launch

Problem reduction often runs into difficulties without specific problem knowledge, as there is otherwise no good reason to attack one interacting conjunct before another. Lack of such knowledge may lead to an extensive search for a sequence of actions that tries to achieve subgoals in an unachievable order.

F. Heuristic State-Space Search

Blind search does not make any use of knowledge about the problem to guide the search. In complex problems, such searches often fail, being overwhelmed by the combinatorial explosion of possible paths. If on the average there are n possible operators that can be applied to a node, then the size of the search space tends to grow as n^d, where d is the depth to be searched. Heuristic methods have been designed to limit the search space by using information about the nature and structure of the problem domain. Heuristics are rules of thumb, techniques or knowledge that can be used to help guide search. Heuristic search is one of the key contributions of AI to efficient problem solving. It operates by generating and testing intermediate states along a potential solution path.

One straightforward method for choosing paths by this approach is to apply an evaluation function to each node generated, and then pursue those paths that have the least total expected cost. Thus, we can calculate the cost from the root to the particular node that we are examining and, using heuristics, estimate the cost from that node to the goal. Adding the two, produces the total estimated cost along the path, and therefore serves as a guide as to whether to proceed from that node or to continue from another, more promising, node among those thus far examined.

Nilsson (1980) and Barr and Feigenbaum (1981) describe the "A* algorithm," which is guaranteed (under appropriate conditions) to find a solution path of minimal cost if any solution path exists. The A* algorithm uses an evaluation function for the n-th node of:

$$f^*(n) = g^*(n) + h^*(n)$$

where $g^*(n)$ estimates the minimum path cost from the start node of the tree to node n and $h^*(n)$ estimates the minimum cost from node n to the goal. For the A* algorithm to find the minimum cost path, the heuristic estimate of $h^*(n)$ of the cost from node n to the goal, must be non-negative and less than the actual cost $h(n)$. An example $h^*(n)$ for our problem of Figure II-3 (whose paths are represented by the tree in Figure II-4) would be the straight line (airline) distance from node n to the goal.

Though the A* algorithm produces a minimum cost path, it does not usually minimize the search effort, in fact usually producing an exponential running time for the search. If one leans more to minimizing the search effort rather than the solution cost, one would put more emphasis on $h^*(n)$, the estimate of the remaining cost to the goal, rather than on $g^*(n)$ the cost from the start node. Barr and Feigenbaum (1981) describe various approaches to this tradeoff of speed versus solution quality, and indicate that a considerable reduction in running time is possible if the optimal solution requirement is relaxed.

G. Game Tree Search

1. Representation

Most games played by AI computer programs involve two players making alternate moves. A game representation must thus take into account the opponent's possible moves as well as the player's own moves. The usual representation is a game tree, which shares many features with a problem reduction representation. A complete game tree is a representation of all possible plays of such a game.

The root node is the initial state, in which it is the first player's (A's) turn to move. The successors of the root node are the states that A can reach in one move. The successors of these nodes are the states resulting from the other player's (B's) possible replies; etc. At each play, the players must take into account all the opponent's possible responsive moves. This can be represented by an AND/OR tree. Figure II-7 is an example of such a tree from the standpoint of player A, who is to move next. Drawn

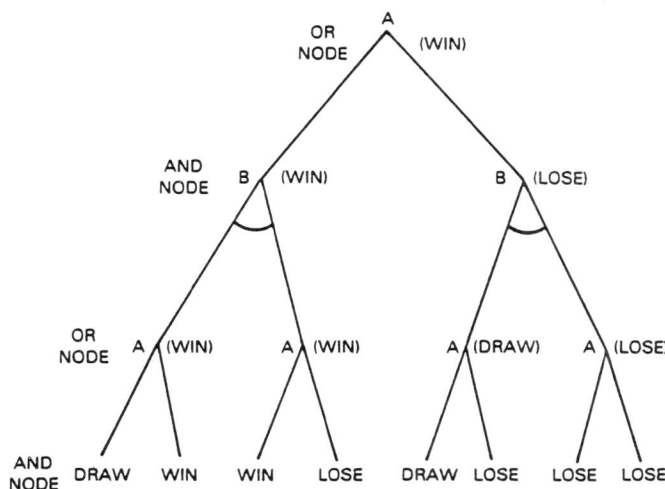

Figure II-7. A Game Tree Drawn from A's Point of View, A's Move

from point A's point of view, A's possible moves under his control are represented by lines leading to AND nodes. These successor nodes are called AND nodes since they control sets of moves all of which A must be able to respond to. A's nodes are called OR nodes, because A can choose any of the moves emanating from these nodes.

2. The Minimax Search Procedure

The minimax procedure is a strategy for playing a two-person game. According to the minimax technique, player A should move to the position of maximum value to him, B responding by choosing a move of minimum value to player A. Given the values of the terminal positions (see Figure II-7), the value (shown in parentheses) of a nonterminal position to player A is computed by backing up from the terminals as follows:

- The value of an OR node is the maximum value of any of its successors.
- The value of an AND node is the minimum value of any of its successors.

3. Searching a Partial Game Tree

For most games, the tree of possibilities is much too large to be generated fully or searched backward for an optimal move. Thus a reasonable portion of the tree is generated starting from the current position, a move is made on the basis of partial knowledge, the opponent reply found, and the procedure recursively repeated from the new position. The minimax procedure thus starts with an estimate of the tip nodes thus far generated, and assigns backed-up values to the ancestors (e.g., values in parentheses in Figure II-7). The value estimates for the tip nodes are generated using a "static evaluation function" based on heuristics.

To reduce the number of nodes that need to be examined, various pruning techniques have been devised, "Alpha-Beta" (see, e.g., Marsland, 1983) being the best known. All these techniques are based on keeping track of backed-up values so that branches that cannot lead to better solutions need not be further explored.

4. Heuristics in Game Tree Search

A "static evaluation function" is one that estimates a board position without looking at any of the positions' successors. The function is usually a linear polynomial whose variables represent various features of the position. For chess, the features of importance include remaining pieces, king safety, center control and pawn structure.

5. Other Considerations

Alternatives to search in choosing moves include opening or end game "book" moves, and recognizing patterns on the board and associating appropriate playing methods with each pattern. The most successful game-playing programs thus far, have made search, rather than knowledge, their main ingredient. Various combinations of more extensive use of specific game knowledge to prune less desirable paths, and increased look-ahead have been utilized in chess in efforts to improve program success.

H. Difference Reduction ("Means-Ends" Analysis) — Another Basic Approach

The difference reduction approach differs from pure search (which usually starts with either the goals or the initial conditions) by instead progressively nibbling away at the problem to reduce the differences between the initial and goal status. Difference reduction was introduced by the General Problem Solver (GPS) Program developed by Newell, Shaw and Simon beginning in 1957 (Ernst and Newell, 1969). This was the first program to separate its general problem-solving method from knowledge specific to the current problem.

Figure II-8 is a simplified flow diagram of the difference reduction approach. The analysis first determines the difference between the initial and goal states and selects the particular operator that would most reduce the difference. If this operator is applicable in the initial state, it is applied and a new current state is created. The difference between this new current state and the goal state is then calculated and the best operator to reduce this difference is selected. The process proceeds until a sequence of operators is determined that transforms the initial state into the goal state.

If at any point, the operator chosen cannot be applied in the current state, a new intermediate goal state is established that is the precondition for the chosen operator to be applied. The difference between the current state and this new intermediate goal state is then used as before. If the new intermediate goal cannot be achieved, a new operator is chosen to reduce the initial difference and the problem proceeds recursively until a solution is achieved.

The difference reduction approach assumes that the differences between a current state and a desired state can be defined and the operators can be classified according to the kinds of differences they can reduce. If the initial and goal states differ by a small number of features and operators are available for individually manipulating each feature, then difference reduction works. However, there is no inherent way in this approach to generate the ideas necessary to plan complex solutions to difficult problems.

I. More Efficient Tactics for Problem Solving

For more efficient problem solving than the methods described above, it is necessary to devise techniques to guide the search by making better use of initial knowledge about the problem or of the information that can be discovered or learned about the problem as the problem solver proceeds through the search. These techniques are reviewed in the Non-Deductive Problem Solving Approaches Section of Chapter III of Part A of this volume.

J. Future Directions for Research

Sacerdoti (1979) suggests the following lines of research as being especially important for the future.

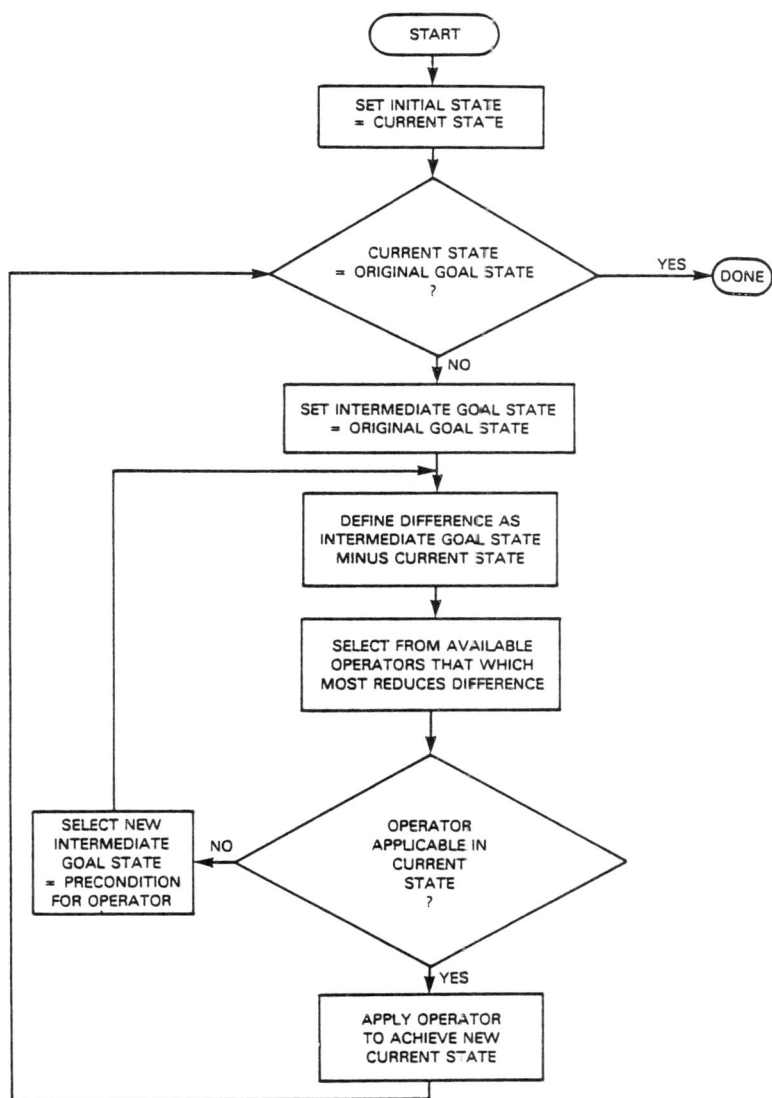

Figure II-8. Simplified Flow Diagram of the Difference Reduction Approach

1. Integrating a Significant Number of Tactics

This approach, if successful, could result in a very powerful problem solver, particularly where hierarchical planning provides the framework and all the other techniques can be applied at each level of planning in the hierarchy. (Some of the more complex expert systems have taken such an approach.)

2. Flexible Control Structure

In the real world, unexpected events occur frequently, so it is often more appropriate to only rough out a plan, creating only its critical components in detail. Then, when the plan is executed, detailed plans can be developed using real world feedback.

3. Planning for Parallel Execution

It appears that problem solvers that distribute plan generation and execution tasks will be one of the major waves of the future. Pseudo-reduction tactics create plans that are partially ordered with respect to time. Therefore they share with hierarchical plan structures the virtue of being particularly amenable to planning in parallel by multiple problem solvers and to execution in parallel by multiple effectors.

4. Partial Goal Fulfillment

Thus far, problem solvers have been designed to fully satisfy their goals. However, in the real world, full goal satisfaction during execution is often impossible. Thus it becomes important to be able to prioritize goals and plan for their partial satisfaction. (This is further explored in Part B, Chapter VI on Problem Solving and Planning.)

5. Feedback of Lessons Learned from Plan Execution to Plan Generation

Lessons learned from plan execution can be extremely valuable for future plan generation. Therefore focussing on integrated systems for plan generation, execution and repair may be one of the best approaches to advancing the state of the art. Particularly, developing catalogs of successful plan generation tactics can be valuable in dealing with complex, interactive environments which have been beyond our capability thus far.

K. Current Research

Table II-1 presents an indication of current research activities in search-oriented automatic problem solving and planning techniques. A more detailed view of current research in this area is provided by the Special Issue on Search and Heuristics of the *Artificial Intelligence Journal* (Pearl, 1983).

L. Current State of the Art

Real, complex problems tend to have the characteristic that their search space tends to expand exponentially with the number of parameters involved. This "NP Complete" type of problem still is out of bounds for searches that do not have powerful heuristics to guide them. Chess has been one indicator of the state of the art in problem solving emphasizing search (though computer capability has been an equally important factor). Berliner (1981) reports that 1981 chess programs (emphasizing look-ahead) had reached an expertise of 2300 points compared with roughly 2500 points for the best human experts.

Current problem solvers emphasizing search have thus far succeeded only in solving elementary or toy problems, or very well structured problems such as games. Thus, the AI community's emphasis has shifted toward expert systems (Duda, 1981) as problem solvers, where the emphasis is on knowledge rather than search.* In addition, there are trends toward distributed problem solving systems and toward interactive problem solving systems where humans make the major decisions and the computer program offers choices and works out the details.

---

* *Even in chess, there is beginning to be an emphasis on knowledge as evidenced by the CHUNKER Program (Campbell and Berliner, 1983) where the incorporation of knowledge about patterns of chess positions drastically reduces search requirements in appropriate situations.*

TABLE II-1. Examples of Current and Recent Research in Search-Oriented Problem Solving Techniques

Technique	Program	Institute	Researcher	Funding
Heuristic Search	Heuristic Search Theory	UCLA	J. Pearl	NSF
	Efficiency in Backtracking	Indiana Univ.	C.A. Brown P.W. Purdom	NSF
	Blockhead	U. of CA Irvine	D. Kibler P. Morris	NOSC
	B Algorithm for Heuristic Search	Hungarian Academy of Science	L. Mero	
	DELTA-MIN for Backtracking	CMU	J. Carbonell	ONR
Constraint Satisfaction and Relaxation Algorithms	Invasion Procedure	UBC	R. Seidel	
Multiple Agent Planning Systems	Distributed AI	SRI	K. Konolige N.J. Nilsson	ONR
Multi-Agent Planning	Synchronization of Multi-Agent Plans	Stanford U.	J.S. Rosenchein	ONR
Parallel Search	Algorithm for Parallel Processing in Heuristic Search	MIT	W.A. Kornfeld	
	Parallel Search Efficiency	Several Canadian Researchers		
Minimax Game Tree Search	Algorithm for Games with Chance Events	Duke	B.W. Ballard	AFOSR
Game Playing Algorithms	SSS* Minimax Algorithm	U. of MD	L. Kanal V. Kumar	NSF
	Brute Force Intelligence SNAC Optimum Search	CMU	H.J. Berliner	ARPA
Branch and Bound	General Formulation	U. of MD	D. Nau et al.	NSF
Analytical Evaluation of Search Methods	Unified Approach	Indiana U.	P.W. Purdom & C.A. Brown	NSF
Generalization of Bayes Rule	A Distributed Hierarchical Approach	UCLA	J. Pearl	NSF
Coordinated Multiple Blackboard Global Data Bases	Unifying Data-Directed and Goal-Directed Control in a Multi-Level Cooperating Knowledge Source Problem Solver	U. of MA	D.D. Corkill V. Lesser	NSF
Distributed Problem Solving	Meta-Level Control	U. of MA	V. Lesser et al.	NSF ARPA
Other	KAMP Planning System Using Procedural Network	SRI	D.E. Appelt	ARPA

M. Forecast

It is expected that within the next five years, the increased speed and capability of computers and the ability to do parallel searches could have as much effect on search performance as new search methods. However, as search usually grows exponentially with depth, heuristics to restrict the paths to be searched will also be of continuing importance. It is also expected that techniques to combine shallow and deep reasoning (e.g., non-monitonic reasoning, causality, first principles, theorem proving) will be major contributors to limiting and guiding search.

Schank (1983) states that "...search is one of the key AI problems. However,...the approaches to search have been inadequate. Searching massive amounts of information requires not efficient algorithms but representations that obviate the need for these algorithms." (Knowledge representation is the subject of the next chapter.)

REFERENCES

- Arden, B.W. (Ed.), *What Can Be Automated*, Cambridge: MIT Press, 1980.
- Barr, A. and Feigenbaum, E.A., *The Handbook of Artificial Intelligence*, Vol. 1, Los Altos, CA: William Kaufman, Inc., 1981.
- Berliner, H.J., "An Examination of Brute Force Intelligence," *Proceedings of the Seventh International Conference on Artificial Intelligence*, August 1981, pp. 581-587.
- Campbell, M. and Berliner, H., "A Chess Program That Chunks," *Proc. of the Nat. Conf. on AI: AAAI-83*, Wash, D.C., August 22-26, 1983, pp. 49-53.
- Duda, R.O., "Knowledge-Based Expert Systems Come of Age," *Byte*, Vol. 6, No. 9, Sept. 1981, pp. 238-281.
- Duda, R.O., "State of Technology in Artificial Intelligence," *Research Directions in Software Technology*, Wegner, P. (Ed.), Cambridge: MIT Press, 1979, pp. 729-749.
- Ernst, G. and Newell, A., *GPS: A Case Study in Generality and Problem Solving*, New York: Academic Press, 1969.
- Graham, N., *Artificial Intelligence*, Blue Ridge Summit, PA: Tab Books, 1979.
- Hayes-Roth, F., "AI: The New Wave—A Technical Tutorial for R&D Management," AIAA-81-0827, Santa Monica, CA: Rand Corp., 1981.
- Marsland, T. A., "Relative Efficiency of Alpha-Beta Implementations," *Proc. of the Eighth Inter. Joint Conf. on AI: IJCAI-83*, Karlsruhe, W. Germany, 8–12 Aug 1983, Los Altos, CA: W. Kaufmann, 1983, pp. 763-766.
- Nilsson, N.J., *Principles of Artificial Intelligence*, Palo Alto: Tioga Publishing Co., 1980.
- Pearl, J. (Ed.), Special Issue on Search and Heuristics, *Artificial Intelligence*, Vol. 21, Nos. 1, 2, March 1983.
- Sacerdoti, E.D., "Problem Solving Tactics," *AI Magazine*, Vol. 2, No. 1.
- Schank, R.C., "The Current State of AI: One Man's Opinion," *The AI Magazine*, Vol. IV, No. 1, Winter/Spring 1983.

III. KNOWLEDGE REPRESENTATION

A. Introduction

Artificial Intelligence views knowledge as the key to high-performance intelligent systems. Thus the representation and management of knowledge is a central topic in AI today.

Newell (1981) defines knowledge as the information used by intelligent agents (human or machine) to make rational decisions.* Further, Newell states that "knowledge is not just a collection of symbolic expressions plus some static organization; it requires both processes and data structures." Thus knowledge representation consists of a system for providing access to a body of knowledge—a data structure for representation in memory and a means (the computational process) for accessing that knowledge.

Structure and access are thus intertwined, with ideally a representation being chosen that simplifies access to the knowledge for the particular task at hand. Thus, a variety of knowledge representations exist, arising from the search for the most useful representation for the class of problems for which they have been devised.

Myopolis (1981, p. 5) states that, "the basic problem of knowledge representation is the development of a sufficiently precise notation for representing knowledge." To this must be added the requirement for efficiency and rapid access.

For the purpose of knowledge representation (KR), Myopolis treats a knowledge base as a model of a world/enterprise/slice of reality. The Heuristic Programming Project (1980, pp. 5-6) indicates that the knowledge base (KB) of AI programs contains both factual knowledge of the task at hand and heuristic knowledge representing the tacit judgmental knowledge comprising domain expertise, and often meta-knowledge of how to solve problems efficiently and effectively.

B. Purpose

The purpose of knowledge representation is to organize the information required into a form such that the AI program can readily access it for making decisions, planning, recognizing objects and situations, analyzing scenes, drawing conclusions, and other cognitive functions. Thus knowledge representation is especially central to "expert systems," "computational vision," and "natural language understanding."

C. Techniques

Representation schemes** are classically classified into declarative and procedural ones. Declarative refers to representation of facts and assertions, while procedural refers to actions, or what to do. It is virtually impossible to come up with a pure system of either type as ultimately both assertions and what to do with or about them are involved in the data structures and the access mechanism in any knowledge representation.

A further subdivision for declarative (object oriented) schemes includes relational (semantic network) schemes and logical schemes.

The principal KR schemes are briefly discussed in the following paragraphs and summarized in Tables III-1.

---

*More precisely, Newell (1981, p. 20) defines knowledge as "Whatever can be ascribed to an agent, such that its behavior can be computed according to the principle of rationality."

**The discussion of KR techniques given in this section is based primarily on Myopolis (1981), Barr and Feigenbaum (1981, pp. 141-222) and Graham (1979, pp. 188-208).

1. Logical Representation Schemes

The principal method for representing a knowledge base logically is to employ first order predicate logic. In this approach, a knowledge base (KB) can be viewed as a collection of logical formulas which provides a partial description of the world. Modifications to the KB results from additions or deletions of logical formulas.

Examples of logical representations are:

IN(SHUTTLE, ORBIT) = The shuttle is in orbit.

$\forall(x)$. EXTRA-TERRESTRIAL BODY$(x) \rightarrow$ POSSESSES $(x,$ NO KNOWN LIFE$)$

= For all x, where x is an extra-terrestrial body, x possesses no known life. Or more simply, all extra-terrestrial bodies have no known life.

Logical representations are easy to understand and have available sets of inference rules needed to operate upon them. Table III-1a summarizes the various aspects of logical KR's.

2. Semantic Networks

A semantic network is an approach to describing the properties and relations of objects, events, concepts, situations or actions by a directed graph consisting of nodes and labelled edges (arcs connecting nodes). Because of their naturalness, semantic networks are very popular in AI.

In a semantic net, the program can start at a node of interest and follow arcs to related nodes, and in turn follow arcs to still more distant nodes. This approach is very natural—being reminiscent of human thinking. However, the multiplicity of pathways, as we go further from the starting node, makes it easy to get lost in the maze, unless a strong organizing or guiding principle is used (such as the "beam-search" approach employed by the HARPY speech-understanding system).

The various aspects of semantic networks are summarized in Table III-1b.

3. Procedural Representations and Production Systems

In procedural representations, knowledge about the world is contained in procedures—small programs that know how to do specific things (how to proceed in well specified situations). Classification of procedural representation approaches are based on the choice of activation mechanisms for the procedures, and the forms used for the control structures.

The two common approaches consist of procedures representing major chunks of knowledge—subroutines (see Table III-1c)—and more modular procedures, such as used in PLANNER (Hewlitt, 1972) and the currently popular production rules. The common activation mechanism for procedures is matching of the preconditions needed for the procedure to be invoked. In PLANNER, this is referred to as "pattern directed procedure invocation." The main difference between PLANNER and the more recent "production rules" is that PLANNER's elemental procedures (called theorems) can communicate directly with each other, while the communication between production rules is only by modification of the pattern in the Global Data Base (GDB) for the individual production rules to observe.

Production rules (PR) are characterized by a format of the type:

> Pattern, Action
> If, Then
> Antecedent, Consequent
> Situation, Procedure

A PR system consists of a knowledge base (KB) of rules, a global data base (GDB) which represents the system status, and a rule interpreter (control structure) for choosing the rules to execute. In a simple production rule system, the rules are tried in order and executed if they match the pattern in the GDB.

TABLE III-1a. Knowledge Representation Schemes
First Order Predicate Logic

Nature of KB	Representation & Applications	Advantages	Disadvantages
A collection of logical formulas which provides a partial description of the world. Modifications of KB occur by the introduction/deletion of logical formulas.	Using quantifiers and logical connectives, one can make a statement about objects, properties, situations and relationships. *Example*: All people have heads = $\forall(x)$. PERSON $(x) \rightarrow$ HAS (x, HEAD)	Simplicity of notation — descriptions are readily understandable. Natural, precise, flexible, modular. Availability of well-understood formal semantics. Each fact need be represented only once. Availability of inference rules for proof procedures. Derivation of new facts from old can be mechanized using automated versions of theorem-proving techniques.	Difficulty in representing procedural and heuristic knowledge. Lack of organizational principles makes a large KB difficult to manage. Weak manipulation (proof) procedures. When the number of facts becomes large, there is a combinatorial explosion in the possibilities of which rules to apply at each step of the proof.

Knowledge Representation 203

TABLE III-1b. *Knowledge Representation Schemes*
Semantic Nets

Nature of KB	Representation	Advantages	Disadvantages
A world described by a collection of nodes representing objects, concepts, events, situations or actions, and arcs or links (binary associations or labeled edges) in a directed labeled graph. Modifications to this network KB occur through the insertion/deletion of objects and the manipulation of associations.	A directed labelled graph that naturally links objects in a relational way: *Example:* [Diagram: SHUTTLE —IS-A→ SPACECRAFT —IS-A→ MAN MADE OBJECT; SPACECRAFT —HAS PART→ BOOSTER ROCKETS —SUBSET OF→ MAN MADE OBJECT; SHUTTLE —ELEMENT OF→ NASA; ASTRONAUT —ELEMENT OF→ NASA; JACK LOUSMA —IS-A→ ASTRONAUT; SHUTTLE —OPERATED BY→ JACK LOUSMA] *Uses:* • Domains where much of the reasoning is based on a very complicated taxonomy. • Domains where it is necessary to represent properties-of or relations-between objects, events, situations, or actions. (Very popular in AI)	Important associations can be made explicitly and succinctly. Relevant facts can be inferred from the nodes to which they are directly linked without a search thru a large data base. Can use ISA and SUBSET links to establish a property inheritance hierarchy in the net. Easy to make deductions about inheritance hierarchies. Can establish states and actions in terms of a small no. of primitive concepts. (Trend towards network schemes with a fixed no. of primitive association types, which have well-defined semantics, and are descriptively adequate)	Inferences drawn by manipulation of the net are not assuredly valid. No standard terminology or conventions about meaning. The interpretation (semantics) depends solely upon the program that manipulates the network. A strong organizing principle is needed to guide search thru the maze. Difficult to represent Boolean relationships other than disjunction.

TABLE III-Ic. Knowledge Representation Schemes
Procedural — Subroutines

Nature of KB	Representation	Advantages	Disadvantages
The KB is a collection of procedures. Modification of KB by addition/subtraction, or modification of subroutines or their access conditions.	Knowledge about the world is contained in procedures — small programs that know how to do specific things, how to proceed in well-defined situations. Control information is inherent in the way one states the facts. *Example*: A subroutine is called when a certain situation occurs.	• Facility for representing heuristic knowledge. • Ability to perform extended-logical inferences like default reasoning. • May have advantages for modeling. • Sometimes much easier to keep track of changes and side effects as the procedure that performs the action can update the data base immediately. • Can do reasoning thru simulation.	• Difficult to verify or change — as knowledge is implicit in procedures. • Control information gets in the way, limiting alternative approaches.

However, in more complex systems, such as used in expert systems, a very complex control structure (see, e.g., Gevarter, 1982) may be used to decide which group of PR's to examine, and which to execute from the PR's (in the group) that match patterns in the GDB. In general, these control structures work in a repetitive cycle of the form:

1. Find the conflict set (the set of rules which match some data in the GDB).
2. Choose a rule from among the conflict set.
3. Execute the rule, modifying the GDB.

Because of their modular representation of knowledge and their easy expansion and modifiability, PR's are now probably the most popular AI knowledge representation, being chosen for most expert systems.

Table III-1d summarizes the central aspects associated with production rule systems.

4. Analogical or Direct Representations

In many instances it is appropriate to use natural representations such as an array of brightness values for an image, or a further reduced sketch map of the scene delineations in a computer vision system. This "homomorphism" (structural similarity) is evident in the use of maps, geometric models, etc. These direct representations are analogous to some properties of the situation being represented.

These natural representations are useful in computational vision, spatial planning, geometric reasoning and navigation. One even notices analogical aspects in musical notation where the rise and fall of the musical frequency is apparent in the representation of the notes in the score.

This form of representation has the advantages of being easy to understand, simple to update, and often allows important properties to be directly observed, so that they don't have to be inferred. A direct or analogous representation can usually be more exhaustive and specific, making for more efficient problem solving. It also can facilitate search and working with constraints. However, this form of representation is clumsy for some tasks, particularly when generalization is needed.

Table III-1e summarizes the attributes of direct representation.

5. Property Lists

One approach to describing the state of the world is to associate with each object a property list; that is a list of all those properties of the object pertinent to the state description. The state and therefore the object properties can be updated when a situation is changed.

Table III-1f briefly indicates the attributes of such a representation.

6. Frames and Scripts

Humans are able to handle with relative ease a large variety of circumstances in everyday life because to a great extent our days are filled with a series of stereotyped situations such as going to work, eating, shopping, etc.

Minsky (1975) conceived of "frames," which are complex data structures for representing stereotyped situations. A frame has slots for objects and relations that would be appropriate to the situation. Attached to each frame is information such as:

— how to use the frame
— what to do if something unexpected happens
— default values for slots.

Frames can also include procedural as well as declarative information. Frames facilitate expectation-driven processing—reasoning based on seeking confirmation of expectations by filling in the slots. Frames organize knowledge in a way that directs attention and facilitates recall and inference.

*TABLE III-1d. Knowledge Representation Schemes
Procedural — Production Systems (PS)*

Nature of KB	Representation	Advantages	Disadvantages
The KB is a collection of loosely coupled production rules (PRs) representing knowledge about the world.	A PS can be represented as:	Modular: Provides a high granularity of information (facts and rules).	Hard to maintain modularity (non-overlap) between rules in large systems.
| These PR's may be organized into sets, called knowledge sources (KS), for particular uses. | ```
      ┌────┐
      │ RI │
      └────┘
        ↑↓
      ┌────┐      INPUT
      │ KB │ ←── GDB ←── DATA
      └────┘
``` | Information can be easily added, removed or updated. | Constraining interactions between rules can lead to inefficiencies. |
| In addition, a global data base (GDB) is used in PS's to represent the system status, and a control structure (rule interpreter, RI) is used to select the rules to activate and execute. | The PR's take the form:

Situation → Action
Antecedent → Consequent
If → Then

PR Example:

If the Shuttle doors fail to automatically close when actuated, and the fault cannot be discovered.

Then disengage motors and close doors manually.

Uses:

• Knowledge about what to do in a specific situation (Expert Systems)

• Domains where:

—the current task is a sequence of transitions from one state to another
—knowledge is diffuse (e.g., medicine)
—knowledge can be easily separated from the manner in which it is used.
—processing can be represented by a set of independent actions | Naturalness.

Facility for representing heuristic knowledge, particularly domain-specific information that might permit more directed deduction processes.

Easy to keep track of changes due to actions.

Useful as a mechanism for controlling the interaction between statements of declarative and procedural knowledge. | Inefficiency of program execution.

Hard to follow the flow of control in problem-solving.

Poor separation of knowledge and control when:
(1) chunks of knowledge are large.
(2) dealing with basically sequential information.

PR's are pure associations, and therefore don't provide substantive explanations. Knowledge about structure is represented in PRs only implicitly.

PR's not too well suited to often-needed structural and causal models.

Problems with consistency and completeness. |

Knowledge Representation 207
```

TABLE III-1e. Knowledge Representation Schemes
Direct or Analogical Representations

Nature of KB	Representation	Advantages	Disadvantages
The knowledge base is a collection of natural representations such as maps, images and geometric models. Modifications to KB occur by updating, adding to or removing representations.	The approach is to use a representation that is analogous with respect to some properties of the situation being represented. The representation is used by direct observation of the information desired such as adjacency, linkages, size, shape, constraints, etc. *Examples* Maps Line Drawings Geometric models.	• Natural representation — readily understandable. • Easy to update. • Important properties often directly observable, so don't have to be inferred. • Usually more exhaustive and specific — making for more efficient problem solving. • Facilitates search and working with constraints.	• Clumsy for some tasks. • May be inappropriate when generalization is needed.

TABLE III-1f. Knowledge Representation Schemes
Property Lists

Nature of KB	Representation	Advantages	Disadvantages
• Lists of properties of objects • KB modified by addition and/or subtraction of properties as appropriate to the state of the system.	State of world is described by obects in the world and lists of their pertinent properties. A property is an attribute-value pair. *Example:* List for a Robot: Attribute / Value in State 1. / Value in State 2. Location / Room A / Room B Holds / Box / Ball On / Floor / Chair Erect / True / False	• All appropriate properties for object grouped into a list. Program need not search a huge DB to find properties of object. • Lists are a natural structure in the LISP programming language.	• Difficult to carry out inferential operations.

An example of a frame is:

Airplane Frame:
Specialization of: Aerospace vehicle
Types:
   range: (fighter, transport, trainer, bomber, light plane, observation)
Manufacturer:
   range: (McDonnell-Douglas, Boeing....)
Empty Weight:
   range: (500 lbs to 250,000 lbs)
Gross Weight:
   range: (500 lbs to 500,000 lbs)
   if needed: (1.6 × empty weight)
Name:
   if needed: (Choose name satisfying type and manufacturer)
Max Cruising Range:
   if needed: (Look up in table cruising range appropriate to type and gross weight)
Number of Cockpit Crew:
   range: (1 to 3)
   default: 2

Scripts are frame-like structures designed for representing stereotyped sequences of events such as eating at a restaurant or a newspaper report of an apartment fire.

Table III-1g summarizes the central aspects of frame representations.

7. Semantic Primitives:

For any knowledge representation scheme it is necessary to define an associated vocabulary. For semantic nets, there has been a real attempt to reduce the relations to a minimum number of terms (semantic primitives) that are non-overlapping. A similar effort has emerged for natural language understanding.

A natural language is an attempt to describe all of the world's aspects important to humans. Unfortunately, as these languages evolved naturally, rather than being scientifically ordained, a great deal of ambiguity has entered the languages, such that the meaning is often dependent on context and background knowledge. Several attempts have been made to describe all of the world's aspects in terms of primitives that are unique, unambiguous representations into which natural language statements can be converted for later translation into another language or for other cognitive actions.

Wilks (1977) has proposed a system designed to be used for language translation. His system is centered around a dictionary for distinguishing among the various senses of the words that can appear in the input text. Definitions in the dictionary are defined in terms of some 80 semantic primitives grouped into the following five classes:

Class	Example Primitives
Entities	man, stuff, part
Actions	cause, be, flow
Cases	to, in
Qualifiers	good, much
Type Indicator	now, kind

TABLE III-Ig. Knowledge Representation Schemes
Frames and Scripts

Nature of KB	Representation	Advantages	Disadvantages

An organized collection of frames.	• A frame is a complex data structure representing a stereotyped situation.
	
	• A frame has slots for:
	  — objects
	  — relations
	
	• Attached to each frame is information such as:
	  — how to use frame
	  — what to do if something unexpected happens
	  — default values of slots
	  — procedures if needed
	
	• Scripts are frame-like structures for representing stereotyped sequences of events
	
	Uses
	
	Stereotyped events and situations such as eating out, identifying standardized manufactured devices, scene analysis, writing stereotyped newspaper reports, analyzing stories, natural language understanding, standardized plans, etc.
		• Facilitates expectation-driven processing.
		
		• Can be designed to determine its own applicability in a given situation, or to suggest other frames if appropriate.
		
		• Organizes knowledge in a way that directs attention and facilitates recall and inference.
			• Many real situations depart considerably from prototypes.
			
			• New situations not easily accommodated.

The completed representation of a text is in terms of semantic formulas constructed from the primitives. For example:

"Some spacecraft sprout large antennas".

```
                              agent ←——→ action ←——→ object
Entities or actions:       [spacecraft]←——→[sprout]←——→[antennas]
                                ↑                          ↑
Qualifiers:                  [some]                      [large]
```

where the terms in square brackets would be replaced by semantic formulas representing their appropriate sense.

Wilks has also incorporated inference rules and other structures to assist in clarification and organization of the resulting text representation.

Schank (see, e.g., Schank and Riesbeck, 1981) has developed a "conceptual dependency" theory as an attempt to provide a representation of all actions in terms of a small number of primitives. Schank's goal is broader than language translation, the representation being task-independent so as to be applicable to inferring, paraphrasing and answering questions as well.

Schank's primitives are intended to be unambiguous and unique. The system relies on 11 primitive physical, instrumental and mental ACTs (propel, grasp, P trans, A trans, speak, attend, etc.), plus several other categories, or concept types.

Detailed rules are provided in conceptual dependency for combining the elements into representations or meaning. There are two basic kinds of combinations or conceptualizations. One involves an actor doing a primitive ACT; the other involves an object and a description of its state. Attached to each primitive act is a set of inferences that could be associated with it.

More recently, Schank has added clarifying elements in terms of goals, scripts, plans, themes and social acts, designed to provide additional meaning, purpose and context to the representations.

An example of a representation in conceptual dependency is:

Armstrong flew to the moon.

Actor:	Armstrong
Action:	flew
Direction to:	the moon
From:	Unknown

The use of semantic primitives allows propositions to be stored in canonical (standardized) form, with resultant computational advantages for many uses.

D. Representation Languages

A number of programming languages have been designed to facilitate knowledge representation. Table III-2 lists some of the more popular ones.

It will be observed that usually one form of knowledge representation (such as production rules or frames) is chosen as central to the language, though some (such as UNITS) provide for multiple representations.

TABLE III-2. Programming Tools Facilitating Knowledge Representation

Tools	Organization	Nature
OPS 5	CMU	A programming language, built on top of LISP, designed to facilitate the use of production rules.
ROSIE	Rand	A general rule-based programming language that can be used to develop large knowledge bases. Translates near-English into INTERLISP.
UNITS	Stanford U.	A knowledge representation language and interactive knowledge acquisition system. The language provides both for "frame" structures and production rules.
KRL	Xerox PARC	Knowledge representation language developed to explore frame-based processing
SAM	Yale	A system of computer programs to analyze scripts.
FRL	MIT	A frame representation language that provides a hierarchical knowledge base format consisting of frames whose slots carry comments, default values, constraints, and procedures that are activated when the value of the slot is needed.
KL-ONE	BBN	A uniform language for representation of natural language conceptual information, based on the idea of structured inheritance networks. Networks use epistemological primitives as links.
NETL	CMU	A comprehensive, domain independent, knowledge-base system. It uses a parallel intersection technique for searching rapidly through large bodies of knowledge.
DAWN	DEC	A general programming and system description language with automated help procedures.
OWL	MIT	A semantic network knowledge representation language for use in natural language question answering and for building expert systems.
FRAIL	Brown U.	A KR language that combines predicate calculus with frame representation for use in natural language understanding.

E. State of the Art

Though production rules have emerged as the dominant KR for expert systems, and semantic networks for image understanding, KR is still in a state of flux with many researchers, various representations, and no clear general understanding of which representations are most appropriate for which problems. As a result, KR research is one of the most active areas in AI today.

F. Issues

SIGART's (1980) "Special Issue on Knowledge Representation," indicates that there are many areas of concern (pp. 114-115). Virtually every aspect of KR still is an issue. A few of these issues are:

1. First Order Predicate Logic (FOPL) as a Standard of Representation.

    Many researchers such as Kowalski (p. 44) feel that FOPL is the only language suitable for KR—whether declarative or procedural. Correspondingly Kowalski maintains there is only one intelligent way to process information—and that is by applying deductive inference methods.

    Others such as Sloman (p. 48) declare that there is "No such thing as an ideal representational formalism...No one formula is equally adequate for all things for all purposes...No doubt all knowledge representation can be embedded in predicate calculus, but this may be of little practical importance."

Zadeh (p. 48) observes that most human knowledge is imprecise in nature. Therefore two valued logic and associated representation techniques are not appropriate—fuzzy logic being necessary.

2. How to provide everyday context and common-sense know-how in representations? Drefus (p. 42) observes that the background context continually varies, while rule behavior tends to assume "everything else being equal."

3. Need to consider representations in a broader sense, such as holograms which can be used to process information, but is not a data structure.

4. Hobbs (pp. 43-44) declares that, "Standard practice in the representation of knowledge is the scandal of AI...Ninety percent of what is done in the representation of knowledge is reinvention, most frequently in predicate calculus." There is a multitude of items for similar aspects. "The consequence is a jungle of incomparable results."

In this regard Newell (1981) observes in regard to the SIGART KR survey that, "The main result was overwhelming diversity—a veritable jungle of opinions. There is no consensus on any question of substance."

5. Doyle (p. 41) declares that there is a need to consider intention, action, purposive communication and the processes of problem solving in KR. Also needed are systems which are self-referent (both to descriptions and parts and to belief systems). Better KR's for learning processes and belief revision also need to be developed.

6. Need to clarify which KR's are best for which purposes.

7. How do we find the most appropriate representation for given problems?

8. Problem of selecting the appropriate level of abstraction for a problem—scope and grain size (Davis, 1982).

9. KR's that facilitate knowledge acquisition.

10. Designing KB's to facilitate updating—modularity.

11. Need for multiple representations for different aspects (or at different stages of problem solving) of the same problem.

12. Problem of incompleteness inherent in all KR's.

13. Understandability—transparency.

14. Lack of a theory of KR.

15. How to represent knowledge so as to enable AI programs to behave as if they knew something about the problems they solve.

16. How best to choose a representation to provide the greatest efficiency in deductive reasoning (Moore, 1982).

G. Some Research Needs:

1. Standardization of nomenclature and techniques
2. Methods of matching representations to problems
3. Methods to handle imprecise knowledge

4. Methods to evaluate efficiency of representation
5. Need to be able to conveniently represent intentions, beliefs, etc. in representations.
6. Methods to provide self-knowledge in representations.
7. Methods for quantification—the ability to specify properties of arbitrarily defined sets.
8. Representation methods for people's beliefs.
9. Representations of processes that consist of sequenced actions over time.
10. Representations for complex and amorphous shapes.
11. Techniques for indexing into a large data base of models.

H. Who Is Doing It

Review of SIGART's (1980) "Special Issue on Knowledge Representation" indicates that the following are the principal organizations involved in KR research.

1. Universities

Stanford University
University of Hamburg (West Germany)
CMU
Simon Fraser University (Canada)
University of Paris
University of Pittsburgh
MIT
Yale
University of Toronto (Canada)
University of Maryland
SUNY, Buffalo
University of Ottawa (Canada)
Rutgers University
University of Amsterdam (Netherlands)
University of Essex (England)
University of California (Berkeley)
N. Dakota State University

2. Other

IBM
DEC
SRI
BBN

I. Future Directions

The knowledge representation field has begun to exhibit some structure—rule-based systems predominating in Expert Systems, but network representations also being important. For image understanding systems, direct representations (such as line sketches) are common, with network representations being widely employed.

In the future, we will probably see increased standardization of terminology, standardized primitives, and the use of multiple types of representations in a single problem. We can also expect increased emergence of self-reflective systems that can reason about their own structure and knowledge.

Also emerging will be knowledge representation systems that are appropriate for learning, generalization and abstraction—currently difficult subjects.

KR languages are on the increase, which should help in constructing knowledge-based systems and encourage standardization of representations.

Within the next five years, we can expect a clearer understanding of which representations are appropriate for which problems.

We can also expect KB's to vastly increase in size with KR techniques being developed to ease the addition of knowledge to them and the retrieval of knowledge from them.

REFERENCES

- Barr, A. and Feigenbaum, E. A., *The Handbook of Artificial Intelligence*, Vol. I, Los Altos, CA: W. Kaufman, 1981.
- Brachman, R. J. and Smith, B. C. (Eds.), "Special Issue on Knowledge Representation," *SIGART Newsletter*, No. 70, Feb. 1980.
- Davis, R., "Expert Systems: Where are We? And Where Do We Go From Here?" *AI Magazine*, Vol. 3, No. 2, Spring 1982, pp. 3-22.
- Gevarter, W., *An Overview of Expert Systems*, National Bureau of Standards, NBSIR 82-2505, May 1982 (Revised October 1982).
- Hewitt, C., "Description and Theoretical Analysis (Using Schemata) of PLANNER: A Language for Proving Theories and Manipulating Models in a Robot," Ph.D. thesis, Dept. of Mathematics, MIT, 1972.
- McCalla, G. and Cercone, N., (Eds.), Special Issue on Knowledge Representation, *Computer*, Vol. 16, No. 10, Oct. 1983.
- Minsky, M., "A Framework for Representing Knowledge," in P. Winston (ed.), *The Psychology of Computer Vision*, New York: McGraw-Hill, 1975, pp. 211-277.
- Moore, R. C., "The Role of Logic in Knowledge Representation and Common Sense Reasoning," *Proc. of the Nat. Conf. on A.I.*, CMU/U. of Pittsburgh, Aug. 1982, pp. 428-433.
- Myopoulis, J., "An Overview of Knowledge Representation," *SIGART Newsletter*, No. 74, Jan. 1981, pp. 5-12.
- Newell, A., "The Knowledge Level," Dept. of Computer Science, CMU, Rept. No. CMU-CS-81-131, July 1981.
- Schank, R. C. and Riesbeck, C. K., *Inside Computer Understanding*, Hillsdale, N.J.: Lawrence Erlbaum, 1981.
- Wilks, Y., "Knowledge Structures and Language Boundaries, *IJCAI 5*, 1977, pp. 151-157.

IV. COMPUTATIONAL LOGIC

A. Introduction

It is frequently necessary to develop computer programs to deduce facts that are not explicitly represented but that are implied by other represented facts. An intelligent robot may have to use logical facts about its environment, e.g., to deduce when a goal state has been reached or how to reach the goal state in the first place. A data base query system may have to deduce desired information from other information in the data base.

Computational logic has been developed to address such problems. In addition, the associated predicate calculus expressions have proven to be a powerful means for knowledge representation for AI programs. Computational logic is thus an important AI area and is briefly reviewed in this chapter.

Raphael (1976, pp. 110-111) states:

> A typical task posed for a logical system is the following. Given some logical sentences representing premises, and a sentence called a theorem, which represents some assertion whose truth we wish to determine, demonstrate whether the theorem is guaranteed to be true provided only that the premises are true. If such a demonstration can be obtained, it is called a proof of the theorem from the given premises, and we say that the premises imply the theorem.
>
> There are two approaches to attempting to construct proofs. One, called the semantic approach, depends heavily upon the meanings of the symbols in the [logical statements]. In a sense, when we use a semantic proof, we reason primarily by considering all the possible interpretations of the logical statement to be proved. In the other approach, called syntactic, we totally ignore the meanings of the symbols; instead, we use formal symbol-manipulation rules of the logical system to construct new [logical statements] out of old ones. The syntactic approach is frequently easier to use, especially for a computer, because one can apply rules in a mechanical way without having to think about what they mean.
>
> A logical system consists of both a specification for the structure of the [logical statements] of the system, and a set of rules, called the rules of inference of the system, for constructing proofs. Many different logical systems have been invented; in fact, each mathematician is free to invent his own as he sees fit.

Traditional computational logic—a computational approach to logical reasoning—is divided into two principal parts, the simpler *"propositional logic"* and the more complex *"predicate logic."*

B. Propositional Logic

In logic a "proposition" is simply a statement that can be true or false. Rules used to deduce the truth (T) or falsehood (F) of new propositions from known propositions are referred to as "argument forms." The interesting and useful things we can do with propositions result from joining propositions together with connectives such as OR, AND, NOT, and IMPLIES to make new propositions. The symbols for these connectives are given in Figure IV-1.

The simplest argument form is the "conjunction," which utilizes the connective AND. It states that if proposition p is true and proposition q is true, then the conjunction "p AND q" is true. In symbolic form we have

p	(premise)
q	(premise)
p ∧ q	(conclusion).

which simply states that for a conjunction, the conclusion is true if the premises are true.

Connective	Symbol	Meaning
And	∧ or ∩	both
Or	∨ or ∪	either or both
Not	¬ or ~	the opposite
Implies	⊃ or →	If the term on the left is true, then the term on the right will also be true.
Equivalent	≡	has the same truth value

Figure IV-1. Typical Mathematical Logic Symbols.

Deduction means obtaining solutions to problems using some systematic reasoning procedures to reach conclusions from stated premises. (In mathematical logic, deductive procedures are sometimes referred to as "formal inference.")

One simple form of deduction can be represented as a mathematical form of argument called "Modus Ponens" (MP):

p	(premise)
p IMPLIES q	(premise)
q	(conclusion)

An example of MP is:

I'm feeling very sick	(premise)
When I'm feeling very sick, I must call the doctor	(premise)
I must call the doctor	(conclusion)

The conclusion is usually stated as a theorem to be proved.

The method of truth tables is the best-known method for proving theorems in propositional calculus. This is a semantic method, in which all the possible combinations of interpretations for the propositional variables are examined.

Graham (1979, pp. 165-168) enlarges on this:

> Suppose we are given some expression involving propositions and logical connectives. Suppose further that we know whether each individual proposition in the expression is true or false. We would like to be able to calculate whether or not the proposition represented by the entire expression is true or false.

We can do this in two steps. First we assign each proposition in the expression a truth value of either T or F. True propositions get the value T and false ones get the value F.

Second, we treat the connectives AND, OR, NOT and IMPLIES as operators operating on T and F, just like the +, −, ×, and / in an algebraic expression operate on numbers. In other words, we do "logical arithmetic" to calculate the truth value of the entire expression.

The proposition

$$p \text{ OR } q$$

is true if p is true, if q is true, or if both are true. This gives us the following truth table for OR:

p	q	p OR q
T	T	T
T	F	T
F	T	T
F	F	F

Another argument form, the "implication relation" is defined such that if p IMPLIES q then when p is true, q will be true, and nothing more. The implication relation does not say that p and q have any cause-and-effect relationship to one another. When p is false, nothing whatever is asserted about q. Therefore, the only way in which p implies q can be false is if p is true and q is false. The resultant truth table is:

p	q	p IMPLIES q
T	T	T
T	F	F
F	T	T
F	F	T

A large number of argument forms are available in traditional logic. All these forms can be easily verified using simple truth tables.

Raphael (1976, pp. 113-114) observes:

> The task of constructing a truth table can certainly be programmed for a computer, and the truth-table method will work to prove or disprove any theorem of propositional calculus. However, this method is not entirely satisfactory, because it can be extremely inefficient. If n different propositional variables occur in the premises and the theorem, then a table with 2^n rows must be filled out; a problem with ten variables requires more than a thousand lines.

Wang (1960) at Harvard University developed a syntactic method that is about as efficient as any general method for propositional calculus can be. It produces exactly the same results as truth tables, usually requires much less computational effort, and is easy to program.

C. Predicate Logic

Propositional logic is limited in that it deals only with the T or F of complete statements. Predicate logic remedies this situation by allowing one to deal with assertions about items in statements, and allows the use of variables and functions of variables.

Propositions make assertions about items (individuals). The "predicate" is the part of the proposition that makes an assertion about the individuals. A proposition is conveniently written as:

$$\text{Predicate } \underbrace{(\text{Individual, Individual,} \ldots)}_{\text{arguments of the predicate}}$$

(e.g.)
"The box is on the table." (proposition) is denoted as:

ON(BOX, TABLE)

The predicate, together with its arguments, is a proposition. Its value is T or F, and any of the operations of propositional logic may be applied to it.

A variable stands for any individual. Variables allow us to make statements that would not be possible in propositional logic. For a proposition containing variables to be true, it must be true for any individual names that are substituted for the variables.

Using variables, if we want to write the English sentence:

"If x is by y and z is on x, then z is also by y."

as a predicate logic expression, it would take the form:

BY(x,y) AND ON(z,x) IMPLIES BY(z,y).

Substituting the name of a particular individual for a variable is known as "instantiation." It is called instantiation because the individual is a particular "instance" of the variable. We can assert that something exists by making up a name for it (e.g., a, b — individual constants) and use that name in our expression. For example, to state that "a" is a box, we write

BOX(a).

We can instantiate our previous expression (for the case of a window, table and ball) as:

BY(TABLE, WINDOW) AND ON(BALL, TABLE)
IMPLIES BY(BALL, WINDOW)

which translates as: if the table is by the window and the ball is on the table, then the ball is also by the window.

Sometimes the individual whose existence we wish to assert will depend on some other individual; then we can use functions (f, g, h) to do this. For example:

The mother of a = f(a).

More generally, if we want to assert that every person has a mother, we can write:

PERSON(x) IMPLIES MOTHER(f(x),x)

which can be read as:

If x is a person, then there exists an f(x) that is x's mother.

D. Resolution

Resolution has been the primary technique used in modern computational logic programs. Resolution is a syntactic method of deduction which replaces all the many argument forms of traditional logic. Resolution is a simple concept but to discuss it, a few additional definitions will be helpful.

Atom: a proposition that cannot be broken down into other propositions (i.e., a proposition that is not formed from other propositions by using connectives).

Literal: an atom (e.g., q) or an atom preceded by NOT (e.g., NOT q)

Clause: a series of literals joined by OR, e.g.: (NOT p) OR q OR (NOT r)
[Duplicate literals in clauses can be eliminated. This process is called factoring.]

Resolution Principle (R): an argument form that applies to clauses:

p OR l OR m OR...	(premise)
(NOT p) OR n OR o OR...	(premise)
l OR m OR n OR o OR...	(conclusion)

(If the premises are T, then by resolution (the cancellation of contradicting literals between clauses) the conclusion is T.)

Empty Clause: (□) indicates a contradiction:

$$\frac{p,\ \text{NOT } p}{\square \text{ (by R)}}$$

Equivalence: Two propositions are equivalent if they have the same truth value.

Identity: States that two propositions are equivalent (proved by using a truth table):

$$\text{e.g., NOT (NOT p) = p} \qquad \text{(identity)}$$

After first putting the original premises and the conclusion into clause form using standard identities, we are ready to prove the truth of a conclusion from a set of premises using resolution. Start by negating the desired conclusion (the theorem to be proved). Then derive new clauses using unification* followed by factoring and resolution, working toward deriving the empty clause. If the empty clause is derived, then (as a result of this proof by contradiction) the desired conclusion follows from the original premises. If we stop before the empty clause is derived, then either the conclusion does not follow from the premises or we gave up too soon.

Graham (1979, pp. 186-187) observed:

> Resolution is complete in the sense that if the conclusion does follow from the premises, then repeated unification, resolution, and factoring will eventually derive the empty clause.
>
> Resolution can be more easily programmed on a computer, and the resulting program is more efficient than was the case with any previous computational-logic programs.
>
> [At present, resolution programs] cannot handle such complex tasks as proving deep mathematical theorems, verifying computer programs, or aiding a robot to cope with the complexities of the real world (as opposed to a limited laboratory world). For these tasks the resolution program uses up the available time or memory before deriving the empty clause.
>
> The trouble, as is usual in AI, is a combinatorial explosion. Unification, resolution, and factoring derive many clauses that are not relevant to deriving the empty clause. The program wastes its time following lines of reasoning that come to a dead end.
>
> Because of these difficulties some people have given up the possibility that computational logic can handle complex theorem-proving tasks. Others seek restrictions on the way resolution and factoring are done that will reduce the number of clauses generated without destroying completeness. Still others (including the author) feel that the answers lie in using powerful heuristic and planning techniques to guide the resolution program to its goal of deriving the empty clause.

---

*Unification is the name for the procedure for carrying out instantiations. In unification we attempt to find substitutions for variables that will make two atoms identical.

E. Computational Logic Today

Computational logic has evolved into several distinguishable subareas: theorem proving, logic programming, non-monotonic logics, and multi-valued and fuzzy logics.

1. Theorem Proving

This branch of computational logic is an outgrowth of resolution theorem proving with additional techniques and modifications added to attempt to restrain combinatorial explosions. With restrictions on resolution clause generation, theorem proving approaches can be made sufficiently efficient to be used in practical problems. An outstanding example of this is the AURA (AUtomated Reasoning Assistant) theorem proving system (Wos, 1983) that has successfully been applied to real applications in mathematics, formal logic, program verification, logic circuit design, chemical synthesis, database inquiry and robotics.

Three techniques (used in the AURA system) that have had a major impact on making theorem provers practical are:

(1) Demodulation: Employing rewrite rules to simplify or canonicalize the expressions to achieve a normalized form.

(2) Subsumption: A technique that recognizes and discards many equivalent or weaker rules or facts than those that have already been generated.

(3) Strategy Rules: Ordering strategies that direct the system as to what to do next.

These three powerful techniques in AURA are domain independent (though the strategy rules have provision for weighting so that the user can assign priorities to concepts).

Other strategies have been important for further reducing the expressions that are generated or retained during the proof process. One class is restriction strategies which provide guidance as to which operations can be skipped. For example, there is the "set of support" strategy that discourages looking at facts that don't have support (e.g., general information used alone, unsupported by other facts).

There are indications that there remain many important domain-independent inference rules yet to be discovered. Examples of research in theorem proving are given by Table IV-1.

2. Logic Programming

It was realized in the early 1970s that logic representations could also function in a procedural mode by using the technique of unification to search for instantiations that would satisfy stated goals. This has led to the PROLOG programming language (see, e.g., Chapter III, Vol IA).

As the manner in which the representations are written and the order (e.g., top to bottom, and left to right) chosen for the execution of the logic statements can have an important influence on the efficiency and effectiveness of executing the program, such representational and ordering choices can be thought of as a form of programming, hence the name logic programming. PROLOG, and logic programming in general, has become very popular in the last few years.

An indication of current research in Logic Programming is given by Table IV-2.

3. Non-Monotonic Logic

One of the popular issues in AI problem solving has been concerned with how to handle lines of reasoning and conclusions that may have to be retracted when new information is received. For example, it is usually reasonable to conclude that if a creature is a bird, then it can fly. However, if it is later learned that the bird is a penguin or is dead, the conclusion must be reconsidered. Recent research efforts on how to handle such situations are indicated in Table IV-3. Etherington and Reiter's (1983)

TABLE IV-1. Examples of Research in Theorem Proving

Technique	Program	Institute	Researcher
Resolution-based automated reasoning program	AURA (AUtomated Reasoning Assistant)	Argonne Nat. Laboratory Argonne, IL	L. Wos R. Overbeek
Set of procedures for tailoring an automated reasoning machine to given specifications	LMA (Logic Machine Architecture, from which a portable reasoning program, ITP, was built)	NW Univ. Evanston, IL	E. Lusk W. McCune R. Overbeek
A strategy for semantic paramodulation of Horn Sets	NUTS (NW U. Theorem-proving System)	NW Univ. Evanston, IL	W. McCune L. Henschen
Special purpose program for program verification		Univ. of TX Austin, TX	R. Boyer J. Moore
Use of examples in automated theorem proving to help guide proof discovery and to determine instantiation of set variables		Univ. of TX Austin, TX	W. Bledsoe
Many-Sorted Calculus based on resolution and paramodulation		Univ. of Karlsruhe W. Germany	C. Walther
A very fast algorithm for unit refutation for the MKR-Procedure	TERMINATOR	Univ. of Karlsruhe W. Germany	G. Antoniou H. Ohlbach
Superposition-oriented theorem prover		L.I.T.P. Paris, France	L. Fribourg
Associative-commutative operators for a refutationally-complete theorem prover		U. of IL Urbana, IL	N. Dershowitz N. Josephson D. Plaisted
		SUNY Stonybrook, N. Y.	J. Hsiang
Procedures for building non-equational theories into a resolution theorem-proving program		SRI Inter.	M. Stickel
Improving the expressiveness of Many Sorted Logic		U. of Warwick Coventry, England	A. Cohen

Sources: IJCAI-83, AAAI-3

work on providing a formal semantics for networks of inheritance hierarchies with exceptions appears particularly promising.

4. Multi-Valued and Fuzzy Logics

Conventional logics deal with the truth or falsity of statements. However, this binary approach is often inadequate for situations in which degrees of certainty are involved as, for example, in medical diagnosis. Thus, work in multi-valued and fuzzy logics has been undertaken to attempt to address this problem. Table IV-4 provides an indication of research in these areas. Several approaches for handling degrees of certainty have already been successfully incorporated into expert systems such as MYCIN and PROSPECTOR.

F. Future Directions

Moore (1982) argues that a number of important features of commonsense reasoning involving incomplete knowledge of a problem situation can be implemented only within a logical framework. Thus logic-based systems will continue to be an important element of AI.

TABLE IV-2. Examples of Research in Logic Programming

Technique	Program	Institute	Researcher
PROLOG Development	PROLOG	Faculte des Sciences de Luminy Marseille, France	A. Colmerauer
Development of a PROLOG/LISP type of programming language	QUTE	U. of Tokyo Japan	M. Sato T. Sakurai
Inclusion of assertions about equality in PROLOG		M.I.T. Cambridge, MA	W. Kornfeld
Use of PROLOG for semantic code analysis of assembler listings		IBM Poughkeepsie, N.Y.	W. Wilson C. John
Extension of PROLOG to increase range of explanation capability	PROLOG/EX1	IBM San Jose, CA	A. Walker
Augmentation of PROLOG to include uncertainties		Weizmann Inst. Rehovot, Israel	E. Shapiro
Addition of algorithmic control structures to PROLOG	LOGAL	U. of Nottingham Med. School U.K.	D. Dodson A. Rector
A method for building libraries of routines and data in PROLOG		Bell Labs. Murray Hill, N.J.	A. Feuer
Integrating PROLOG into the POPLOG environment	POPLOG	Univ. of Sussex Brighton, U.K.	C. Mellish S. Hardy
An interpreter for logic programs which executes goals in parallel		U. of CA Irvine, CA	J. Conery D. Kibler
An experimental tool for parallel execution of distributed AI problem solvers based on logic programming	PRISM	U. of MD College Park, MD	S. Kasif M. Kohli J. Minker
A simple unification algorithm for infinite trees for structure sharing implementations of logic programming languages		Inst. for New Generation Computer Technology (ICOT) Tokyo, Japan	K. Mukai
A program to debug logic programs		Uppsala Univ. Sweden	A. Edman S. Tarnlund

Source: IJCAI-83

The advent of powerful resolution-based theorem proving systems (such as AURA) — utilizing both domain-independent and domain-dependent inference rules to constrain combinatorial explosions — has resulted in opening up practical applications for such systems. However, much research remains to be done to discover more effective strategies, to devise methods for linking rules together to take larger reasoning steps, to explore parallel processing approaches, to build user-friendly interfaces, and to develop more rapid and improved knowledge representation techniques.

TABLE IV-3. *Examples of Research in Non-Monotonic Reasoning*

Activity	Institute	Researcher
Data Dependencies on Equalities	Yale U.	D. McDermott
Inheritance Hierarchies with Exceptions using Default Logic	Univ. of BC Canada	D. Etherington R. Reiter
Default Reasoning as Likelihood Reasoning	Univ. of TX Austin	E. Rich
Default Reasoning using Monotonic Logic	Tulane U.	J. Nutter
Reason Maintenance	Carnegie Mellon U. (CMU) Pittsburgh, PA	J. Doyle
Semantic Considerations in non-monotonic Logic	SRI International	R. Moore

Source: AAAI-83, IJCAI-83

TABLE IV-4. *Examples of Research in Multi-Valued and Fuzzy Logics, and Plausible Reasoning Techniques*

Activity	Institute	Researcher
Approximate Reasoning Techniques	Universite Paul Sabatier Toulouse, France	H. Prade
Consistency and Plausible Reasoning	Rand Santa Monica, CA	J. Quinlan
Propagation of Uncertainty	Advanced Information & Decision Systems Mt. View, CA	R. Tong D. Shapiro J. Dean B. McCune
Heuristic Reasoning about Uncertainty	Stanford U. Stanford, CA	P. Cohen M. Grinberg
"Evidence Space" for Dealing with Uncertain Reasoning	Tech. Univ. of Berlin Fed. Rep. of Germany	C. Rollinger
Use of Baysian Statistics in Common Sense Reasoning	Brown U. Providence, R.I.	E. Charniak
Fuzzy Logic	U. of CA Berkeley, CA	L. Zadeh
A Method for Computing Generalized Bayesian Probability Values for Expert Systems	SRI International	P. Cheeseman

Source: IJCAI-83

The advent of portable theorem proving systems opens up the opportunity for much increased experimentation, which should be instrumental in rapidly advancing the field. Wos (1983) predicts that as a result, automated reasoning systems with the capability for being used in a wide variety of real applications will be commonplace within five years.

As expert systems technology pushes forward toward employing causality and structure, in addition to empirical association rules, deeper levels of reasoning will be required. It is anticipated that advanced theorem proving systems will play an important role in this arena.

PROLOG, the rapidly proliferating language for logic programming, has been earmarked for the Japanese Fifth Generation Computer project. The powerful inference rules (such as the set of support strategy) used in advanced theorem provers are now being considered for use with PROLOG. These, coupled with domain-specific control strategies and making provisions for taking advantage of many of the features of LISP (as in LOGLISP) may well make a hybridized PROLOG the dominant AI language within the next decade.

Examination of Tables IV, and the associated textual comments, indicate that the basic reasoning problems of non-monotonic reasoning and reasoning in the presence of uncertainty, are beginning to succumb to some of the recent research. We can thus conclude that computational logic, which earlier appeared doomed by the combinatorics generated by the pure resolution approach, has become revitalized with new representational approaches, inference rules, domain heuristics, and advanced computers and will play an increasingly important role in future AI applications.

Additional material on computational logic from an AI point of view can be found in Boyer and Moore (1979), Kowalski (1979), Nilsson (1980), Clocksin and Mellish (1981), Robinson and Sibert (1981), Cohen and Feigenbaum (1982), Clark and Tarnlund (1982), Rich (1983), and Wos et al. (1984).

REFERENCES

- Blasius, K., et al., "The Markgraf Refutation Procedure," *Proceedings of the Seventh International Joint Conference on Artificial Intelligence,* Vancouver, Aug. 1981, pp. 511-518.
- Boyer, R. and Moore, J., *Computational Logic,* New York: Academic Press, 1979.
- Clark, K. and Tarnlund, S. (Eds.), *Logic Programming,* New York: Academic Press, 1982.
- Clocksin, W. F. and Mellish, C. S., *Programming in PROLOG,* Berlin, Springer-Verlag, 1981.
- Cohen, D. N., *Knowledge Based Theorem Proving and Learning,* Ann Arbor: UMI Press, 1981.
- Cohen, P. R. and Feigenbaum, E. A., *The Handbook of Artificial Intelligence,* Vol. 3, Los Altos, CA: W. Kaufmann, 1982.
- Graham, N., *Artificial Intelligence,* Blue Ridge Summit, PA: Tab Books, 1979.
- Hayes-Roth, R., "AI: The New Wave — A Technical Tutorial for R&D Management," Santa Monica: Rand Corp., 1981 (AIAA-81-0827).
- Kowalski, R., *Logic for Problem Solving,* New York: North Holland, 1979.
- Moore, R. C., "The Role of Logic in Knowledge Representation and Common Sense Reasoning," *Proc. of the Nat. Conf. on A.I.,* Pittsburgh, Aug. 1982, Los Altos, CA: W. Kaufmann, 1982, pp. 428-433.
- Nilsson, N. J., *Principles of Artificial Intelligence,* Palo Alto: Tioga, 1980.
- Raphael, B., *The Thinking Computer,* San Francisco: Freeman and Co., 1976.
- Rich, E., *Artificial Intelligence,* New York: McGraw-Hill, 1983.
- Robinson, J. A. and Sibert, E. E., Logic Programming in Lisp, RADC-TR-80-379, Vol. 1, Syracuse U., School of Computer and Information Science, Syracuse, NY, Jan. 1981.
- Wang, H., "Toward Mechanical Mathematics," *IBM J. Research and Development,* Vol. 4, 1960, pp. 2-22.
- Wos, L., "Automated Reasoning: Real Uses and Potential Uses," *IJCAI-83,* pp. 867-876.
- Wos, L., Overbeek, R., Lusk, E., and Boyle, J., *Automated Reasoning: Introduction and Applications,* Englewood Cliffs, N.J.: Prentice Hall, 1984.

- *IJCAI-83: Proc. of the Eighth Inter. Joint Conf. on AI,* 8-12 Aug. 1983, Karlsruhe, W. Germany, Los Altos, CA: W. Kaufmann, 1983.
- *AAAI-83: Proc. of the Nat. Conf. on AI,* Aug. 22-26, 1983, Wash., D.C., Los Altos, CA: W. Kaufmann, 1983.